Water, Whiskey, and Vodka

Water, Whiskey, and Vodka

A Story of Slavic Languages

Danko Šipka

GEORGETOWN UNIVERSITY PRESS | Washington, DC

The publisher is not responsible for third-party websites or their content. URL links were active at time of publication.

Library of Congress Cataloging-in-Publication Data

Names: Šipka, Danko, author.
Title: Water, whiskey, and vodka : a story of Slavic languages / Danko Šipka.
Description: Washington, DC : Georgetown University Press, 2023. | Includes
    bibliographical references and index.
Identifiers: LCCN 2023016677 (print) | LCCN 2023016678 (ebook) | ISBN 9781647123741
    (paperback) | ISBN 9781647123734 (hardcover) | ISBN 9781647123758 (ebook)
Subjects: LCSH: Slavic languages—History. | Language and culture—Slavic countries.
Classification: LCC PG45 .S53 2023 (print) | LCC PG45 (ebook) | DDC 491.8—dc23/
    eng/20230517
LC record available at https://lccn.loc.gov/2023016677
LC ebook record available at https://lccn.loc.gov/2023016678

♾ This paper meets the requirements of ANSI/NISO Z39.48-1992 (Permanence of Paper).

24 23   9 8 7 6 5 4 3 2   First printing

Printed in the United States of America

Cover design by Martyn Schmoll
Interior design by Matthew Williams

Contents

Illustrations

Acknowledgments

I would like to thank to the two anonymous reviewers of the book proposal and the two readers of the final draft. All of them provided most useful comments. Georgetown editor Hope LeGro, who has encouraged me to embark on this project, is also to be thanked for her invaluable suggestions that have significantly improved the text and for her overall guidance in this project. I would furthermore like to thank Sonya Manes, a copy editor at Georgetown, for her fine final edits.

I am furthermore indebted to the following colleagues and friends who have provided superb feedback on earlier drafts of the text: Wayles Browne, Motoki Nomachi, Robert Niebuhr, Đorđe Otašević, L'upčo Spasovski, Mladen Šašić, and Ljiljana Šipka. I am also grateful for excellent English-language editing at various stages of the project to Olja Šipka and Kimberly Koerth.

An earlier draft of this book was piloted in the course History of Slavic Languages at Arizona State University (ASU) in the fall semesters of 2020, 2021, and 2022, as well as in the course titled The Slavs at Columbia University in the spring of 2021. I am grateful to those students who provided anonymous feedback on the manuscript.

Several institutions have supported my research that led to the publication of this book. I am grateful to all of them. Hokkaido University, Sapporo, Japan, enabled my research in August, September, and October of 2017. Ss. Cyril and Methodius University, Skopje, Macedonia, enabled my training and research in 2018. The School of International Letters and Cultures at ASU provided a grant for research in Vienna in January 2019 (with Royal and State archives of Austria enabling access). The Social Science Research Council and Melikian Center at ASU funded my trip to Slovenia (partially also supported by the Slovenian Research Council) and Croatia in May of 2019. The University of Illinois enabled my library research in 2021. The Fulbright Foundation funded my research in Serbia in May and June 2022 (with the Serbian Academy of Sciences and Arts kindly enabling access to its archives); the US State Department funded my trips to Bosnia and Albania in the same period.

Abbreviations

Below is a list of abbreviations and other linguistic signs that I have used at various points throughout the text.

___	underlining, used to emphasize the focus of the discussion; e.g., _o_ is underlined in _məlʌko_ to show where the stress falls in discussing stress placement.
*	reconstructed (not attested), e.g., *_mạti_ in Proto-Slavic, which was not attested in writing.
<=	comes from _burmistrz_ <= _Bürgermeister_.
=>	yields, develops into, e.g., long (_ā_, _ō_) => long _ā_.
( )	1. Origin of the sound (in formulas), 2. Evidence for the PIE sound (in PIE to PSL examples) 3. Examples (in PLS to Slavic languages changes)

A	Accusative
Bel.	Belarusian
Bul.	Bulgarian
Cze.	Czech
D	Dative
G	Genitive
Ger.	German
Gre.	Greek
I	Instrumental
Lat.	Latin
L	Locative
N	Nominative
PIE	Proto-Indo-European
Mac.	Macedonian
Pol.	Polish
PSL	Proto-Slavic
Rus.	Russian
S-Cr (B/C/S)	Serbo-Croatian (Bosnian/Croatian/Serbian)

Slo.	Slovene
Slk.	Slovak
Sor.	Sorbian
Ukr.	Ukrainian
V	Vocative

Introduction

This is a gateway book. In it I strive to provide an accessible introduction to the history of Slavic languages for anyone who is interested. It may, for example, be instructive to those new to learning a Slavic language, as a first step in exploring the world of Slavic languages and cultures. It may also help someone whose relatives speak a Slavic language. Slavic languages are more complex and interesting than they may appear at first glance. Although they are quite complicated, my aim is to share with you my excitement and not to present overly technical information, to attract you to explore beyond what I present here. The chapter and section titles serve as teasers and clues to what is to come, rather than summaries of what is discussed. At the end of each chapter is a list of suggested sources where you can read more about some of the details of historical developments. Similarly, all technical terms of linguistics, when needed, will be explained in simpler terms. While I include several maps and tables showing relevant facts about Slavic languages, readers can find more elaborate information in the various recommended readings.

The book comprises ten main chapters. The opening chapter, titled "What Is a Slavic Language and How Do Language and Culture Interact?," gives you a general lay of the land, both providing initial basic information about Slavic languages and discussing several key anthropological and linguistic concepts that will follow the journey throughout the book. The remaining nine chapters are organized in three parts.

Part I, "Nuts and Bolts," presents the major historical developments of Slavic languages and the traditions in the scholarly study of these developments. Then I take you through an exploration of the sounds of Slavic languages, some of which are special to these languages, and the unique way that Slavic words form to convey gender and other things.

In Part II, "Words, Words, Words," I focus on the development of the vocabularies of Slavic languages. We explore the development of the words Slavic languages inherited from their common ancestor language and then the similarities and differences between Slavic vocabularies. In the final chapter of this part, chapter 7, I look at how Slavic languages lent words to and borrowed words from other languages.

In the final part of the book, "Part III: Languages as Tools of Cultures," I examine the cultural history of Slavic languages. Every language has standard varieties, those that are accepted by everyone, and less standard varieties, those that may be understood but are not considered to have as much weight. I begin by diving into the evolution of the standard language variety in Slavic cultures. Taking that a step further, I explore the dynamics of the relationship between language authorities—perhaps those who decide what the "official language(s)" are for a given culture—and the general body of speakers in Slavic languages. As in English-speaking communities, in Slavic language communities there is debate and sometimes disagreement about what a language *is* and what it is *not*. I end this part by illuminating some of the disputes about Slavic languages and Slavic dialects.

To help you along the way, I have provided a transcription and pronunciation guide for Slavic letters old and new, a list of abbreviations, and an index. In addition, there is a bibliography. It is divided into three sections: references cited, which are those works mentioned in each chapter's selected readings; a list of comparative grammars of Slavic languages, which allow you to get into much more detail about the similarities and differences between the Slavic languages; and etymological dictionaries of Slavic languages, which show you more detail about the origins of the languages. The latter two lists are meant to be a point of departure for those with a reading knowledge of Slavic languages.

I hope that after reading this book you can begin to appreciate the deep connection between the Slavic languages and, yet, how each one is unique. In Slavic languages one can trace various historical processes and cultural circles that have influenced Slavic peoples. There are also internal linguistic developments that seem to follow a logic of their own. Over the centuries, speakers of Slavic languages have changed their habits as to which sounds they use or how they inflect their words. These processes do not have a straightforward connection to the cultural and historical background of Slavic languages. Last but not least, various forms of Slavic languages reveal influences of various ideologies and political programs.

1 What Is a Slavic Language, and How Do Language and Culture Interact?

Slovaks and Slovenes, Serbs and Siberians

The word *Slav* is not exactly a household name in English-speaking cultures. More often, one hears a reference to *Russian*, a subset of Slavs, or to *eastern European*, which includes Slavs and speakers of other languages. In the perception of an average English-speaking person, Russian culture eclipses all other Slavic cultures due to the size of Russia; the number of its speakers; the political weight it has within the English-speaking world; and the prominence of its historical figures, from Ivan the Terrible to Vladimir Vladimirovich Putin, and cultural icons, from Pyotr Ilyich Tchaikovsky to Anton Pavlovich Chekhov. At the same time, Russians and other Slavs are typically labeled as eastern Europeans. The category of eastern Europeans encompasses a diverse assembly of Slavic and non-Slavic languages, the latter being Lithuanian, Latvian, Romanian, Albanian, Hungarian, and Estonian. The perception of homogeneity might have been amplified by the fact that all major Slavic nations were a part of the so-called Eastern Bloc during the 1945–89 Cold War period. However, this misunderstanding is older than the Cold War and is related to the history of immigration to the United States, beginning in the late nineteenth century. One can see unrelated ethnic groups merged under the disparaging term *Bohunk*, first documented in 1903, to refer to an immigrant from central Europe. The word is a clipping from *Bohemian* (i.e., a Czech, a speaker of a Slavic language) and *Hunk*, a variant of Hungarian (i.e., a speaker of Hungarian, a completely unrelated language). To this day, the people from eastern Europe are merged into one "ethnic" category, while countries and regions within that rough geographic area are confused. Slovenia, for example, is commonly confused with Slovakia, Serbia with Siberia, and Sorbians with Serbians. As often happens, perceptions live a life that is not in sync with the facts. And the facts are as follows.

Slavs are 360 million people who currently occupy vast areas of central Europe, southeastern Europe, eastern Europe, and Eurasia: Russians, Ukrainians, Poles,

Figure 1.1. Slavic Languages, Major and Minor

Czechs, Slovaks, Serbs, Croats, Bulgarians, and others. They are the largest sub-group of Indo-European peoples in Europe. The languages of the Indo-European peoples encompass 46 percent of the world's population—3.2 billion people—distributed from the northernmost to the southernmost tip of the Americas and from Iceland to India. All Slavic peoples have a common heritage as descendants of Old Slavs. Likewise, all Slavic languages have developed from the same ancestor language, Proto-Slavic. Their present distribution is presented in figure 1.1. More widely spoken languages are named in the map, whereas those with fewer speakers are marked with numbers. If the names of only a few of them are familiar to you, you are not alone, and worry not—we will come to all of them in due course.

The etymology of the word *Slav* is murky. There are several competing hypotheses about it. One of them claims that this ethnic name is related to the word *slovo* 'word'; that is, Slavs are those who speak, who could be understood. This hypothesis is supported by the fact that most Slavic languages refer to Germans with a word such as the Russian term *nemets,* literally a mute person. So, Slavs are one's own people who can be understood, and neighboring ethnic groups, like Germans, are those who cannot speak, that is, impossible to understand. There are also theories that link the etymology of the term *Slav* to *slava* 'glory.' On the opposite end of the spectrum of hypotheses is that the word comes from the Greek and Latin words for a 'slave,' or a 'prisoner of war.' Needless to say, Slavs prefer the former hypotheses, and the latter ones have been disputed for some time now anyway.

What Is Culture, and What Are Some Differences between Cultures?

To better understand Slavs and their languages, let's look at the role of culture in language. Languages are embedded in the social fiber of their respective cultures. Slavic languages are no exception. Language and culture are indeed elusive concepts. Understanding and defining a culture together depend not only on the content of the definition but also on where the definer is coming from. The definitions of culture, dispersed across the vast literature on the subject, exhibit a stunning degree of variation. Among the things we look at to understand a culture are shared knowledges, beliefs, morals, customs, laws, behavioral patterns, values, ideas, attitudes, and collective memories. Scholars such as Helen Spencer-Oatey also point to the fact that these shared basic assumptions, values, orientations, beliefs, policies, and procedures form a fuzzy set of knowledge shared by a group of people that influence (but do not determine) any individual member of that group.

For the manner in which various languages function in their respective cultures, the differences between various cultures are more important than the definition of what a culture is. Academics who study culture as a concept and compare cultures agree that there are key ways that cultures can be the same or differ. Let's look at some of the ways that Slavic cultures compare with non-Indigenous North American cultures. The pioneering cross-cultural researcher Harry Triandis brought to our attention the differences between collectivist cultures, which consider the group to be more important than the individual, and individualist cultures, which consider the individual to be more important than the group.

Compared with mainstream non-Indigenous North American cultures, Slavic cultures are more collectivist, while North American, English-speaking, and western European cultures tend to favor individualism. Edward T. Hall, another influential cross-cultural researcher, differentiated between monochronic and polychronic cultures. Monochronic cultures construe time as one clear line. As a consequence, schedules are prominent in their time management and they are more likely to separate personal time from work time. In polychronic cultures, there are multiple timelines—the past, the present, and the future coexist. In consequence, their time management is determined by interpersonal relations rather than by schedules, and they are less likely to separate work from personal issues. Slavic cultures are more polychronic, while mainstream non-Indigenous North American cultures are typically monochronic. Hall's classic pattern of cross-cultural differences also includes a distinction between high- and low-context cultures. In high-context cultures, most things are not expressed directly. Instead, they need to be inferred from the context. In low-context cultures, direct statements that do not require a context are more common. While mainstream non-Indigenous North American cultures and Slavic cultures alike are low context compared to Japanese and other East Asian cultures, Slavic cultures are much closer to the low-context end of the scale when compared with mainstream American culture.

Dutch social psychologist and cultural researcher Geert Hofstede has identified six dimensions along which cultures vary. Along with the aforementioned individualism, he has identified power distance, the level of tolerance for unequal distribution of power in the society; masculinity, tolerance for violence in the society; uncertainty avoidance, how tolerant the society is toward ambiguity and uncertainty; long-term orientation, the belief that one needs to be prepared for change; and indulgence, whether the culture in question celebrates fun and good things in life without any restrictions. Mainstream non-Indigenous North American culture is individualistic (an individual is more important than community, and competition is more valued than cooperation) and tolerant of unequal distribution of resources (it is fine that some members of the society are much richer than others). These non-Indigenous Americans tend to accept a high amount of violence (e.g., carrying and using weapons are generally fine), tend to be very tolerant of ambiguity and uncertainty (they prefer opportunity over security), and tend to want and seek out self-gratification in life rather than practice restraint (in other words, fun is highly valued). On all of these dimensions, Slavic cultures are comparatively closer to the opposite end of the scale. In its long-term orientation dimension, a measure of how prepared for change a culture thinks it should be, non-Indigenous North American cultures are in the middle of the scale, and Slavic cultures are closer to the lower end (i.e., they do not feel they should be prepared for change). These cultural nuances are embedded within each language. Knowing these differences and understanding a culture are crucial to understanding its language. Languages contain various idioms, proverbs, and other elements that reflect the predominant cultural values of their societies. For example, the high masculinity of mainstream North American cultures is reflected in countless idioms containing firearms, such as *gun shy, trigger happy, straight shooter*, to *shoot oneself in the foot*, and many others.

Languages serve their respective cultures—typically, one language is in service of multiple cultures. Although the key parameters of the dominant culture are mirrored in various elements of the language, most notably in its lexicon or vocabulary, this does not change the fact that there may be other cultures a language serves. Thus, in Russian, the dominant culture is that of ethnic Russians, but that does not change the fact that numerous Ukrainians, Belarusians, and members of various Indigenous nations of Russia and central Asia use Russian as their primary or secondary language, embedding in it some of their own cultural heritages, if only ever so slightly.

How Do Slavs Write?

Slavic people belong to the cultural spheres of Eastern and Western Christian churches and, to a more limited degree, to Islam. As a consequence, various written alphabets or scripts reflecting this cultural heritage have been used in Slavic languages. The initial script was the Glagolitic script, a specifically Slavic script, which emerged in 862–63 CE. It was invented by Slavic brothers from the hinterland of Thessaloniki in today's Greece. Their work was commissioned by Rastislav, the prince of Great Moravia (a powerful state encompassing vast areas of central Europe). The Glagolitic script was used to write Old Church Slavonic language, the first Slavic literary language (i.e., the language variety used in formal writing of sacred and other literary texts). The two Slavic brothers created this language also as a tool of Christianization in service of Rastislav and his principate. The Glagolitic was a native script of unclear origin, but more than one half seems to be derived from the Greek alphabet. For example, the letter *L* looks like ⰾ in the Glagolitic script, and its Greek equivalent is Λ; the letter *D* looks like ⰴ in the Glagolitic script, and its Greek equivalent is Δ. As one can see, there is a faint similarity in the top-pointed shape and the fact that the letters represent roughly the same sounds. However, the similarity is not so pronounced as to prove the origin of the Glagolitic letters beyond a reasonable doubt.

The Slavic Cyrillic script, which many readers may associate with Russian, because it is the script used in that language (and several other Slavic languages) even today, appeared in the late AD 800s and early 900s. The Slavic Latin script was then added around the year 1000. These three scripts coexisted for a while, but in the fourteenth century the Glagolitic script was displaced by the other two.

During the Ottoman Turkish rule in the Balkans, from the fifteenth to nineteenth century CE, as well as in the sixteenth century in Belarus, an Arabic script that was modified to include specific Slavic sounds was also used and was subsequently replaced with the Latin script. The Gothic version of the Latin script was used among Sorbians and Czechs but was also eventually replaced by the mainstream Latin script; the Greek script was used among Slavic Macedonians at one point in time and then switched to the Cyrillic script; and the Hebrew script was even used in texts of the extinct West Slavic Knaanic language. Today, most of the major Slavic languages—including Russian, Ukrainian, Belarusian, Bulgarian, and Macedonian—use the Cyrillic script. The Serbian variant of Serbo-Croatian (Bosnian/Croatian/Serbian) uses both Cyrillic and Latin scripts, whereas all other aforementioned languages use the Latin script. The story of these alphabets' incorporation into Slavic cultures and their export to non-Slavic peoples will be discussed in chapter 8. These alphabets and the letters used in various Slavic languages are presented in table 1.1 (note: approximate most common pronunciation is given).

How Many Slavic Languages Are There?

The Russian language is known throughout the English-speaking world. Many people are also familiar with Polish, but what about other Slavic languages? How many of them are there, and what are their relationships to one another? Traditionally, three groups of Slavic languages are differentiated: East Slavic languages, which include Russian, Ukrainian, and Belarusian; West Slavic languages, which include Polish, Czech, Slovak, and Lower and Upper Sorbian; and South Slavic languages, which include Serbo-Croatian (Bosnian/Serbian/Croatian), Slovenian, Bulgarian, Macedonian, and the extinct Old Church Slavonic (the first Slavic literary language used in the ninth through eleventh centuries). These three groups of Slavic languages, with their thirteen major languages, are defined by the features found only in each group and then by two additional sets of features: those common to East and West Slavic languages but not South Slavic languages and

Table 1.1. Slavic Alphabets and Their Letters

Latin	Cyrillic	Glagolitic	Gothic	Arabic	Hebrew	Greek	Sound
A a	A a	⊹	𝕬a	ٲ	א	A α	a as in art
Ä ä					א		a as in bad
Ą ą	Ѫ	Ⰵ	𝕬á				on (o as in over, n as in no)
Ã ã							an (a as in alpha, n as in no)
B b	Б б	Ⰱ	𝕭b	ب	ב	B β	b as in boy
C c	Ц ц	Ⰲ	𝕮c	ج	צ	Tσ, τσ	ts as in blitz
Č č	Ч ч	Ⰳ	𝕮č	ج		Tσ, τσ	ch as in cheese
Ć ć (ci)	Ћ ћ		𝕮ć	ج			ch as in cheese
Cz cz							ch as in cheese
D d	Д д	Ⰴ	𝕯d	د	ד	Δ δ	d as in day
Đ đ	Ђ ђ	Ⰼ		ج			j as in jack
Ď ď			𝕯'ď'		ד		j as in jack
Dž dž	Џ џ			ج		Tζ, τζ	j as in jack
Dż dż							j as in jack
Dź dź (dzi)							j as in jack
E e	E e	Ⰵ	𝕰e	ه	'	E ε, H η	e as in echo
Ě ě			𝕰ě		'		ye (y as in yes, e as in echo)
Ę ę	Ѧ	Ⰵ					en (e as in echo, n as in no)
É é							ey (e as in echo, y as in yes),
F f	Ф ф	Ⱇ	𝕱f	ف	ף	Φ φ	f as in fat
G g	Г г	Ⰳ	𝕲g	غ	ג	Γ γ	g as in go
H h	X x	Ⱈ	𝕳ħ	ح	ה	X χ	h as in hot
I i	И и	Ⰻ	𝕴i	اِی	'	I ι	i as in igloo
J j	Й й		𝕵i	يِ	'	I ι	y as in yes
K k	К к	Ⰽ	𝕶ł	ق	ק	K κ	k as in kilo
L l	Л л	Ⰾ	𝕷l	ق	ל	Λ λ	l as in lip
Ĺ ĺ							l as in lip
Ł ł			𝕷ł				w as in wine

Table 1.1. Slavic Alphabets and Their Letters (*continued*)

Latin	Cyrillic	Glagolitic	Gothic	Arabic	Hebrew	Greek	Sound
Lj lj	Љ љ			لَ			*l* as in *lip*, *y* as in *yes*
M m	М м	𑍣	𝔐𝔪	م	מ	Μ μ	*m* as in *me*
N n	Н н	Ⱀ	𝔑𝔫	ن	ן	N ν	*n* as in *no*
Ń ń (ni)			𝔑ń				*n* as in *no*, *y* as in *yes*
Ň ň			𝔑ň		ן		*ny*, *n* as in *no*, *y* as in *yes*
Nj nj	Њ њ			نُ			*n* as in *no*, *y* as in *yes*
O o	О о	ⱁ	𝔇o	ۏ	ו	O o, Ω ω	*o* as in *on*
Ó ó							*oo* as in *book*
Ò ò							*we* (*w* as in *we*, *e* as in *echo*)
P p	П п	ⱂ	𝔓p	پ	פ	Π π	*p* as in *pot*
Q q							*q* as in *quiet*
R r	Р р	Ⱃ	𝔑r	ر	ר	P ρ	*r* as in *room*
Rz rz							*s* as in *pleasure*
Ř ř			𝔑ř				*rs* (*r* as in *red*, *s* as in *pleasure*)
Ŕ ŕ					ר		*ry* (*r* as in *red*, *y* as in *yes*)
S s	С с	Ⱄ	𝔊s	س	ס	Σ σ/ς	*s* as in *sit*
Š š	Ш ш	Ⱎ	𝔊š	ش	שׁ	Σσ σσ, Σι σι	*sh* as in *ship*
Ś ś (si)			𝔊ś				*sh* as in *ship*
Sz sz							*sh* as in *ship*
T t	Т т	Ⱅ	𝔗t	ت	ט	T τ	*t* as in *top*
Ť ť					ט		*ty*, *t* as in *tip*, *y* as in *yes*
U u	У у ꙋ	𑍫	𝔘u	وُ	ו		*oo* as in *book*
Ů ů							*oo* as in *book*
Ù ù							*woo* (*w* as in *we*, *oo* as in *book*)
V v	В в	ⰲ	𝔙v	و	ו		*v* as in *vine*
W w			𝔚w				*v* as in *vine*

Table 1.1. Slavic Alphabets and Their Letters (*continued*)

Latin	Cyrillic	Glagolitic	Gothic	Arabic	Hebrew	Greek	Sound
X x			𝔛𝔵				x as in x-ray
Y y	Ы ы		𝔜𝔶			Υ υ	a sound between i as in sit and oo as in pool
Z z	З з		3ȝ	ﺝ	ז	Ζ ζ	z as in zebra
Ž ž	Ж ж		3̌ȝ̌	ﺝ	שׁ,ז	Ζ ζ	s as in pleasure
Ż ż							s as in pleasure
Ź ź (zi)			3̇ȝ̇				s as in pleasure
	Ѕ ѕ					Τζ τζ	d as in day, z as in zebra
	Оу оу						oo as in book
	Ю ю						y as in yes, oo as in book
	Я я						y as in yes, a as in art
	Ё ё						y as in yes, o as in on
	Ъ ъ						back semivowel (as if pronouncing an ultrashort oo as in book)
	Ь ь						front semivowel (as if pronouncing an ultrashort i as in bit)
	Э э						e as in echo
	Щ щ					Στσ στσ	sht, sh as in ship, t as in tip (South Slavic), shch (sh as in ship, ch as in chip)
	Ќ ќ					Κι κι	ky (k as in kit, y as in yes)
	Ѓ ѓ					Γι γι	gy (g as in go, y as in yes)
	Ў ў						w as in wine
	Ґ ґ						g as in go
	Ї ї						i as in bit

Table 1.1. Slavic Alphabets and Their Letters (*continued*)

Latin	Cyrillic	Glagolitic	Gothic	Arabic	Hebrew	Greek	Sound
	W	ꙩ					ot (*o* as in *over*, *t* as in *top*)
	Ѣ ь	Ⰰ					ya (*y* as in *yes*, *a* as in *bad*)
	Ѥ						ye (*y* as in *yes*, *e* as in *echo*)
	ІА	Ⱔ					yen (*y* as in yes, *e* as in *echo*, *n* as in *no*)
	ІЖ	Ⱘ					yon (*y* as in *yes*, *o* as in *over*, *n* as in *no*)
	ѯ					Ξ ξ	Ks (*k* as in *kit*, *s* as in *sit*)
	ѱ					Ψ ψ	ps (*p* as in *pit*, *s* as in *sit*)
	Ѳ	Ⱚ				Θ θ	*th* as in *this*
	V	Ⱛ					*i* as in *it*
	Ҁ						*no sound value*

those common to East and South Slavic languages but not West Slavic languages. However, these are linguistic minutiae that are not of immediate interest.

You may have heard of many—maybe all—of the languages I just mentioned. Like all language groups, however, there are so many more languages than just the most common ones—some of them with more speakers and more scholarship, and others with far fewer speakers and fewer studies about them, as you could see from figure 1.1. One type that you may not be familiar with are languages/dialects with a disputed status. Often, the dispute concerns whether it is a language or a dialect. For example, there are those who would say that Rusyn (in southern Poland, in Slovakia, and in northern Serbia) is a separate language, but there are also those who believe it is a dialect of Ukrainian. Linguists love to categorize languages and to group them. They have come up with many different types of Slavic languages. There are what linguists call Slavic literary microlanguages, which are languages in a close relationship with a major Slavic language. For example,

Slavic literary microlanguages called Pomak Bulgarian and Banat Bulgarian stand in close relationship with Bulgarian, a major Slavic language. Similarly, Resian and Venetian Slovene are related to Slovene, a major Slavic language. Typically, these languages are located in a community that is outside of a larger Slavic community but is self-contained or near a larger Slavic language. These microlanguages are a subset of small literary languages. They, in turn, feature a limited number of speakers and do not fulfill all the functions of more established languages (e.g., they may be mostly used at home or in literary works). There are additional extinct Slavic languages, and there are Slavic artificial languages (or planned languages), that is, languages that did not emerge spontaneously but instead were intentionally created. While more than ten artificial Slavic languages have been proposed, two have the highest name recognition. One is Slovio, based on the principles of Esperanto (an artificial international language based mostly on words common to the chief European languages); the other is Interslavic (or Mezhduslo-vyanski), which relies on Old Church Slavonic, and thus has a hybrid, semiconstructed nature. In addition to these artificial languages, there are Slavic hybrids (mixed forms of two Slavic languages). Then, there are mixed languages of Slavic and non-Slavic materials called pidgins that do not have native speakers and that have emerged for the purposes of trade or other kinds of communication between Slavic (as a rule, Russian) and non-Slavic speakers. Finally, there are the so-called macaronic languages, used in code-switching, which is switching back and forth between two languages, most notably in works of literature.

Next, let's look at various examples of disputed languages, extinct languages, hybrid languages, small literary languages, and microlanguages in each of the three groups of Slavic languages, starting with the Eastern group. If you are just interested in major languages in each group, read those sections and skip sections about other languages.

Major East Slavic Languages

The East Slavic branch includes three major languages—Russian, Ukrainian, and Belarusian—as well as a number of their smaller kin. Russian is by far the best-known Slavic language globally. This recognition is evident in Slavic departments in the English-speaking world, where Russian is obligatory and other Slavic languages are optional complements, if not mere adornments. This emphasis comes as no surprise, given that Russia covers the largest territory and that the Russian language features the largest number of speakers of all Slavic languages. The power of the global military and political presence of Russia and the influence of its potent culture contribute further to the dominance of Russian among Slavic languages. This eastern European language features over 150 million native speakers and over 100 million second-language speakers. It ranks seventh among world languages, with only Mandarin Chinese, Spanish, English, Hindi, Bengali, and Portuguese having more native speakers. Native speakers of Russian are concentrated in Russia (which is twice the size of the United States) and its surrounding post-Soviet countries, such as Latvia, Ukraine, and Kazakhstan. It features two major dialects, northern and southern, which are not very different from the standard language.

Ukrainian is the second-largest East Slavic language, with approximately 35 million native speakers and an additional 5 million second-language speakers. The native speakers are mostly concentrated in western and central Ukraine, but there are sizeable groups of speakers in eastern and southern Ukraine and in several Balkan countries, as well. Ukrainians also have a strong diaspora presence in Canada and the United States. There are three main dialects of Ukrainian: Northern, Southwestern, and Southeastern.

Belarusian is a much smaller cousin of the East Slavic branch, with some 5 million native speakers and 6 million second-language speakers (most of which have Russian as their first language). It is spoken in Belarus, and it has a minority presence in eastern Poland, Ukraine, and the Czech Republic. It features four major dialects: Northeastern, Middle, Southwestern, and West Polesian. Because of the dominance of the Russian language in Belarus, Belarusian is listed as vulnerable, which is the first out of four levels of endangerment as defined by the United Nations Educational, Scientific and Cultural Organization (UNESCO).

Other East Slavic Languages

Rusyn (Ruthene) is an example of a disputed Slavic microlanguage. It is disputed because there are those who would claim that it is not a separate language but rather a dialect of the Ukrainian language. It has more than half a million estimated total speakers. Its main varieties are Carpathian Rusyn in Ukraine, Slovakia, Hungary, and Poland (in Poland, it is known under the name of Lemko) and Pannonian Rusyn in northern Serbia and Croatia. Just like Belarusian, Rusyn is listed as vulnerable by UNESCO. There are further microlanguages in this Slavic group, such as West Polesian (in Belarus and Ukraine), Podlachian (in Poland), and Elshanian (in Lithuania).

Ruthenian is an example of an extinct language in the East Slavic branch—these were Western East Slavic forms in official use in the Grand Dutchy of

Lithuania from the thirteenth to the seventeenth century. Its colloquial form was gradually replaced with today's Ukrainian, Belarusian, and Rusyn. It is unclear whether it was a separate literary language or a western form of Old Russian (recently also known as Old East Slavic), a colloquial form used in Kievan Rus' in the tenth through the fifteenth centuries.

The East Slavic group is also known for two hybrid language forms: Surzhyk (a mixture of Russian and Ukrainian) and Trasianka (a mixture of Russian and Belarusian). The very names of these varieties mean that these forms are perceived as a mix of something. *Surzhyk* means a flour or bread made of mixed grains (e.g., wheat and rye), and *Trasianka* means a low-quality mix of fresh grass and last year's hay. These forms are considered colloquial and nonstandard, and the frequency of their use varies based on the speakers' educational status and their region, as well as the social context of the conversation. Balachka, a group of Ukrainian dialects spoken by the Cossacks along the Kuban River, also features a certain degree of hybridization through the incorporation of Russian words. The Motolian dialect, spoken in West Polesia, features some hybridization as well through the incorporation of elements from all three main East Slavic languages in addition to Polish.

As we have discussed, languages are embedded in the social fiber of their cultures. When those languages begin to be spoken outside of their native cultures, they can change. Russian and all other Slavic languages have heritage language forms used by the second and further generations of immigrants. These are hybrid forms that mix elements of the Slavic language in question and the main language or languages of the country of immigration. Traditionally, Slavic immigrants are found in the greatest numbers in English-speaking and German-speaking countries, and less so in the French-speaking world. These heritage language forms will consequently be Slavic-based hybrids with English, German, or French elements, for example.

There are other kinds of hybrid forms, too. In the sphere of high culture, there are the Russian redaction of Old Church Slavonic and various East Slavic redactions of Church Slavonic, which became the language of Orthodox Christian rites. The term *redaction* (used in the subject literature synonymously with the term *recension*) is used to denote a version of Old Church Slavonic or Church Slavonic in which some elements of local languages are incorporated. The Russian redaction of Old Church Slavonic was a starting point for the incorporation of some features of local languages, starting from the late tenth and early eleventh century. The version that incorporates Russian language features is called the

Russian redaction. Old Church Slavonic is extinct, and it only lives in preserved manuscripts. Church Slavonic, a continuant of Old Church Slavonic after the eleventh century, in contrast, is a living hybrid language, although its use is rather limited. It features several East Slavic redactions: Synodal Russian, Standard Russian, Ukrainian, Rusyn, and Old Moscow (used by Old Believers, i.e., those who follow religious practices before the seventeenth-century reforms in the Russian Orthodox Church). The incorporated elements of local East Slavic languages pertain mostly to their pronunciation (other than that, Old Church Slavonic is considered a South Slavic language).

There have been well over a dozen Russian-based pidgins that have emerged out of necessity between Russian traders, fishermen, and other people in similar roles and the individuals who speak non-Slavic languages in various areas of the vast Russian Empire. Such pidgins include combinations of Russian with Norwegian, English, Chinese, various Indigenous languages of Russia, and even some Indigenous languages of Alaska (from when it was a part of Russia).

Finally, there is also a macaronic variety of Runglish, or Rusenglish—a variety of World Englishes—that is, English with some typically Russian features. Rusenglish is prominently featured in a novel titled *Everything Is Illuminated* by Jonathan Safran Foer. Alex Perchov, one of the two lead characters in the book, repeatedly uses an imaginary English verb *to bile* following the Russian pattern *zholch* 'bile': *zholchit* 'to gall, to irritate,' literally 'to bile.' If the East Slavic language situation looks complicated, the West Slavic branch will add confusion to the complication.

Major West Slavic Languages

There are three distinct subgroups of West Slavic languages: Lechitic, Czecho-Slovak, and Sorbian. Each of these subgroups has its own structural features. For example, the Lechitic languages have retained nasal vowels (*ę* and *ǫ*, which are pronounced like *e* and *o* but with an added feature of pushing the air through the nose). The largest language of the Lechitic subgroup, and the second-largest Slavic language, right after Russian from the East Slavic branch, is Polish. It has 45 million native speakers and more than 5 million second-language speakers. Most Polish speakers are, naturally, in Poland. There also are minority speakers in Lithuania, Belarus, and Ukraine, and there exists a large Polish diaspora in North America and western Europe. The four major Polish dialects are Greater Polish, Lesser Polish, Masovian, and Silesian. There are also what are called New Mixed dialects in the west and north regions of the country, where Poles from various regions of today's Poland, Ukraine, and Lithuania came to replace Germans at the end of World War II.

Czech is the larger of the two living languages from the Czecho-Slovak subgroup. It has over 10 million native speakers, most of them in the Czech Republic, with a minority presence in all neighboring countries and the Balkans, and some diaspora in North America. Colloquial and formal Czech are further apart than in most other related Slavic languages. Two major Czech dialectal groups are Bohemian, spoken in the west and the center of the country, and Moravian, spoken in the east.

Slovak is the smaller brother of this subgroup, with more than 5 million native speakers in Slovakia. It has a minority presence in all neighboring countries and the Balkans, and there is also a Slovak-speaking diaspora around the world. Slovak has three dialects: Western, Central, and Eastern.

There are two Sorbian languages, which are also known as Lusatian languages and were historically additionally known as Wendish; both are spoken in the south of eastern Germany. The first is called Upper Sorbian, spoken in the hilly region in the upper flow of the Spree River and with 40,000 speakers, and the second, spoken to the north of it, is called Lower Sorbian, in the lower flow of the same river and with 10,000 speakers. They have not been disputed, and they are generally not considered microlanguages because they do not stand in a close relationship with a major Slavic language. They definitely belong to small literary languages, given the fact that they do not function in all spheres as do more established Slavic languages and that their realm largely remains restricted to home use. Both languages are currently classified as "definitely endangered" (which represents the second out of four levels of endangerment as defined by UNESCO).

Other West Slavic Languages
The status of Kashubian, from the Lechitic group, with some 100,000 native speakers, spoken in north-central Poland, was disputed until the early twenty-first century. Today, most scholars consider it a separate language and a small literary language, but there are still those who consider it an external dialect of Polish. Sometimes Kashubian is referred to as an ethnolect, a more neutral term that avoids calling it a language or a dialect. Kashubian is listed as "severely endangered" (the third of four categories of endangerment as defined by UNESCO). Recently, there has also been an attempt by its speakers and some linguists to declare Silesian, generally considered a dialect of Polish (and partly of Czech), a separate language. There are extinct Lechitic languages, such as Polabian, which

was spoken by the Slavs along the Elbe River in today's Germany, and Slovincian, spoken in Pomerania, today's northwestern Poland. Polish was combined with Latin in the so-called macaronic Latin in the sixteenth-to-seventeenth-century Polish-Lithuanian Commonwealth. Latin was the lingua franca of the commonwealth, and literary traditions have recorded hybrid Latin-Polish texts in which the authors freely switch between Latin and Polish.

Recently, there have been attempts to declare Moravian, generally considered a dialect of Czech, a separate language. There are similar claims made about Lachian dialects, which are spoken along the border between the Czech Republic and Poland, that they are separate microlanguages. These claims about Lachian are made solely based on the literary work of just one author.

Some consider East Slovak, a literary tradition based on dialects spoken in eastern Slovakia, a separate microlanguage based on an eighteenth-century Protestant literary tradition. In the past, there were unsuccessful attempts to merge Czech and Slovak into the Czecho-Slovak language. This subgroup also has an extinct language, which is called Knaanic, also known as Judeo-Czech or Judeo-Slavic, which was used by the Jews in the Czech region. As intricate as the West Slavic situation appears, it is dwarfed by the complexity of the South Slavic group.

Major South Slavic Languages

There are two major subgroups of South Slavic languages: Western and Eastern. The larger of the two main languages in the Western branch is Serbo-Croatian (Bosnian/Croatian/Serbian), with 21 million speakers in Croatia, Serbia, Bosnia, and Montenegro, with minority speakers in the neighboring countries, as well as a sizeable diaspora all around the world, most notably in Austria, Germany, and the United States. Its major dialects are Kajkavian in the northwest corner of Croatia, Chakavian in the Croatian south, and Shtokavian everywhere else in Croatia, Serbia, Bosnia, and Montenegro.

The other Western South Slavic language is Slovene (or Slovenian), with 2.5 million speakers worldwide. Most of them are in the Republic of Slovenia, and there is a strong minority presence in neighboring Austria and Italy. Its colloquial form is rather far apart from its formal form. As already mentioned, Slovene is marked by a high dialectal fragmentation (as many as seven dialectal groups and thirty-seven dialects).

The largest Eastern South Slavic language is Bulgarian, with some 9 million native speakers in Bulgaria and minorities in neighboring counties. The two major dialectal groups are Western and Eastern. Another living Eastern South Slavic language is Macedonian. There are over 2 million speakers in Macedonia, with minorities in neighboring countries and diaspora all around the world, most notably in Australia and North America. Although most scholars consider it a separate language, historically there were attempts to treat it as a Bulgarian dialect (this will be addressed in chapter 10). Its main dialectal groups are Northern, Southern, Western, and Eastern.

The extinct Old Church Slavonic also belongs to the same subgroup. There is additionally the Bulgarian redaction of Old Church Slavonic and the Bulgarian redaction of Church Slavonic. Church Slavonic texts are encountered in truly unusual spaces in history, such as the Reims Gospel (known also as Texte du Sacre—'sacred text'—in French). This document comprises 47 double-sided pages: 16 in the Cyrillic and 31 in the Glagolitic script and is kept in the cathedral of the French city of Reims. The origin of the document is unknown. It first surfaced in the late fourteenth century, when Charles IV gifted it to the Emmaus Monastery in Prague. It was lost in Prague during the fifteenth-century Hussite Wars and resurfaced in Istanbul, where Charles, Cardinal of Lorraine, bought it in the sixteenth century and donated it to the Reims cathedral. A story, perhaps apocryphal, claims that Henry III of France and several of his successors, including the infamous Louis XIV, took their oath on it. Another story told about the document is that Russian czar Peter the Great visited Reims in 1717 and was able to read the text's Cyrillic segments. To add to the controversy, it is unresolved to which redaction the text belongs. A rich tapestry of history, real and possibly imagined, envelops this short parchment manuscript.

Other South Slavic Languages
The description of Western South Slavic languages is much more complicated than it was presented in the previous section. First, there is debate over the formal status of the language traditionally called Serbo-Croatian (in recent decades also known as BCS for Bosnian/Croatian/Serbian or BCMS for Bosnian/Croatian/Montenegrin/Serbian). It features four ethnic standards—Serbian, Croatian, Bosnian (also known as Bosniak), and Montenegrin. Linguistically, they are less different from each other than are British and American English—there are only a handful of marginal structural differences, and there are approximately 2 percent to 3 percent lexical differences, where in many instances a difference is a matter of preference for one form over another, rather than acceptance of one form and rejection of another. Politically, however, they are considered separate standard languages. Those who are more linguistically minded consider Serbo-Croatian to

be a polycentric language with several ethnic standards (i.e., a standard variety that is normed in several separate centers, just like English). Those who are more politically minded consider it a macrolanguage that encompasses several ethnic standard languages. This controversy over the status of the language will be explored in depth in chapter 10. I will henceforth use both the traditional linguistic term that many linguists still use and the most common political designation, hence: Serbo-Croatian (Bosnian/Croatian/Serbian), abbreviated S-Cr (B/C/S).

There are, furthermore, various microlanguages in the Western South Slavic subgroup: Resian Slovene, Venetian Slovene, and Molise Croatian in Italy; Burgenland Croatian in Austria; and Prekmurje Slovene (normally considered a dialect of Slovene) in the northeast of Slovenia and neighboring Austria. There are Bunjevac (in northern Serbia) and Shokac (in northeastern Croatia and northern Serbia), both generally considered a part of the Shtokavian dialect, but there have been attempts to elevate them to microlanguages. In addition, Croatian Kajkavian and Chakavian dialects have also developed literary traditions, so they are also considered microlanguages by some. Hybrid languages also exist in this group—Serbian, Croatian, and Bosnian reductions of Old Church Slavonic. There is also the Serbian redaction of Church Slavonic, still used in the Orthodox Church rites. Among extinct languages, most notably there was a hybrid called Slavonic-Serbian, which was used in the Habsburg Empire from the sixteenth to the nineteenth century. Incorporated in it were the features of the Russian reduction of Church Slavonic, the Russian language, and the local Serbian dialects.

There are four microlanguages in the Eastern South Slavic subgroup—Banat Bulgarian, used since the eighteenth century in the Banat region split between Serbia and Romania; Pomak Bulgarian, used by Bulgarian-speaking Muslims in Bulgaria, Greece, and Turkey; Aegean Macedonian, spoken by Slavic Macedonians in northern Greece; and Gora (known also as Gorani, Goranski, and Nashinski), spoken by Slavic-speaking Muslims in Albania, Macedonia, and the disputed territory of Kosovo.

It should be obvious to you now that the question posed at the beginning of this section is unanswerable. If we talk only about living languages defined by linguistic criteria that perform a full range of social functions the way English and many similar languages do, we can say that there are ten Slavic languages: Russian, Ukrainian, Belarusian, Polish, Czech, Slovak, Serbo-Croatian (Bosnian/Croatian/Serbian), Slovenian, Bulgarian, and Macedonian. However, if microlanguages are added to the mix along with small literary languages (Sorbian languages therein), political languages, planned languages, extinct languages, and the hybrid language forms, then that number is five times higher.

All these Slavic languages have developed in their cultural environment, as previously discussed. However, they have also been following their own internal logic of development, seemingly without any relation to their cultural backgrounds. What disappears and emerges are languages and their dialects. What changes are particular elements of the language mechanism.

Chapter Takeaways

We have seen in this chapter that in addition to ten full-blown Slavic languages and two major small literary languages (Upper and Lower Sorbian), there exist myriad other language forms: microlanguages, hybrid language forms, constructed languages, dead languages, disputed language forms, and so on. It should also be clear that there are some cultural differences between mainstream Slavic cultures and their mainstream English-speaking counterparts. These differences are, among other things, reflected in languages that serve those cultures. In their history, Slavic peoples have been exposed to various cultural influences. One consequence is that throughout history they have used various writing systems (Glagolitic; Cyrillic; Latin, including the Gothic variant; Arabic; Hebrew; and Greek), which were eventually reduced to just two: Cyrillic and mainstream Latin.

Chapter Readings

Hall (1959, 1966), Hofstede (2020), and Hofstede and Hofstede (1994) provide theoretical foundations for the parameters relevant in cross-cultural research. Spencer-Oatey (2012) defines culture. Triandis (1995) discusses individualism and collectivism. Two collected volumes offer reviews of individual Slavic languages: Comrie and Corbett (1993) and Sussex and Cubberly (2006). In them, an interested reader will find extensive information about the status of these languages and also about a variety of phenomena in their structures. Introduction to Slavic languages can also be found in Jakobson (1951) and De Bray (1951). Proshina (2012) discusses Slavic Englishes. Rusenglish is prominent in Foer (2002). Kempgen (2015–16) provides tables with various script and fonts used in the history of Slavic languages. Greenberg et al. (2020), an unfolding encyclopedia of Slavic languages and linguistics, provides increasingly encompassing insights into various issues surrounding Slavic languages as new articles are added to it in the years to come.

Nuts and Bolts

2 Water, Whiskey, and Vodka: How Slavic Languages Came to Be

Time as an Axe and a Measuring Tape

Historical linguists are engaged in reconstructions, attempts to establish language forms without their attestation in writing. Historical reconstructions are certainly not photographs of the past stages of development. They are more like idealized representations that make sense based on the limited data we have—something like artists' representations of faraway galaxies and exoplanets. Any language is constantly in a state of flux. Reconstructing language forms that stretch across vast expanses of time and space certainly entails various generalizations.

In historical linguistics, space and time—the two categories that are intricate in and of themselves—need to be construed in terms of their relationship to the generations of speakers of the languages in question. Let us start with time. As Saint Augustine observed, "And each hour passes away in fleeting particles. Whatever of it has flown away is past, whatever remains is future." This notion construes time like an invisible axe that divides the past from the future. This idea needs to be expanded into categories that can account for time as the measure of change, as Aristotle has defined it.

In historical linguistics, two extended notions of time are used. First, there is expanded time. Expansion is based on objective measures (days and/or years) or those that are purely conventional (weeks, months, and centuries). It is also possible to define these units of time based on similarities of the features within a unit of time and their differences toward preceding and following units of time. That is how we speak about old, middle, and modern ages. Historical linguistics uses this latter notion of time. The difference between the mechanistic and substantive division of time can be seen in the disparity between the traditional notions of the nineteenth and twentieth centuries on the one hand, and Eric Hobsbawm's idea of the long nineteenth century (1789–1914) and short twentieth century (1914–91) on the other. The latter notion is based on pivotal historical events—the French

Revolution; the beginning of World War I, during which major European empires would disappear; and the fall of the Communist Bloc. Historical linguistics uses periods and ages; they are not marked by pivotal events. Instead, the mass of critical changes is what separates one historical linguistic period from another. The borders between periods and ages are soft and fuzzy. The changes are constant, and, for long periods of time, new forms coexist with those that they are eventually going to replace. The idea of historical linguistic periods and their succession is akin to Thomas Kuhn's idea of normal science versus the paradigm shifts. Kuhn believed that there are time periods in which there is relative stability, what he called normal science. In contrast, there are periods in which the existing paradigms of thinking are replaced with new ones. He called these periods paradigm shifts. In historical linguistics, the replacement of one period with another is akin to Kuhn's paradigm shifts.

Time can also be construed to include a social context. In this approach, time is determined by what is new in it. This is the neoteric time, the second important extension of time in historical linguistics. For example, if we think about the 1970s, particular hairstyles and apparel come to mind. Similarly, in historical linguistics, we can talk about the periods of rapid lexical changes caused by technological developments or the patterns of regional and global dominance.

These two notions of time, expanded and neoteric, are at the heart of two approaches to linguistic changes: internal and external language histories. The former approach focuses on the internal language changes that happen without straightforward societal triggers. Changes in sound, inflections, and syntax are mostly of this nature. Except for some marginal contact-induced phenomena, it is impossible to say why languages abandon certain sounds and acquire new ones or why they simplify or lose inflections of their words. In external language history, the focus is on the changes triggered by the sociocultural context of a language in question. These mostly concern the lexicon—new words appear and old ones disappear as a result of technological progress, new ideas in society, changes in social organization, and so on. Similarly, words are lent and borrowed as a consequence of various conquests. For example, the English lexicon is largely Romanized as a result of the Norman Conquest. There are also patterns of regional and global dominance. For instance, various languages have borrowed English words because of the relatively recent global dominance of the English language. External language history is also connected to some epilinguistic elements, that is, those elements that do not belong to the linguistic system but still have some relation to it. These are elements like gestures and writing scripts, which are traded between cultures just like words are.

Both external and internal language histories are so-called diachronic linguistic approaches because they investigate language changes over time. Studying the contemporary state of a language, in contrast, is called synchronic linguistics. Famous early twentieth-century structuralist linguist Ferdinand de Saussure compared the diachronic approach to making a lengthwise cut through the stalk of a plant so that we can see how the plant has grown. The synchronic approach is making the lengthwise cut on the top of the stalk so that we can see the relationships between the parts of its structure.

In the history of Slavic languages, one typically differentiates three major periods: the Proto-Indo-European, the Proto-Slavic (some also call it Common Slavic; others reserve this designation just for a later phase of Proto-Slavic, usually calling this later phase Late Common Slavic), and then the periods of individual Slavic languages that are typically divided into old and modern periods (e.g., Old Russian and Old Polish vs. Modern Russian and Modern Polish). Various timelines have been proposed over the course of Indo-European and Slavic research. The timeline that has the most proponents claims that Indo-European unity existed by the end of the third millennium BCE, after which that language community split into various families during the second and first millennium BCE. The common Slavic period then lasted from the end of the third millennium BCE until the fourth through the sixth century CE, when the migrations of the group that would eventually be known as Southern Slavs from eastern to southern Europe caused the split of the Common Slavic community. The aforementioned controversial Balto-Slavic community would be situated in the second millennium BCE.

Change as the Only Steady Thing

The basic unit of historical linguistics is change. Change assumes that in the same context, a unit that existed at an earlier point in time is replaced by another unit. For example, if we compare the modern standard English *I was* with the Middle English *Ich wæs*, a previous stage in the development of English, we can see that the *ch* sound in *ich* was replaced with nothing (i.e., it was dropped) and that *æ* (as in *cat*) was replaced with *a*, pronounced as either *wʌz* (as in *sun*), or *wɒz* (as in *wash*), or unstressed *wəs* (as in -*er* in words like *better*). The initial unit (a sound, an ending, a word, etc.) that can be found at an earlier point in time is called the source; the unit that replaces it at a later point of time is its reflex. In this example, *ch* has Ø (i.e., nothing) as its reflex (i.e., it turns into nothing), and *æ* (as in *cat*) is the source for three different reflexes ʌ (as in *gut*), ɒ (as in *wash*), and ə (as in *-er* in words like *better*). It can also happen that several different sources merge into one reflex. For example, in some Slavic languages, the sound *e* comes from the Proto-Slavic *e*, from *ę* (nasal e, as in the French word for hand: *main*), and from *ě* (the so-called *yat'*, probably a sound akin to *a* in the English word *bad*, with the previous very short *y* sound as in *yes*). Linguistic changes are nothing like political regime changes—they do not happen abruptly, and a typical scenario is a period of coexistence of the new form with the old. One can see this in today's English. The object relative pronoun *whom* is in the process of being replaced with the *who* form. Most speakers today say, *the friend who I met* but there will still be some users of English who say, *the friend whom I met*. We are thus in the process of change, and it is likely that the number of speakers using *who* instead of *whom* will grow until *whom* is phased out altogether.

All changes are not equal. Some of them just change the frequency of the elements in the system. For example, the fact that some speakers of English pronounce the word *picture* in the same manner as the word *pitcher*, that is, they drop the *k* sound, does not really change anything in the system. The sound *k* still exists in words like *cat*, *rock*, and twice in the word *click*. These changes are known as quantitative changes because they only change the frequency (i.e., the quantity) of the elements of the system.

In contrast, some changes do alter the nature of the system. For example, almost all Slavic languages lost the aforementioned *ę* sound (nasal *e*, as in the French word for 'hand': *main*) and replaced it with a simple vowel or a sound sequence in all of its positions. This is an example of a qualitative change because a unit has been eliminated from the system and the quality of the system has been changed. This kind of qualitative change is called reduction. The opposite is also possible—that the essence of a qualitative change is an emergence of a new unit. The same sound *ę* was not present in the Proto-Indo-European period, and it emerged as something characteristic of Proto-Slavic. This is called extension in the sense that the system extended the repertoire of its units. The situation of going from the Proto Indo-European state without nasality via the Proto Slavic state with nasality back to the present-day state in almost all Slavic languages without nasality is known as a linguistic cycle. These processes are not limited to the sounds or inflectional forms. The meanings of words follow the same principles—new ones emerge, typically by semantic transfer (as in calling a new appliance a *printer* because it does the same job as the craftsman), broadening (e.g., calling any adhesive bandage a Band-Aid), or narrowing (e.g., *deer* used to mean 'animal,' and then its meaning narrowed down to a specific species). Certain kinds of meaning also disappear, as can be seen in the example of the 'animal' meaning for *deer*. The simplest possible model of semantic transfer postulates the source domain (the initial meaning), the target domain (the new meaning), and the link between them. For example, the source domain of 'human leg' has yielded the target domain of a 'table leg,' and the link between them is that the leg of the table looks roughly like a human leg and partially serves the same purpose (supports something).

The Space of Speaking: The Not-So-Ultimate Frontiers

Languages exist not only in time but also in space. In space, languages are areas in which various key linguistic features overlap. For example, if we look at the English-French linguistic border in Canada, we find scores of features that define the border—certain words are used and others are not, certain sounds are pronounced and others do not exist, grammatical features are different, and so forth. Thus, the area of the French language will be defined by the overlapping features of certain words that are used (e.g., *main* and not *hand*), certain sounds (e.g., vowels pronounced with concurrent passage of the stream of air through the nose, as in *main* 'hand'), the widespread presence of the grammatical gender (*main* 'hand' is feminine, i.e., 'she,' not 'it'), and many, many others that do not cross into the territory of the English language.

There is an eternal, unanswerable question of what the difference between a language and a dialect is. As will be discussed in chapter 10, Max Weinreich, a scholar of Yiddish, supposedly once noted that a language is a dialect with an army and a navy, which points to the fact that the distinction is indeed arbitrary and nonlinguistic because it depends on political power. With this in mind, we can think of dialects as tied to geographical areas where certain linguistic features are found. For example, in most of Canada and parts of eastern New England, diphthongs (complex vowels) found in, say, the pronunciation of the words *price*, *hike*, or *about* is somewhat higher (narrower) than in regions farther south, which makes *about* pronounced by Canadians who have this feature sound like *a boot* to speakers of American English. In fact, the real pronunciation is different from the impression the speakers of American English have, but that is a side issue here. This phenomenon is called Canadian raising. There is an area where this phenomenon has spread and that area is encircled by a line, which separates it from other areas where that phenomenon cannot be found. That line is called the isogloss.

In the case of dialects and languages, areas of many critical features typically overlap, and the area of the language is encircled with a bundle of isoglosses. However, it is also common for isoglosses to cross language borders and dissect language areas. For example, in the East South Slavic area, there is a bundle of isoglosses that clearly separates Serbian from Bulgarian dialects and a fan of isoglosses in the realm of Macedonian dialects, where some features are shared with Serbian and others with Bulgarian.

What Are Linguistic Spaces Made of?

Numerous factors determine the geographical spread of languages and dialects and their fragmentation. Slavic languages are very different in terms of how fragmented their dialects are. Russian (in a country two times bigger than the United States) features only two major dialects, whereas Slovene (in a tiny country almost 500 times smaller than the United States) is highly fragmented into seven dialectal groups with seemingly countless dialects. The spread and the fragmentation of the dialects and languages are influenced by the following factors.

First, the nature of the terrain plays an important role. In vast flatlands, the speakers spread more and language forms tend to be less fragmented because there is more contact between the speakers. In rugged insurmountable areas, the speakers are more likely to stay in place with a separation from other speakers, leading to a higher degree of fragmentation as each of the separated communities starts to develop its idiosyncratic linguistic features. Economic resources are also important factors in the spread and fragmentation of dialects and languages. If these resources are abundant, people stay in place and eventually become more isolated from other speakers. If the resources are scarce, they move and mix with other people. The same is true of political circumstances; people tend to move during times of war and stay in place in peaceful times. Another key factor is the existence of a central authority or absence thereof. Areas encompassed by some central authority (using the language in question) make their language less fragmented due to the influence of such an authority. Some of these regularities may not be true anymore in some societies due to the effects of globalization. However, they were certainly at work when Slavic languages and their dialects were formed.

These factors can explain the difference between the low fragmentation in Russian (Rus.) versus the high fragmentation in Slovene. Russia (more precisely, its European part, which is the homeland of the Russian language) is mostly flat, whereas Slovenia is mountainous. The Russian statehood is very old, whereas the first Slovenian central authority was established in the 1990s. Wars and quests for resources were more common in Russia than in Slovenia. Another example of how these factors interplayed in the spread of dialects is provided by the so-called East Herzegovinian dialect of S-Cr (B/C/S). It spread along the north-south axes because of economic factors (descending from the austere Dinaric Mountains into fertile plains) and along the east-west axes for political reasons (fleeing from the Ottoman Turkish Conquest).

Linguists as Biologists and Romanticists

We tend to talk about languages as if they were people. There are language families with their genealogical trees, and with mother and sister languages attached to them. For example, there is a family of Germanic languages, to which English, German, Dutch, and many other languages belong. One can draw a tree, where Proto-Germanic—a mother language for all of them—branches into English, German, Dutch, and other sister languages. We also talk about language death and dead languages. One such language is Sanskrit, a language of ancient sacred scripts of India. This anthropocentric perspective is a consequence of a prevailing biologism in the science of the late eighteenth century and early nineteenth, when learned heads of the period took interest in the relations between some of the world's 7,000 languages.

The interest in the study of languages at that time was a direct consequence of the previous colonial conquests and contacts with Indigenous populations. It is then no wonder that the first impulse for the study of kinship ties and family resemblances between some of the world's languages came from the British Empire, on which the "sun never set" in those times. It was Sir William Jones, a learned man and philologist with a record of service as a judge in Bengal, who, in a lecture at the Asiatic Society in London in 1786, postulated that Sanskrit, Greek, Latin, Old Persian, Gothic, and Celtic may have a common ancestor. Although there were some earlier stipulations in a similar vein, such as the ones by an early seventeenth-century Dutch professor at Leiden University, Marcus Zuerius van Boxhorn, it is Jones's lecture that initiated a tradition of scholarship in documenting kinship between languages and their families.

This extended language family stretches, in its precolonial expanse, from Iceland to Sri Lanka. Eventually, this language family was named Indo-European, after the southeasternmost and the northwesternmost territories of its wide geographical spread. The colonial interest in all things exotic and "Oriental" encountered the fertile ideological ground of early Romanticism of that time, which, in the context of the study of languages was represented in the ideas of Johann Gottfried von Herder and, in particular, Wilhelm von Humboldt. They claimed that each language encapsulates a view of the world characteristic of its ethnic group. The Romanticist idea of the naturalness of ethnic groups and their conception of letters (including folklore and belles lettres) as ultimate forms in which the ethnicities express themselves are together another powerful source that gave rise to an anthropocentric and biological view of related languages.

A cohort of nineteenth-century scholars—such as Danes Rasmus Rask and Karl Verner, along with Germans Jacob Grimm, Franz Bopp, and August Schleicher—should be credited for developing scientific principles in linguistic analysis. Slavic languages are one of the families within this vast Indo-European clan.

Until the mid-twentieth century, the interest in Slavic languages remained dominated by the study of historical links between Slavic languages and their broader Indo-European context. Among the prominent scholars were Josef Dobrovský, Pavel Jozef Šafárik, August Leskien, Aleksey Shakhmatov, Antoine Meillet, André Vaillant, and many others (some Slavs, and some not, as one can infer from their names). These linguistic investigations were largely based on Romanticist ideas about the closeness of Slavic peoples, culminating in the political agenda of a Slavic unity, called Pan-Slavism, with Šafárik as one of its early proponents.

Brotherhood Imagined

Linguistic kinship is then just a part of general ethnic brotherhood. A serious challenge to this understanding of the Slavic ethnic identity was recently offered by Florin Curta, who showed that the idea of Slavic ethnicity was far younger and much less clear than previously believed: "The first clear statement that 'we are Slavs' comes from the twelfth-century *Russian Primary Chronicle*" (Curta 2001:350). The idea of Slavdom is based on genetic and structural similarities between Slavic languages and, to a lesser extent, cultures. The range of this concept is not problematic—it extends to cover the speakers of all Slavic languages. The problematic question at hand is if linguistic similarities mean cultural similarities. The territories of Slavic languages feature a high degree of diversity. Geographically and climatically, they range from Mediterranean landscapes in the south to polar tundra in the north. Historical differences are no less important—Slavic peoples were a constitutive part of various European, Middle Eastern, and central Asian empires, and they exhibited considerable differences as to the emergence and duration of their own statehood. Finally, among Slavic peoples we find Orthodox Christianity, Catholicism, Protestantism, Islam, and various less commonly practiced religious systems. The question is then if one can talk about Slavdom as a cultural category and a type of identity. Mere structural and genetic similarities of languages surely do not suffice to prove cultural similarity. One should note that during human events, one can find areas and periods of strong feelings of Slavic unity (in many areas in the context of the nineteenth-century national revivals of Slavic peoples and their resistance to Germanization or German geopolitical influences) but also ongoing conflicts between Slavic peoples (e.g., rebellions of Poles against Russian rule). It is important to realize that the idea of Slavic cultural unity is complicated and even controversial.

Slavic Cousins and Indo-European Second Cousins Once Removed

What remains uncontested is the genetic similarity of the Slavic languages (i.e., that they have developed from the same ancestor language) and the similarities in their vocabularies and grammars. The same is true for their overarching clan of Indo-European languages. Major Indo-European families include Germanic languages (English, German, Dutch, Swedish, etc.), Italic languages (Spanish, Italian, French, Romanian, and many others), Slavic languages (Russian, Polish, Bulgarian, and others), Iranian languages (Persian, Dari, etc.), and Indo-Aryan languages (Hindi/Urdu, Bengali, Sinhalese, etc.—called "Indian" on the map). In addition to these families, there are also language families with a limited number of languages—such as Anatolian, Celtic, and Baltic—and also languages that form a family on their own (e.g., Armenian, Greek, and Albanian). The maps with the geographical distribution of Indo-European language families are provided in figure 2.1.

It should be stated that the upper map in figure 2.1 reflects the distribution of Indo-European language groups prior to European colonial expansions, which considerably enlarged the territory where Indo-European languages are used. Spanish spread to Central and South America, Portuguese to South America, English to North America and Australasia, and Russian to Asia. Spanish, Portuguese, and English, along with French, are also present in Africa. As a matter of fact, the very state depicted in the upper map in figure 2.1 is a result of various movements of people, such as enormous expansion of Italic languages from a

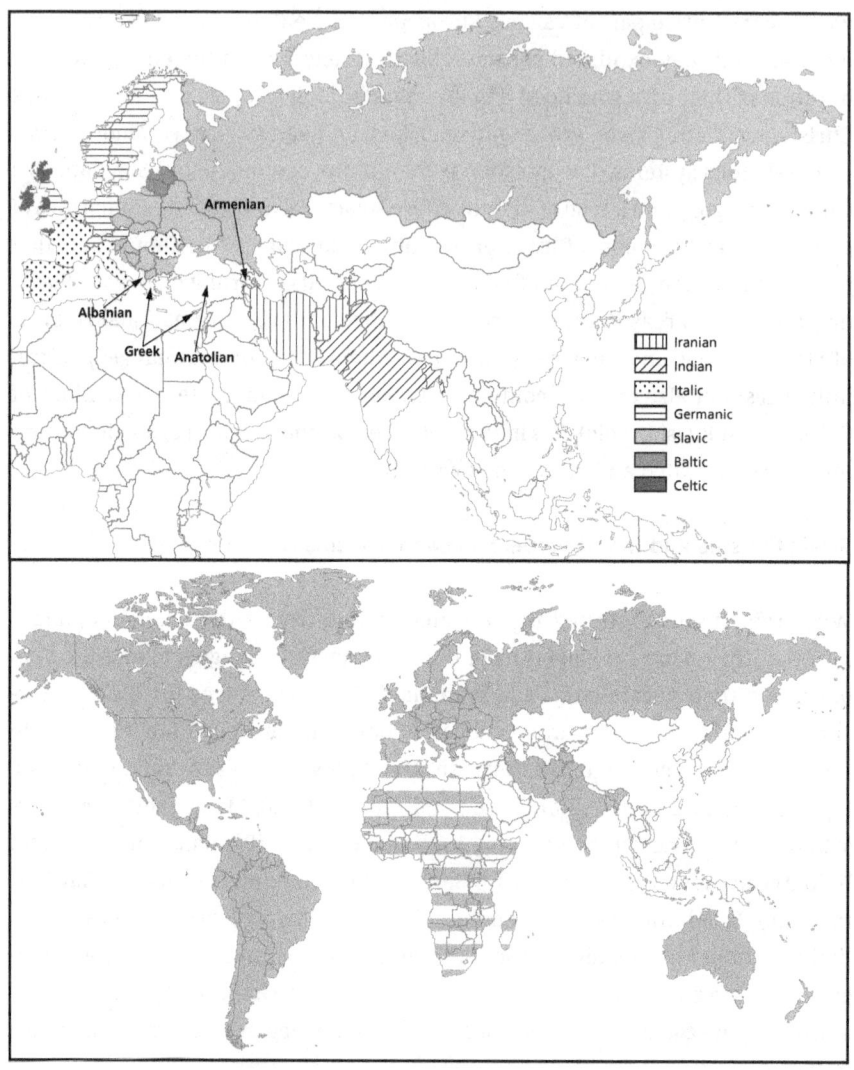

Figure 2.1. Geographical Distribution of Indo-European Languages

limited area in today's central Italy to nearly the entire region of southern Europe and vast westward and southward movements of the Slavic peoples originating from an area on the border between today's Belarus and Ukraine.

While the division into families like Germanic, Slavic, and so on is more widely known, there is another binary division of Indo-European languages primarily based on one development in phonology. In one group of Indo-European languages, the sounds $\acute{k}$ and $\acute{g}$ (palatalized k and g, pronounced with concurrent softness on the hard palate, as if pronouncing the y sound, as in *yes*, right after the k and g) have lost their softness and turned into a sound pronounced in the back of the mouth cavity like h and g, respectively. Meanwhile, in the other group, they turned into the consonants pronounced by friction of the stream of air further to the front of the mouth cavity, on the teeth as in s and z. The first group is called Centum languages and the second Satem languages. The terms themselves come from the word for 100—*centum* (pronounced: *kentum*) in Latin, and *satem* in Avestan (an ancient Iranian language). With some minor exceptions, Centum languages are in the west of the Indo-European space, and Satem languages are in the east. One can see this in English-Russian word pairs that have developed from the same root and have the same meaning, for example, h̲eart: s̲erdce. Of the major families, Germanic, Italic, and Celtic are Centum; whereas Slavic, Baltic, Iranian, and Indo-Aryan are Satem. It is interesting to note that in this Centum-versus-Satem classification, Slavic languages stand closer to Hindi than to English.

Kinship Disputes

When Slavic linguistic kinship is discussed, there exists a controversial issue of the so-called Balto-Slavic community. What is disputed here is the claim that Baltic languages (Lithuanian, Latvian, and the extinct Old Prussian) formed a linguistic community with Slavic languages. What is undisputed is that there are numerous phonological and inflectional features shared by Baltic and Slavic languages, so among Indo-European second cousins the Baltic languages are the most closely related to Slavic languages. What has been controversial is the question of whether the similarities are the result of the previous Balto-Slavic community or a function of the adjacency of the two separate communities (Baltic and Slavic) and their contacts.

The relationships between the languages within the Indo-European family are generally accepted and uncontroversial. There is also a hypothesis about the genetic links between the Indo-European family and various other language families within the so-called Nostratic macrofamily. This term was proposed by Holger Pedersen, a Danish linguist, more than one hundred years ago. It remains controversial. According to Pedersen and his followers in the intervening period, Indo-European languages form the Nostratic macrofamily with the Uralic (including Finnish, Hungarian, etc.), Altaic (Turkish, Mongolian, etc.), Kartvelian (Georgian, etc.), Afroasiatic (Arabic, Hebrew, etc.), Koreanic (Korean and some extinct relatives), and Dravidian (Tamil, Telugu, etc.) families (with other families added by some researchers).

Some examples, even within the broader Indo-European family let alone the Slavic one, offer strikingly obvious examples of kinship. For example, the English word *three* sounds very similar to *tri* found in Sanskrit and many Slavic languages; *tre* in Italian, Albanian, and Tocharian; and *tres* in Latin and Spanish. Nevertheless, establishing kinship ties between Slavic and Indo-European languages is a result of the painstaking work of many generations of linguists, which will be discussed in the next section.

Drawing the Genealogical Tree

What has attracted early comparativists to the study of the Indo-European languages and then Slavic and other Indo-European branches is similarities in the lexicon. The several areas of widespread Indo-European similarities include kinship terms, body parts, animal and plant names, basic features and actions, numbers, and pronouns. In some cases, these similarities are evident right away and even to an untrained eye. In other cases of widespread resemblances, establishing cross-linguistic connections may include accounting for phonological and semantic changes. To take body parts as an example, the similarity between English *nose* and Slavic *nos* (well-known from an eponymous Gogol short story) is visible to the naked eye. In contrast, English *eye* vs. Slavic *oko* and English *ear* vs. Slavic *uho* are explained by phonological changes that have made these English-Slavic equivalents, which stem from the same Indo-European root, so different. The phonology of English *water* vs. Slavic *vodka* is rather straightforward, whereas the semantic aspect of these two cognates is more complicated. Things get dramatically more complicated if we add Celtic *whiskey*, which has developed from the same source, because this word does not sound very similar to either *water* or *vodka*. The same is true of English *tooth* and Russian *desna*, or gums, where one needs to explain the different meaning in addition to the different sound. A further example of the same category is offered by the English *queen* and its Slavic cognate *žena* 'wife/woman.'

Following are some further examples of material from various Indo-European languages that a historical linguist might encounter in making reconstructions. (For the pronunciation of various sounds, see the appendix.) There are English-Slavic pairs in which we can see straightforward links between the form and meaning. In other Indo-European examples, provided after English-Slavic pairs, the meaning could be different, which is appropriately indicated (otherwise, the meaning is the same as in the English-Slavic pairs). The first pair is *mother* vs. *mater* 'mother'; Proto-Indo-European (henceforth, PIE) *$méh_2tēr$ 'mother,' Hindi/ Urdu *mā*, Persian *mādar*, Gre. *mitéra*, Lat. *māter*, Ger. *Mutter*, Albanian *motër* 'sister,' Latvian *māte* 'mother,' Rus. *mat'* 'mother.' The second example of this category is *milk* vs. *mleko* 'milk'; PIE $h_2melĝ$- 'milk,' Albanian *miel* 'to milk,' Lithuanian *melžti* 'to milk,' Lat. *mulgeō* 'I milk,' Ger. *Milch* 'milk,' Rus. *moloko*. Further examples include *sister* vs. *sestra* 'sister,' *son* vs. *sin* 'son,' *me* vs. *me* 'me,' *new* vs. *nov* 'new,' *water* vs. *voda* 'water,' and *three* vs. *tri* 'three.' There are also English-Slavic pairs where the meaning is straightforward, but the form is quite different. The first example of this is *feather* vs. *pero* 'feather'; PIE *$péth_2r̥$ 'wing, feather,' Danish *fjer* 'feather,' Armenian *t'er* 'leaf,' Lat. *penna* 'wing, feather,' Irish *éan* 'bird,' Gre. *pterōtós* 'winged,' Rus. *pero* 'feather.' In these examples, obfuscating phonological changes are mostly in English, with one reduction in Slavic. Semantic changes are present but not in English or Slavic. (Slavic languages do have extensions into 'quill' and 'pen,' but a principal PIE sense is preserved.) The significant differences in form with similar meanings are also found in *four* vs. *četyre* 'four'; PIE *$k^ṷetṷores$ 'four,' Albanian *katër* 'four,' Armenian *čʿors* 'four,' Latvian *četri* 'four,' Welsh *pedwar* 'four,' Lat. *quattuor* 'four,' Ger. *vier* 'four,' Persian *čahâr* 'four,' and Sanskrit *catur* 'four.' Further examples include *name* vs. *imja* 'name,' *who* vs. *kto* 'who,' *two* vs. *dva* 'two,' *hundred* vs. *sto* 'hundred,' *tongue* vs. *jazyk* 'tongue,' and *heart* vs. *serdce* 'heart.'

Contrary to the previous examples, in the next two examples involving various Indo-European languages, the forms of the words are similar but the meanings quite different. The first example of this category can be seen in the English-Slavic pair *mead* vs. *med* 'honey'; PIE *$méd^hu$ 'honey, honey wine,' Gre. *methu* 'wine,' Welsh *medd* 'mead,' Swedish *mjöd* 'mead,' Latvian *medus* 'honey, mead,' and Sanskrit *madhu* 'mead, honey.' Out of the two PIE senses, one became dominant in English, the other in Slavic languages. The second example is the English-Slavic pair *same* vs. *sam* 'alone, self'; PIE *$somHós$ 'same,' Scottish *samin* 'same, like, together,' Dutch *samen* 'together,' Danish *samme* 'same,' Gre. *homos* 'same,' Sanskrit *sama* 'same, like, smooth,' and Persian *ham* 'also, same.' In this case, semantic changes happened within the Slavic languages. Further English-Slavic examples include *wit* vs. *videt'* 'to see,' *bear* vs. *brat'* 'to take,' and *meal* vs. *melju* 'I grind.'

Finally, to make things miserable for historical linguists, there are cases, like the two that follow, in which the form and the meaning alike are very different.

The first example of this challenging situation is the English-Slavic pair *timber* vs. *dom* 'home'; PIE **dem-* 'to build,' **dōm-* 'home,' Lat. *domus* 'home,' Gre. *dōmos* 'house,' Sanskrit *dām* 'house,' Armenian *tun* 'building,' Icelandic *timbur* 'timber,' Ger. *Zimmer* 'room,' and Albanian *dhomë* 'room.' The difference is a consequence of the initial PIE differentiation and further changes in English, both semantic and phonological. The second English-Slavic example of this category is *quick* vs. *živ* 'alive'; PIE **gʷihₐṷos* 'alive,' Dutch *kwik, kwiek* 'quick,' Swedish *kvick* 'quick,' Gre. *bíos* 'life,' Lat. *vivus* 'alive,' Lithuanian *gývas* 'alive,' Welsh *byw* 'alive,' Kurdish *jîn* 'to live,' Sanskrit *jīva* 'living,' and Albanian *nxit* 'to urge, stimulate.' In these examples, the Slavic languages feature substantial phonological changes, whereas semantic change is found in English. Further cases of this English-Slavic situation are, among others, *kind* vs. *žena* 'wife,' *can* vs. *znati* 'to know,' *foot* vs. *pod* 'under,' *tooth* vs. *desna* 'gums,' *corn* vs. *zrno* 'seed,' and *eastern* vs. *jutro* 'morning, tomorrow.'

Just like in any other genealogical tree, the idea is that what is related developed from the same source. Some of the interesting examples of cognates between English and Slavic languages that have undergone semantic changes include English *same* vs. Slavic *sam* 'self, alone,' *corn* vs. *zrno* 'grain,' *meal* vs. *mleti* 'grind,' *quick* vs. *živ* 'alive,' *wit* vs. *wiedzieć* 'to know,' *can* vs. *znati* 'to know,' *light* vs. *luč* 'torch,' *timber* vs. *dom* 'house,' *home* vs. *sem'ya* 'family,' and *eastern* vs. *jutro* 'morning' (the Slavic examples are from various present-day Slavic languages). Sometimes, the links between words are unexpected. Thus, as already noted, English *water*, Celtic *whiskey*, and Slavic *vodka* all stem from the same Indo-European word for water (whiskey is from *uisge beatha* 'the water of life,' *vodka* is 'small water').

The Guesswork Network

The process of determining a common source for related words is called reconstruction. Reconstruction assumes that the form being established is not attested (not found in records such as written documents). The periods of unity of Indo-European and Slavic languages alike fall into the confines of time without literacy in those language families. With no written records, historical linguists resort to a range of reconstruction techniques to establish the lexical sources underpinning the similarities within language families.

The first of these techniques is an obvious one—the comparative method, that is, using the hypothesis about genetic relationship between languages within the Indo-European family to account for similarities in examples from these languages. This method eventually leads to finding the hypothetical source by comparing related words from the same language family. For example, if we look at the words for 'nose' in Indo-European languages, we will find a great number of languages where this word starts with the sound *n*, e.g., *nos* in Slavic languages, Sanskrit *nāsa*, Ger. *Nase*, Lat. *nasus*, and Lithuanian *nosis*. It is reasonable to assume that their protolanguage had the *n* sound. The chance that all these languages have developed that sound independently from one another is slim to none. Nevertheless, in most cases, reconstruction by the comparative method is more complex than in the presented case. As noted, the phonology and the semantics of the corresponding words thought to be developed from the same source are often different, sometimes very different. This difference necessitates the establishment of phonological and semantic correspondences and their contexts. If we compare English *ten*, *two*, and *tooth* with Russian *desjat'*, *dva*, and *desna* (or Lat. *decem*, *duo*, and *dent-*, or the same roots in many other Indo-European languages), we eventually conclude that the initial *t* in English corresponds to the initial Russian or Latin *d*. The next step is then to determine the mechanisms of change in one or more observed languages (in this case, the change was in English). To summarize, reconstruction using the comparative method relies not only on mere comparison of related words but also on linguistic laws of changes in certain contexts. The form and meaning of the reconstructed root need to equally include similarities in descendant words as well as phonological and semantic changes over a course of time.

Historical Linguists' Toolkit

A range of other reconstruction tools are also used. Commonly, languages with early writing, which are often sacral tongues, tend to be rather conservative about keeping previous stages of language development. One such Slavic language is called Old Church Slavonic, a common Slavic literary language of the ninth to eleventh century CE. There were the aforementioned national redactions of Church Slavonic later on, but its original version has preserved many features of Proto-Slavic, an ancestor language of all the Slavic languages of today. Similarly, Sanskrit has a comparably special place in Indo-European studies as an ancient and sacred Indo-European written language of India. The speakers of English are certainly familiar with this phenomenon given the conservative forms of pronouns like *thou*, *thy*, *thee*, and *ye* in the Bible (such as the King James version). Another reason Old Church Slavonic texts were important is the mistakes made by the scribes while transcribing texts in that language. These mistakes show that certain changes happened in the living language that the scribes used daily. For example, the two semivowels (sounds akin to the one represented by *e* in the English word *hunter*); the hard (as if an extra short *u* sound, as in *put*), written in the Cyrillic script as ъ; and the soft (as if an extra short *i* sound, as in *pit*), written as ь, are often mixed up in Bosnian, Croatian, and Serbian redactions of Old Church Slavonic and Church Slavonic manuscripts. Their confusion (and the pronunciation of both as an extra short *a* sound, as in *pat*) started in the tenth century, showing that the difference between them was lost in the living language of those scribes.

Additionally, certain conservative living languages tend to keep a record of the previous stages of development—Slovene and Sorbian are such languages in the Slavic branch. For example, they feature three numbers: singular, dual (used for two persons or things), and plural. All other Slavic languages have had this distinction, but then almost all of them reduced it to just singular and plural. Rural dialects are another invaluable source of information for reconstruction because some of them tend to be conservative. For example, in the standard variants of S-Cr (B/C/S) and many dialects, at one point in their history the word stress placement has moved toward the beginning of the word in a host of words. However, certain dialects retain the original word stress placement akin to that in Proto-Slavic, which then provides data for the reconstruction of the previous stress placement.

Place-names are extremely important in historical reconstructions. If they are used long enough, they may represent fossils of the previous stages of development or point to the distribution of speakers in an earlier period. For example, the name of the river Thames probably comes from the Brittonic Celtic *Tamesas*, an Indo-European root related to the Slavic words for *dark* (*taman*, *temny*, etc.). The origin of this and many other place-names can point to a broader distribution of Celtic speakers in previous times.

Internal reconstruction is another common technique. In it, some of the present-day features may point to processes in the past. For example, Slavic languages have an alternation of *a*, *e*, or *o* with zero (i.e., no sound in that place) in the forms of the same word. Thus, in Russian *son* 'a dream,' *sna* 'of a dream,' Polish *sen* vs. *sna*, and S-Cr (B/C/S) *san* vs. *sna* (with the same meaning as in the Russian pair), in the same place in the word, there is an *o*, *e*, or *a* (depending on the language) in the form meaning 'a dream' and Ø (i.e., no vowel) in the form meaning 'of a dream.' For example, Russian has *son* 'a dream' vs. *sØna* 'of a dream.' It turns out that the vowel appears if its syllable is at the end of the word. If there is another vowel behind, there will be no vowel, hence the zero. Knowledge of this present-day alternation has helped to establish the historical development of the so-called *yers* (ъ and ь), that is, the semivowels (previously mentioned ultrashort sounds akin to the sound represented by the letter *e* in the English word *hunter*) that were vocalized in certain positions and that got lost in others.

A neighboring language with an earlier written tradition can also help the language without such a tradition. For example, when the Southern Slavs moved to the Balkans in the sixth and seventh centuries CE, they were several centuries away from having literacy, but Latin, which was also used in the region, had written fixation. Thus, one can judge if a certain historical change has happened or not based on the Latin recordings of Slavic names. For example, Slavic languages featured the process of denasalization, in which nasal vowels *en* and *on* (*e* and *o* pronounced with a concurrent passing of the stream of air through the nose, as the French do to this day) were replaced with a nonnasalized vowel (in the case of Central South Slavic, *e* and *u*, respectively). Thus, depending on the recording that Latin had chronicled at a given moment in time of the Slavic name as *Montimeros* or *Mvtimeros*, one can see if its form was *Mǫtimirə* (with no denasalization) or *Mutimirə* (with the denasalization process completed).

Another productive method for reconstructing the timeline of historical development is the so-called relative chronology. In it, the results of two or more historical processes are used to determine a sequence in time. An example of this reconstruction technique used in Slavic phonology to determine the order of the so-called palatalizations is provided in chapter 3.

Finally, the evidence from nonlinguistic scholarship (archaeology, history, genetics, etc.) is often useful in reconstruction. Most notably, archaeological findings provide helpful insights. Thus, if there exist archaeological findings attesting to, for example, burning a certain kind of wood or using certain animals for food, one can assume that the people in question had the words for that kind of wood or animals. In recent years, genetic data have become increasingly important in tracing historical changes. The same is true for statistical methods. For example, a Bayesian statistical method was used on various occasions to test hypotheses about the location of the Indo-European ancestral lands (Bayes's theorem describes the probability of an event based on the prior knowledge of the conditions that may be related to the event).

Deconstructed Reconstructions

Some reconstruction techniques remain controversial. The best known of those is lexicostatistics, especially deployed in the field of glottochronology. Lexicostatistics relies on creating lists of basic concepts (numbers, pronouns, body parts, etc.) in two or more languages and then looking into the level of their similarities to determine the relationship between the languages. Glottochronology, a step further, determines the time when these languages that are thought to be from the same source separated. The method was proposed by Morris Swadesh in the 1950s. He created a list of 207 very basic concepts (including body parts, colors, actions, and adjectives) that are supposedly culturally neutral. By calculating the percentages of cognancies between the words in the related languages, one can draw their family tree and then determine the glottochronology, the time when they split (the less cognancies, the earlier the split). The general idea is that the more similarities on these lists, the closer the relationship between the languages in question, suggesting that they split from one another closer to the present day. This method remains controversial because it is difficult to create a culturally universal list. Additionally, lexical borrowing, which is random, exists even in a basic vocabulary, and many concepts have synonyms rather than just one word to represent them—all these factors can skew the results.

The Branches of the Tree and Their Leafing

The general idea behind the trees of language families is that two or more languages that bear more similarities than other related languages developed from the same source. Thus, if we look at Russian and Polish, they share more similarities with each other than either of these two shares with Spanish, German, or Hindi, which all also belong to other Indo-European language families. These nonincidental similarities support the idea that Russian and Polish belong to a subgroup within the Indo-European family that is known as Slavic languages. While languages share various similarities—which words they have, what sounds they use to pronounce them, how they string their words together, and so forth— the systems of inflections play a particular role in establishing genetic relationships between languages. Similarities in the development of inflections have been used to assign languages to the Indo-European family and its subgroups ever since William Jones, the first comparativist, began this tradition. The similarities from other areas (sound, meaning, etc.) are also used as supporting evidence.

Among Indo-European languages, the families differ in the time of their first attestation and thus in the moment of time before a need existed to reconstruct previous stages of development. Slavic languages are latecomers to the world of literacy, so reconstruction plays a very prominent role in establishing their historical development. The Anatolian subgroup was the first to have attestation in Hittite cuneiform clay tablets around 1800 BCE. Greek and Indic families followed in 1400 BCE; Romance, Iranian, and Celtic in 500 BCE; Germanic and Armenian in 500 CE; and Slavic as late as 900 CE. However, there are first attestations at an even later point in time—these came from the Baltic subgroup and Albanian around 1500 CE.

The genealogical tree of the Indo-European language family and its Slavic subgroup is difficult to draw because languages change over time and their speakers disperse over time. This will be the topic of the next chapter.

Where Do They All Come From?

Another important and never fully settled issue in Indo-European and Slavic studies concerns the location of the ancestral lands of the Indo-Europeans and Slavs (i.e., the source area of their migrations). Over the years, various theories about the location of the Indo-European homeland (i.e., *Urheimat*) have been proposed based on lexical evidence and archaeological data. Most widely accepted is the so-called Steppe Hypothesis, which places the homeland in the Pontic Steppe between the Dnepr and Ural Rivers north of the Black and Caspian Seas. The best-known competing theory is the Anatolian Hypothesis, which postulates that the dispersion of Indo-European people started in Anatolia, a part of today's Turkey (i.e., somewhat to the southwest from what the Steppe Hypotheses suggests). Figure 2.2 shows the homeland regions as advocated by the two aforementioned theories.

Regarding the Slavic homeland, the theory with the most traction is the so-called Middle-Dnepr Hypothesis, which places Slavic ancestral lands in today's south Belarus and north Ukraine. The most prominent competing theories place the Slavic homeland between the rivers Oder and Vistula (the Oder-Vistula Hypothesis) or in the Pannonian Basin along the Danube River (the Danube-Pannonian Hypothesis). Figure 2.3 shows a map with the areas of the three hypotheses about the Slavic homeland marked. The reason all these are considered merely hypotheses and why there are multiple theories is aptly summarized by Dolukhanov (2013:144): "In summing up the evidence of written sources, linguistics and

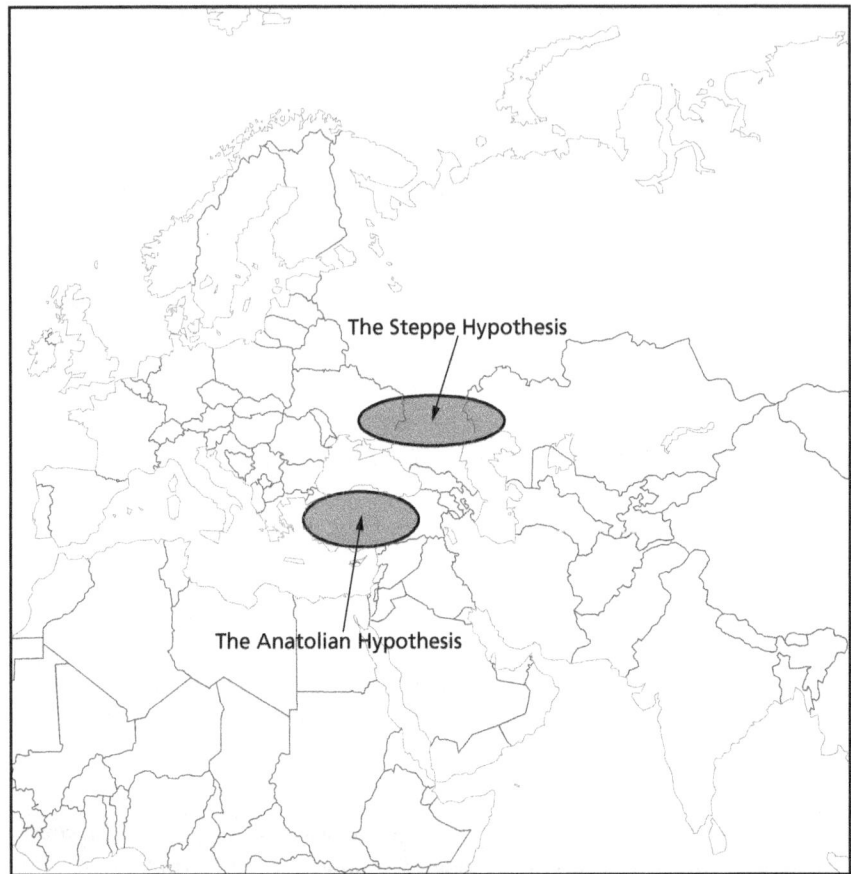

Figure 2.2. Theories about the Indo-European Homeland

physical anthropology one has to emphasize yet again that, in their own right, they fail to provide a reliable basis for a solution to the problem of Slavic origin."

Chapter Takeaways

Linguistic changes happen over time and within a distinct territory. The time segments delimited by a substantive number of changes are called periods. Various historical processes cause a higher or lower density of changes in a unit of space, resulting in a more or less pronounced fragmentation of linguistic varieties, such as dialects. Linguistic changes are typically gradual; the old feature typically

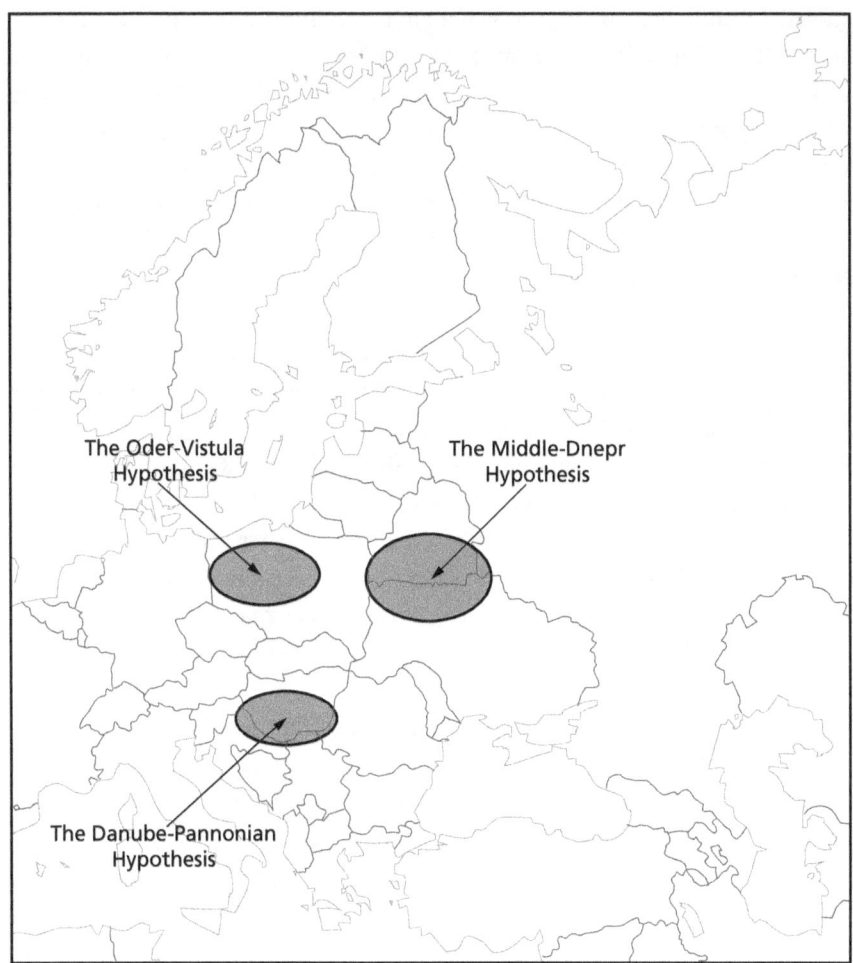

Figure 2.3. Theories about the Slavic Homeland

coexists with the new one for a long period of time. Linguists have developed various techniques to account for similarities between various languages and to group these languages into language families. Slavic languages form a family that has developed from the ancestor language called Proto-Slavic. Along with various other languages of Europe, the Middle East, and India, they belong to an even broader family of Indo-European languages—all of which have developed from the ancestor language called Proto-Indo-European. The most common hypothesis claims that Proto-Indo-European originates from the steppes of today's southern

Russia and Ukraine. This area was monolithic until the end of the third millennium BCE, and it started to disintegrate into Proto-Slavic, Proto-Germanic, and ancestor languages of other Indo-European families during the second and first millennium BCE. Proto-Slavic had its period of unity in its homeland on the border of today's Ukraine and Belarus until the fourth through sixth century CE, when it started to disintegrate into what would eventually become Slavic languages.

Recommended Chapter Readings

There exists a rich body of literature, primarily in Slavic languages, as well as in German and French, relating to the content of this chapter, but here I will include only sources in English because it is the language most accessible to the readers of this book. The quote about time is from Augustine (2006:XV:20).

The notions of the long nineteenth and short twentieth century are discussed in (Hobsbawm 1995, 1996). Paradigm shifts are discussed in Kuhn (1962). A structuralist model of linguistic change is presented in Saussure (1972). Hock (1986) offers a review of methods in historical linguistics. Language change is explored in Bybee (2015). A reader in nineteenth-century historical Indo-European linguistics is offered in Lehmann (1967). Clarkson (2007) and Beekes (2011) represent solid introductory texts to Indo-European linguistics. Schenker (1995) explores the world of Proto-Slavic. Curta (2001) offers further interesting insights into the early world of the Slavs. Dolukhanov (2013) offers a broad review of archaeological data about early Slavs. Another insight into the world of early Slavs is provided by Barford (2001). Dvornik (1956) offers an insight into the state of Slavic studies in the mid-twentieth century. Greenberg et al. (2020) provide increasingly encompassing insights into various issues regarding the historical study of Slavic languages as new articles are added to their text.

3 The Sounds of the Slavs: Like Dancing in the Air

Rustling Russians

To most speakers of English, the sounds of Slavic languages have a rustling (leaves, not cattle) quality. When overhearing a conversation between two speakers of Slavic languages, many inquisitive speakers of English will ask if they speak Russian. This has happened to me about 10,000 times. Russian is, of course, the best-known Slavic language; it eclipses all others. More significantly, large differences in the sounds of Slavic languages will be disregarded, and the massive presence of palatal consonants will lead speakers of English to equate whatever Slavic language they hear with Russian. This equation is obviously wrong, but the rustling part is true. Starting with the disintegration of the Indo-European community at the beginning of the first millennium BCE (as discussed in the previous chapter), the sounds of Slavic languages have departed from those in English and other Germanic languages. Then, starting with the third to fourth century CE, an additional Interslavic differentiation took place, which made the languages' sounds different in the same way we can find, say, between English and Dutch, both Germanic languages that sounded the same during the Proto-Germanic era (from about 500 BCE to 500 CE).

Vowels and More Vowels

If we compare today's Slavic languages with English, we will notice several important differences, such as a very rich system of vowels in English as opposed to systems with a limited number of vowels in Slavic languages or the rustling character of Slavic languages. They are a consequence of diverging lines of development in the time since the disintegration of the Proto-Indo-European language mentioned in the previous chapter. Let us, then, investigate these and other lines of development. The presentation of these developments here is merely a teaser—comprehensive and rigorously presented scholarly information about the sounds of Slavic and Indo-European languages can be found in the sources listed in the recommended chapter readings section.

In this review it is important to keep in mind some of distinctions that you have learned in high school but most likely have forgotten in the intervening period. The sounds of human languages can be vowels or consonants. In vowels, such as *a* in the word *art*, the stream of air does not encounter obstacles on its way out of our mouth or nose. Such obstacles do exist in the case of other sounds, called consonants, such as *b* in *bet*. In this example, our lips form and then abruptly release that obstacle. Many vowels and consonants are pronounced in the mouth cavity. Some of them are pronounced in its front, others in its back. For example, the vowel *u* in *bull* is pronounced in the back and *i* in *bill* in the front. If you pronounce these two sounds one after the other, you will feel your tongue move back and forth. Similarly, the consonant *k* as in *kill* is pronounced by pressing the back of the tongue against the back palate, while *ch* as in *chill* is pronounced by pressing the front of the mouth toward the front palate. Again, when pronouncing them one after the other, you will feel your tongue move back and forth. It is easier to pronounce a sequence of a front consonant and a front vowel, then a back consonant and a front vowel. In the former case our tongue does not have to move; in the latter it does.

The reconstructed PIE sound system featured an extremely high number of vowels. Their variety was equally impressive. First, there were five basic vowels: *a, e, i, o, u*, all of which can be long or short. The next element of the PIE system is reduced vowels (akin to the *e* sound in the English word *hunter*). There were two of them, called schwa primum (transcribed *ə₁*) and schwa secundum (transcribed *ə₂*). Then, there were diphthongs in spades. These are the vowels, such as *y* in *my*, that require a change in the position of speech organs during their pronunciation. In their first part, all of the diphthongs had the vowel *a*, *o*, or *e*, which could be long or short in all cases. What differentiated them was the second part. First, there were vocalic diphthongs, which had the vowels *i* and *u* in the second part. These were nonsyllabic; they were more like *y* in *day* and *w* in *wet*, which is noted as *i* and *u*. Second, there were nasal diphthongs, with *m* and *n* in their second part (nasal, or *nose*, consonants, pronounced with additional passage of the air through the nose). Third, there were liquid diphthongs, with *l* and *r* in the second part (i.e., consonants that "flow" as they are pronounced with only a partial closure of the air passage). There were, finally, liquids and nasals that functioned as vowels when they were not in contact with vowels, schwas, and diphthongs. They are called vocalic liquids and nasals. Functioning like a vowel means that they can form syllables. Their functioning as vowels is marked by a line below them. There were short vocalic liquids and nasals *r̥, *l̥, *m̥, and *n̥ and their long variants *r̥̄, *l̥̄, *m̥̄, and *n̥̄. In most Slavic sources, a ring below is used instead of the line, so *r̥, *l̥,*m̥, *n̥ and r̥̄, *l̥̄, *m̥̄, and *n̥̄. This brings the repertoire of PIE vowels to an impressive sum of twenty-seven or, if we count long and short vowels separately, then it is a staggering fifty-four.

Say It in the Back of Your Mouth and with a Puff

The main features of PIE system of consonants were a large concentration of sounds in the back of the mouth cavity (pronounced by pressing the back of the tongue on the soft palate, i.e., the back part of the palate) and many accompanying features, especially for the consonants *k* and *g*. The most widespread accompanying feature was aspiration. Many consonants had a nonaspirated version (e.g., *p, *t, *b, and *d) and an aspirated version, pronounced with a puff after it, as if saying an ultrashort *h* as in *hot* after the consonant (or the way some English speakers pronounce *p* in *part*), which is marked by a superscript ʰ: *pʰ, *tʰ, *bʰ, and *dʰ. Then, *k* and *g* could be aspirated (kʰ, gʰ), but they could also have palatalized versions (pronounced by pressing the tip of the tongue against the front part of the palate) marked like *ḱ* and *ǵ*, and labialized versions (rounding lips while pronouncing them), marked as: *kᵘ and *gᵘ.

Airy and Laissez-faire Indo-Europeans

There are thus twenty-eight PIE consonants, with a vowel to consonant ratio of 27:28, that is, .96. This reconstructed language was extremely vocalic, even if we do not count short and long vowels separately. Namely it is so because anything above .3 is considered vocalic, and anything below it consonantal. One should also say that there is a hypothesis, widely and increasingly accepted, that PIE also had three laryngeal consonants, produced in the larynx (the voice box) and transcribed as *h₁, *h₂, and *h₃. In this theory, the schwas (*ə₁, *ə₂) are used to represent the laryngeals between the consonants, that is, in the vocalic position. This would make the system slightly less vocalic but still very prominently on the far end of the vocalic spectrum. The reconstructions with the inclusion of the laryngeals are henceforth provided within parentheses in case there is a difference between the reconstructions with and without them. Older works of Slavic scholarship (e.g., various comparative grammars of Slavic languages, a publishing staple in the Slavic world) typically feature reconstructions without the laryngeals.

PIE featured both closed and open syllables (the former end in a consonant, the latter in a vowel). Thus, the syllable in the reconstructed root *$d\underline{u}o$ (*$d\underline{u}oh_1$) that yielded both English *two* and its Proto-Slavic (PSL) counterpart *dva, is open, given that it ends in a vowel. In contrast, the PIE root *$k^u et\underline{u}er$, which yielded the English *four* and PSL *$četyre$, features two closed syllables, each ending in a consonant (*t* and *r*, respectively): *$k^u et | \underline{u}er |$ (the vertical lines here represent division of syllables). In other words, they have had a laissez-faire attitude toward syllable formation.

Leafy and Picky Slavs

During the early part of the first millennium BCE, in the centuries in which the Slavs developed their own linguistic profile, a number of changes in the habits of the speakers thoroughly reshaped the sound system. They parted ways with other Indo-Europeans, whose community split into Germanic, Romance, Celtic, Indo-Arian, and other families. First, the number of vowels and their categories were dramatically reduced. Most notably, the process called monophthongization happened as the Slavs replaced diphthongs with simple vowels (called monophthongs, hence the term for the process) or vowel combinations. This is apparent in examples like the Proto-Slavic root for 'ear,' which is reconstructed as *$\underline{au}s$ (*$h_2\underline{au}s$) and thus contained a diphthong (underlined as are its reflexes). Some language groups retained diphthongs, so Latin had *$\underline{au}ris$* and Greek had *$\underline{oũ}ς$* (*$oũs$*). Proto-Germanic had *$\underline{au}zon$, which yielded the English *$\underline{ea}r$*. In contrast to all these, the PSL form is *$\underline{u}ho$, with a simple vowel in that place rather than a diphthong. This is visible in a number of other examples when we compare Slavic forms with their counterparts in Baltic languages, which have preserved diphthongs: PSL *$r\underline{o}ka$ (without a diphthong) and Lithuanian *$r\underline{an}ka$*, with the *an* in the same position. An additional example is provided by the masculine plural ending, which is *-*i* in some endings in PSL and *-a$\tilde{\imath}$* in Lithuanian, with the diphthong in the position where PSL has a simple vowel.

Second, the Slavs started linking quantity (the length of the vowels) to quality (the way they sound). In PIE, each vowel could be long and short. Their further development in Proto-Slavic depended on their length, that is, quantity. They would evolve into one vowel if they were short and another if they were long, so the quantity determined the resulting vowel type, or the quality. The story of the

PIE sounds *o* and *a* is illustrative in this regard. What used to be a long *o* and long *a* in PIE became a long *a* in PSL. What was a short *o* and short *a* evolved into an *a* in PSL. So, the formula was as follows: long (*ā*, *ō*) => long *ā*; short (*a*, *o*) => short *o*. Thus, if we compare Latin, which preserved the original length in these examples, with PSL, we can see that in the word for 'mother' it has *māter*, whereas PSL has **mati*, and that it has *dōnum* 'gift,' whereas PSL has **dati* 'give.' By the same token, 'eye' is *okulis* in Latin and **oko* in PSL, while 'I plough' is *aro* in Latin and **orǫ* in Slavic. The same thing happened with other vowels. Short *u* evolved into the back semivowel, also known as back or hard *yer* (like an ultrashort *u*, or a schwa pronounced in the back of the mouth), marked as *ъ*; long *u* turned into the *yery*, a sound between *i* and *u* but pronounced somewhat lower (thus, we have Latin *tū*, PSL **ty* 'you'; and Latin *nurus*, PSL **snъxa* 'daughter in law'). Long *i* continued to be an *i*, and its short counterpart turned into the front semivowel, also known as the front or soft *yer* (like an ultrashort *i*, or a schwa pronounced in the front of the mouth), marked as *ь*. Hence, 'alive' is *vīvus* in Latin and **živъ* in PSL, and 'fog' is *migla* in Lithuanian (another language that retains the original PIE length), and its PSL counterpart is **mьgla*. Finally, short *e* continued to be an *e*, and long *ē* evolved into the *yat'*, a complex sound of not fully understood nature, probably somewhere between the *a* and *e* sounds with a preceding element akin to *y* in *yes*, marked as *ě* (or *ѣ* in Cyrillic script). Latin *fero* 'I carry' corresponds with PSL **berǫ* 'I pick, I take.' On the other hand, 'seed' is *sēmen* in Latin and **sěmę* in PSL.

Third, two qualitatively new sounds have emerged: the front nasal (the *e* sound pronounced with an accompanying passage of the stream of air through the nose) marked as *ę* and the back nasal (the *o* sound pronounced with an accompanying passage of the stream of air through the nose) marked as *ǫ*. The novelty of this development is that no PIE simple vowels have had accompanying pronunciation features. One can see the emergence of the Slavic nasals when comparing their position with the Lithuanian cognates, where there is the reflex akin to the PIE situation. The number five is thus **pętъ* in PSL (with a nasal), and it is *penki* (with the *en* sequence) in Lithuanian. Similarly, 'to blow' is **dǫti* in PSL, and its Lithuanian counterpart in form albeit not in meaning is *dumti* 'to rush, to rip, etc.'

The Paths of Pulling Out Puffing

Another process that has shaped PSL and consequently the present-day Slavic languages was deaspiration (the loss of that puff that used to be pronounced after various consonants). The widespread PIE feature of aspiration was completely abandoned—this separates Slavic languages from the PIE languages of the Indian subcontinent, which have retained aspiration. The loss of aspiration was straightforward. For example, in pairs *b* vs. *bʰ* and *p* vs. *pʰ*, the aspirated ones simply lost their aspiration, and, as a result, both members of the pair yielded the nonaspirated version. Thus, in the end only *b* and *p* remained with no additional phonological value created. Here are some examples: In the word for 'brother,' Sanskrit (an ancient, now dead, language of India with literacy starting as early as in 1500 BCE) has retained aspiration in *b͟hrātr̥*, while PSL has the deaspirated (puffless) **b͟ratrъ*. Similarly, Sanskrit has *mádhu* and PSL *med͟ъ* for 'honey.' In general, aside from the shift toward the front of the mouth cavity, there is a straightforward line of retaining consonants and losing their accompanying features, which separates Slavic from Germanic languages (including English). In the latter language family, there was an intricate consonant shift (called the first Germanic sound shift), so much so that there is a law that explains it, called Grimm's law, also known as Rask's rule. For example, in the word *p͟od* 'under, floor,' Slavic languages retain the original PIE **p*, while there is a shift to *f* in the English cognate *foot*. Similarly, in Slavic, the word *t͟ri* 'three' retains the original PIE **t*, while English shifts to *th* (θ): *t͟hree*. So, Slavic and Germanic peoples have followed very different paths to get rid of their puffs.

The Roots of Rustling

Finally, we get to why Slavic languages sound like rustling. While the PIE velars (*k* and *g*, on their own, or various accompanying features) have changed into something else in other language families (with palatalization disappearing as an accompanying feature), Slavic languages had a series of profound sound changes that converted PSL *k*, *g*, and *h* into palatal consonants, pronounced in the front of the mouth cavity (akin to *sh* in *ship*, *ch* in *chair*, *j* in *jet*, and *s* in *measure*, as well as some additional ones that English does not have). This process is called *palatalization*, where *palatal* means pronounced on the front palate. In addition to affecting single consonants, these changes have affected their clusters, resulting in sequences of rustling sounds. The frequency of such sounds was very high in Slavic words, which further underlines their rustling character. English had palatalizations, which can be seen in examples like English *church* (which used to be *cirice* in Old English) versus Dutch *kerk* 'church.' The Old English has palatalized the back *k* sound into the front *ch* sound, which was not the case in the Dutch language for this word. However, the scope of palatalization in English was severely limited compared to its scope in Slavic languages.

In the Slavic world, there were palatalizations that affected the PSL sounds *k, *g, *h in the positions before or behind front vowels. For example, k, which is pronounced in the back section of the mouth cavity, if positioned in front of the e, which is pronounced in the front of the mouth cavity, will turn into a č (pronounced ch as in chat), also pronounced in the front of the mouth cavity. Among other situations, this happens when adding the calling suffix -e (the equivalent of putting hey in front of a noun in English). Thus, the word for 'hero' in Proto-Slavic was *junakъ in its basic form. However, when they wanted to say 'hey, hero,' the back semivowel (pronounced, as one can infer from its name, in the back of the mouth cavity) was replaced with the -e, pronounced in the front of the mouth cavity, and that form of this word was *junače, with the k changed into a č. The type of change in the first and the second palatalization is the one in which a back consonant (i.e., k in the aforementioned example, pronounced in the back of the mouth cavity) turns into a front consonant (pronounced in the front of the mouth cavity) before a front vowel, also pronounced in the front of the mouth cavity (into a ch in front of an e in this case). The third palatalization was a change in which the front vowel before the back consonant has caused it to change into a front consonant. For example, in borrowing the Germanic word for prince *kuningaz, the Slavs changed the g sound, pronounced in the back of the mouth cavity, into dz, pronounced in the front, because it was after the front ę, also pronounced in the front, so the form in Proto-Slavic was *knędzъ. In all three palatalizations, the resulting sequence is the one of a front consonant and front vowel, which is easier to pronounce than when the vowel and the consonant are pronounced in different parts of the mouth cavity, as the tongue does not have to move much. The first and second palatalizations were named after their sequence in time. The first palatalization happened first, then the process of monophthongization (replacing diphthongs, as ay in word day with simple vowels, as a in dam), and only then the second palatalization. This is the relative chronology of those events, mentioned in chapter 2. Here is how this relative chronology can be established based on the material from present-day Slavic languages (needless to say, accompanied with a treasure throve of other relevant information). In present-day S-Cr (B/C/S), the word for 'wolf' is vuk, but one possible plural is vuci, and then the vocative—that is, the form used to call the wolf—is vuče. Reconstruction techniques show that the origin of these forms is as presented in table 3.1.

In this case, there were three relevant processes since PSL split from PIE: The first palatalization, which changed k into č' (ch as in chip, just a bit softer) in front of any front consonant; the monophthongization, which changed the diphthong

Table 3.1. The Origin of S-Cr (B/C/S) Forms for 'Wolf'

	PIE	PSL	S-Cr (B/C/S)
Singular	*wĺkʷos	*vьĺkъ	vuk
Plural	*wĺkʷoⁱ-	*vьĺc'i	vuci
Vocative	*wĺkʷe	*vьĺč'e	vuče

oⁱ- into i; and the second palatalization, which changed k into c' (tz as in blitz, just a bit softer). The only way to explain the result that we can see in present-day S-Cr (B/C/S) is as follows: The first palatalization happened first and changed *wĺkʷe into *vьĺč'e. Nothing happened to *wĺkʷoⁱ- given that the diphthongs are still around and that their first part is a back vowel. The period of the first palatalization ended, and the diphthongs were then replaced with simple vowels in the process of monophthongization. This changed *wĺkʷoⁱ- into *wĺki. At that point, the second palatalization happened, changing *wĺki into *wĺc'i. To make a long story short, how these processes played out relative to each other, that is, their relative chronology, matters. The second palatalization happens only if the front vowels i and yat' (ě) come from the diphthongs oⁱ- and aⁱ-. The first palatalization, in contrast, encompasses all front vowels except those originating from the diphthongs.

The third palatalization happened when k, g, and h were after ь, i, and ę and there were no ъ or y after them. The results were identical to the second palatalization. For example, in the word for 'path,' the initial *stьga has changed into *stьdz'a. An example of evidence that the sound was initially g is Old High German, which has retained the inherited PIE sound and where steg (ending in a g) meant 'bridge, path.'

Rustling Goes Wild

There were also palatalizations that encompassed practically all nonpalatal consonants—*k, *g, *h, *t, *d, *s, *z, *r, *l, *n, *m, *p, *b, and *v—turning them into palatals. So, compared to many other languages, palatalization went wild. This happens when these consonants come in contact with a lingual glide *i̯ behind them or, much less commonly, before them. For example, the S-Cr (B/C/S) word for house is kuća, which comes from kut 'corner,' derived with the suffix -i̯a, so it literally means 'the thing with corners.' The suffix changes the nonpalatal *t* into the palatal *ć* (pronounced as *ch* in *chip*). This kind of palatalization is called iotation after the name of the Greek letter ι, iota, that represents this sound.

These palatalizations also encompassed groups of consonants. For example, *sk* and *zg* would change into **š'č'* (a softer *sh* followed by a softer *ch*) and **ž'dž'* (*s* as in *pleasure* but softer, followed by *j* as in *jet*). This can be seen in the PSL words for 'whistle,' which is reconstructed as **piš'č'el*, and for 'yeast,' which is **drož'dž'e*.

While PSL was still a vocalic language, the vowel-to-consonant ratio has dropped substantially to 10 vowels versus 26 consonants, that is, .54, almost one-half of that found in PIE. One issue in Slavic phonology that has commanded the attention of Slavic historical linguists for over a century is the exact phonological value (i.e., the way it sounded) of the yat' sound (*ě*). It has disappeared from all present-day Slavic languages, yet the variety of its reflexes (*e, i, je, ije*, etc.) has given rise to various competing theories about its PSL phonological value. For example, what used to be **mlěko* in PSL is *mleko, mliko, mljeko*, or *mlijeko* in various dialects of just one language, S-Cr (B/C/S). The most broadly accepted of these theories claims that its sound was somewhere between *a* and *e* with a previous palatalization, which would be rendered in English as a very short *y* (as in *yes*) followed by a long *a* (æ, as in *bad*).

It should be clear that the changes occurring since PSL split from PIE were along the lines of simplification (toward fewer units and a less-diversified system) and facilitation of pronunciation (front consonants now combine with front vowels and open syllables are easier to pronounce than their closed counterparts). That this change is so logical begs the question of why only certain PIE speakers followed this route, whereas others stuck with their diphthongs (as we can see in English and many other languages) and aspirations (as seen, among others, in Hindi/Urdu, the most populous language of India and Pakistan). That is the million-dollar question that still awaits its bold explorers. Processes in the sound systems that have transpired in the dissolution of the PSL speech community were not as turbulent as those in the breakup of the PIE community.

Slavic Phonological Divorces

The serial divorces of the Proto-Slavic marriage were, generally speaking, amicable. Many things stayed the same. Of those that changed, some did so in precisely the same manner in all Slavic languages or in most of them, with some marginal exceptions. Other things changed so as to make the three groups of Slavic languages and the languages within those groups more distant from one another. Old Church Slavonic has a special place in all this evolution because its inventories correspond with PSL, with some minor exceptions.

The system of vowels generally underwent further simplification. The yat' (the mysterious sound between *a* and *e* mentioned in the previous section) has disappeared everywhere; the semivowels (like *e* in *hunter*), the vocalic liquids (*r* and *l*), and the nasals were abandoned in a vast majority of languages; and even yery (the sound between *i* and *u* mentioned in the previous section) has been lost in many of them. In some languages, such as Upper and Lower Sorbian as well as Slovene, there was a contrary process of developing additional distinctions in the middle vowels range: closed *o* and *e* and their counterparts led to open *o* and open *e* (spelled the same but pronounced differently). This distinction is something akin to the difference between the vowel in the English *man* (open, more space between the tongue and the ceiling of the mouth cavity) and *men* (closed, less of that space). Nevertheless, the number of units and their diversity in any individual present-day Slavic language are lower than in PSL. Consonantal changes were mostly quantitative (changing the frequency but not the variety of sounds). While all Slavic languages have retained rich palatal distinctions, there is a range of various configurations. The main development in the syllabic organization was the abandonment of the open syllable principle. Unlike PSL, the present-day Slavic languages have both open and closed syllables, as can be seen in the Russian word *zaum* (a concept of 'being beyond the mind' in Russian futurist poetry), where the first syllable, *za*, is open and the second, *um*, closed. This is an example of a linguistic cycle, which goes from open and closed syllables in PIE to open syllables in PSL, to finally return to the point of departure—open and closed syllables in today's Slavic languages.

Three major changes that have made the phonology of the present-day Slavic languages distinct are the fall and vocalization of yers, the liquid metathesis and pleophony, and the further development of the palatalizations. Their technical linguistic names may sound scary at this moment, but fear not—we will get back to them. These three processes are special in that they clearly demonstrate the principles of change in historical linguistics: the importance of the position of the sound, the significance of how the sounds are ordered, and the import of how precise the distinctions in some areas are. The speakers of Slavic languages have also had diversified paths of developing other phonological features and of shaping their patterns of stress.

Pesky Little Critters

The pesky little critters are the two PSL semivowels, back and front, also called yers (the first of the three triggers that have shaped the sounds of the present-day Slavic languages), which could either turn into a full vowel or disappear. Their fate depended on their position in the word. According to the rule known as Havlík's law (after Antonín Havlík, who established that rule in 1889), there were two possible positions: weak, in which they have eventually disappeared, and strong, in which they have mostly turned into full vowels. The strong position was before the syllable with another semivowel; any other position was weak. This law is illustrated in table 3.2 with the lost semivowel marked with zero in descendant languages and the one that was vocalized bolded.

The divergent development of the yers in their strong position was one of the factors that made Slavic languages different from one another. The following paths of development have been attested. First, there are languages like Bulgarian and Slovene that still have a yer in their system (a central one, neither front nor back, despite the way it is spelled and transcribed). The word for 'sleep' in Bulgarian is thus *sъn* (<= *sъnъ*). Not all strong semivowels will remain semivowels; some of them will vocalize, as in Bulgarian *den* (<= *dьnъ*) 'day.' Second, in some languages, such as S-Cr, the two semivowels merged into one full vowel, *a* in this case: *san* (<= *sъnъ*), *dan* (<= *dьnъ*). Third, in West Slavic languages, they also merged into one vowel, but the consonant before the front semivowel is palatalized and the one before its hard counterpart is not, for example, in Polish: *sen* (<= *sъnъ*), *dzień* (<= *dьnъ*)—*dzi* represents the sound *j* as in *jet*. Finally, in East Slavic languages and Macedonian, they vocalize into a front and back vowel, respectively.

Table 3.2. Strong and Weak Yers

PSL S—strong position W—weak position	Russian	Polish	S-Cr (B/C/S)	Meaning
S W ↓ ↓ sъnъ	sonØ	senØ	sanØ	dream
W ↓ sъna	sØna	sØna	sØna	of dream

Thus, Russian has *son* (<= *sъnъ*), *d'eń* (<= *dьnъ*). Three things can be seen from the fall and vocalization of the yers—the position mattered, the loss was possible because descendant Slavic languages abandoned the open syllable principle, and languages differed in whether they maintained the difference between the semivowels and full vowels and also whether they kept the difference between the yers in their reflexes.

Moving and Shaking

The Slavic liquid metathesis and pleophony, the second trigger—an additional important process in the Slavic serial divorces—affects the PSL roots borrowed from the PIE that contained the sequences *or*, *ol*, *er*, and *el*, either between two consonants (which is represented by *TorT*, *TolT*, *TerT*, and *TelT*, where the capital *T* stands for any given consonant) or at the beginning of a word before a consonant (represented as *orT*, *olT*, *erT*, and *elT*). For instance, **gordъ* 'castle' would be an instance of a *TorT* sequence and **ordlo* 'plow' would be an instance of an *orT* sequence. What is moved and shaken is the order within these sequencies. The problem with these was that they made their respective syllables closed, something untenable in the PSL system, which only allowed open syllables. For example, in **melko* (and the English cognate *milk*, which reflects the IE distribution of the sounds), the first syllable was closed: **mel-ko*. There were two possible manners in which these sequences could be made compliant with the open syllable principle (the rule that each syllable must end in a vowel). The first one relies on transposition of the liquids (*l* and *r*), so **mel-ko* would yield **mle-ko* and both syllables would be open. This is the liquid metathesis (the etymology of which is 'change place') that has happened in the Slavic south and west. The second possible resolution is the insertion of another vowel behind the consonant, so **mel-ko* would yield **me-le-ko* (with three open syllables, which then further evolves into *moloko*, as we find it in today's Russian). This change has happened in the Slavic east only between two consonants (not at the beginning of the word), and it is called pleophony (etymologically: many-sound-ness). Slavic languages and their groups differ in additional details in the process of liquid metatheses—most notably if it was accompanied by vowel lengthening or not. Take, for example, in **gordъ* 'castle' (with English cognate *yard*—both were enclosed and guarded): In S-Cr there is a lengthening into *a*, resulting in *grad* 'city.' In contrast, Polish *gród* 'castle' does not have such lengthening. Liquid metathesis and pleophony show the importance of syllabic organization in shaping Slavic phonology.

I Softened It My Way

We finally get to the third trigger: Slavic languages soften their sounds each in its own way. Starting from the same initial values of PSL palatalizations, the present-day Slavic languages have evolved further in creating their distinctive systems of palatal consonants. For example, originating from the PSL words *svĕt'a* 'candle' and *med'a* 'border' (with soft *t* and *d*, as if pronouncing *y* as in *yes* very quickly after them), Slavic languages have developed a variety of values. In some languages, these sounds were made even softer. Thus, in formal S-Cr (B/C/S), the words are *sveća/svijeća* and *međa* (they turn into a softer *ch* as in *chip* and *j* as in *jeep*), so the value of *ć* (soft *ch*) is different from *č* (hard *ch*, in words like *čist* 'clean'). In Slovene and some S-Cr (B/C/S) dialects, the *đ* sound further evolves into a *y* as in *yes*, while the difference between the *t'* and *č* is eliminated. These words are *sveča* (the same *č* as in *čist*) and *meja* (pronounced *meya*). Macedonian speakers have shifted their pronunciation toward the palatalized velars *ḱ* and *ǵ* (as if pronouncing a *y* as in *yes* quickly after *k* and *g*), so the words are sveḱa and *meǵa*. Bulgarians (with Old Church Slavonic, i.e., OCS, following suit) have developed these into consonant sequences, so the words are *svešta* and *mežda* (the sequences are *sh* as in *ship* followed by a *t* and *s* as in pleasure followed by a *d*). East Slavic languages keep them soft, but their value has merged with the palatalization of *k* and *g*, so it is *sveča* (*ch*, just like *č* in *čistyj*, which comes from a *k*) and *meža* (*s* as in *pleasure*, just like *ž* in *žoltyj*, which comes from a *g*). Finally, West Slavic languages have depalatalized those consonants (moved their pronunciation from the front palate to the teeth), so they are pronounced on the teeth, for example, in Polish *świeca* (the *tz* sound as in *blitz*) and *miedza* (*d* as in *day* and *z* as in *zebra* pronounced quickly one after the other). To sum it up, the development of palatalizations in individual Slavic languages tells a story about how speakers of individual languages make more or less precise distinctions in certain parts of their mouth cavities.

All these processes and many others have shaped phonological systems in Slavic languages. In all these differences, there is a high degree of family resemblance. Slavic sounds show unity in diversity.

Do All Slavs Sound Alike?

Assorted Russian villains in recent Hollywood movies have often been performed by the actor Rade Sherbedgia (or Rade Šerbedžija in the original rendering).

Speakers of Russian will immediately recognize his accent in English as non-Russian (even if they haven't heard him speaking his accented Russian). And indeed, he is neither Russian nor a native speaker of Russian but, rather, an ethnic Serb and a speaker of Serbo-Croatian (Bosnian/Croatian/Serbian). His accent in English is quite different from that which one would find among Russians. If we take the phrase *police lies* (something a Russian mafioso or any other mafioso would be likely to utter) and represent the standard American English pronunciation as *puhlees lahyz*, Sherbedgia's pronunciation would be *polees lahyz* while the common Russian accented pronunciation would be *palyis lays*. Reasons for the differences are that speakers of Russian do not distinguish between short and long vowels, and speakers S-Cr (B/C/S) do; Russian speakers have the so-called positional palatalization, where consonants would be softened before the *i* and *e* sounds, which is absent in S-Cr (B/C/S); and Russian devoices its consonants (e.g., turns *z* into *s*) at the end of words, which is not the case in S-Cr (B/C/S). But the Hollywood entertainment industry does not care. As long as a nonnative speaker does not differentiate between *bed* and *bad* or *color* and *collar*, pronounces the *r* sound in a certain distinctive manner, and so forth, general public perception is that nothing else matters. "They are all the same anyway." The "others" are always the same.

Yes, these are stereotypes, and we will confront them with reality here. But first, it is important to note that there are also inter-Slavic stereotypes. Speakers of Slavic languages will also have some impressions about other Slavic languages. Thus, Poles might find the pronunciation of Czech and Slovak languages funny because they feature long vowels, which are absent from Polish. S-Cr (B/C/S) and Slovene, which have tones (pitch) on their vowels, would sound like singing to Poles. Slovene, with its free stress placing and open and closed vowels, sounds like the jingling of bells to speakers of S-Cr (B/C/S).

Forceful, Long versus Short, and Musical

Enough stereotypes—on with reality. The first feature that differentiates Slavic languages prominently is their word stress pattern. Some of them rely just on a force of pronunciation in stressed syllables; others distinguish between short and long vowels; yet other have tones, just like in music. In East Slavic, Eastern South Slavic, and most West Slavic languages, the stress is dynamic. This means that stressed syllables are stronger than those that are not stressed, and they are all the same length and tone. Russian is illustrative in this regard. Its stress is so strong that some vowels get reduced when they are not stressed. Thus, in the word *moloko*, there are three letter *o* sounds, but only the last one is stressed and consequently pronounced as an *o*. The one before it (in the middle of the word) is in the first stage of reduction, pronounced as *u* in the English word *but* (ʌ). The one at the beginning of the word is in the second stage of reduction, pronounced like *e* in the English word *higher* (ə). So, *moloko* is pronounced as məlʌk<u>o</u>, with the stressed vowel underlined. Then, there are Czech and Slovak, where vowels are additionally differentiated by whether they are long or short. For example, 'airplane' is *letadlo* (with a short *e*, which is the default in writing), but 'to fly' is *létat* (with a long *é* marked with the slanted line above it). Finally, S-Cr (B/C/S) and Slovene additionally have pitch (or tone). For example, in the S-Cr (B/C/S) word *luka* 'port,' the pitch rises like an airplane taking off, while in the word *Luka* 'Lucas,' it briefly rises then falls precipitously, like an airplane that crashes shortly after taking off. In linguistic texts, this change of pitch is noted quite intuitively: *lúka* (rising), *Lûka* (rising, then falling). Further differences in the stress concern its placing. There are languages like Russian, Slovene, and Bulgarian in which placing the stress is free. There are also those Slavic languages in which the place of the stress is fixed: on the first syllable of the word in Czech, Slovak, and Sorbian languages; on the penultimate syllable (i.e., the one next to the last) in Polish; and on the antepenultimate (i.e., the one before the next to the last) in Macedonian. There are also cases like S-Cr (B/C/S) where it is free with some limitations (most notably that the last syllable as a rule does not bear stress).

The Sounds and Their Clusters

Another prominent difference between the sound systems of Slavic languages is the level of tolerance speakers exhibit toward consonant clusters. West Slavic languages are generally more tolerant than their Eastern and Southern counterparts. One systematic difference between the west on the one hand and the other two groups on the other hand is preservation versus simplification of the groups *dl* and *tl*. Thus, 'plough' is *radło* and 'she knitted' is *plotła* in Polish. The first word is *ralo* (without the *d* sound) in S-Cr (B/C/S) and Russian. The second one is *plela* (i.e., without the *t* sound) in these two languages. Polish is especially tolerant toward consonant clusters; for example, the word for 'bee' is *pszczoła* (pronounced *pshchowa*), whereas Russian and S-Cr (B/C/S) have *pčela* (pronounced *pchela*). S-Cr (B/C/S) is on the other side of the spectrum—among other things, it does not allow geminates (sequences of two identical consonants). For example, 'wounded' is *ranny* in

Polish and 'early' is *rannij* (read *rannyiy*—both *y* as in *yes*) in Russian. S-Cr (B/C/S) has just one *n* in both words: 'wounded' is *ranjen*, 'early' is *rani*.

Yet another point of divergence for Slavic languages are positional variants of their sounds. Most Slavic languages have final devoicing, which causes the Russian words for 'Serb' (*serb*) and 'sickle' (*serp*) to be pronounced the same, like *syerp* (*y* as in *yes*), given that voiced consonants (*b*, *d*, *g*, *z*, etc.) turn into their voiceless counterparts (*p*, *t*, *k*, *s*, etc.) at the end of the word. There are, however, outliers such as S-Cr (B/C/S) and Ukrainian, where this does not happen. One can see that in the Russian pronunciation of the word for sickle, *serp*, there is a soft *s* (which is marked by a *y*). In contrast, *sambo*, the word for a Russian martial art, is pronounced just like that, without the softening. The softening of the *s* in the former example is called positional palatalization—the consonant is softened by a front vowel behind it. In *sambo*, the *a* behind the *s* sound is central rather than front, so there is no positional palatalization. Again, S-Cr (B/C/S) is on the other side of the spectrum from Russian because it does not have positional palatalization. The *s* sound in *sit* 'full, not hungry,' *set* 'set, in tennis,' *sat* 'watch, clock, hour,' etc., is roughly the same. Some of these positional changes happen to sequences of sounds. Thus, the initial sequence *je-* (pronounced *ye-*, *y* as in *yes*), which is preserved in the Slavic south and west, evolves into an *o-* in the east. For example, 'lake' is *jezero* in S-Cr (B/C/S), *jezioro* in Polish, and *ozero* in Russian.

Finally, the way in which the palatalizations evolved has shaped up very different systems of palatal consonants. Some of them are more palatal, meaning the area of the tongue touching the palate is broader—we will call them soft palatals. The other ones are less palatal, meaning the area of the tongue touching the palate is narrower—we will call them hard palatals. To take one language from each of the three subgroups, Polish distinguishes hard and soft *sh* (written *sz* for hard and *ś* or *si* for soft), *s* as in *pleasure* (written *rz* or *ż* for hard and *ź* or *zi* for soft), *ch* (written *cz* for hard and *ć* or *ci* for soft), and *j* (written *dż* for hard and *dź* or *dzi* for soft). S-Cr (B/C/S) distinguishes the latter two (*č* for hard, *ć* for soft *ch*, and *dž* for hard, *đ* for soft *j*) but not the former two (it only has *š*, pronounced *ch*, and *ž*, pronounced *s*, as in *pleasure*). Russian has only the first three sounds (*š*, *ž*, and *č*), and the fourth (*dž*) can only be found in foreign words and is not a part of the system. But Russian has a range of positionally palatalized consonants. The development of the soft *r'* is illustrative in showing different paths of development. It is preserved in languages like Russian, so *more* 'sea' is pronounced as *morye* (*y* as in *yes*, merged with the *r*, so the *r* is soft). In Czech, it evolves into something between *r* and *ž* (spelled *ř*, *moře*, pronounced as *r* merged into one sound with the *s* from *measure*). In Polish, the process goes further, and the sound changes into a *ž* (pronounced as *s* in pleasure and spelled as *rz*). This *ž* sound that stems from a soft *r* is written *rz*, and the one that was originally the *ž* sound is written *ż*. Thus, 'sea' is *morze* and 'it can be' is *może*, both of which are pronounced with an *s* as in *pleasure*.

A Not-So-Fake President and a Completely Fake Russian

The sound differences between standard S-Cr (B/C/S), Polish, and Russian have led National Security Agency (NSA) analysts to a conclusion that Marshal Tito, a mid-twentieth-century leader of Yugoslavia (a real president), was in fact not a Yugoslav but rather Russian or Polish. This erroneous conclusion disregarded the fact that the phonetics of dialects may deviate from that of the standard language, which is the case with Tito's Kajkavian dialect on the border of Croatia with Slovenia. In other words, there are features such as positional softening and final devoicing, which the Kajkavian dialect shares with Russian and Polish, but not with standard S-Cr (B/C/S).

The faux Hollywood Russian Rade Sherbedgia does not have many pronunciations that a veritable Russian man would have: positional palatalization, final devoicing, reductions in nonstressed vowels, to name a few. Yet, on another level, all Slavic languages sound like rustling leaves because they have a high number of soft consonants that have emerged from various palatalizations. Slavic speakers will notice that the leaves are knee-deep in Polish, ankle-deep in S-Cr (B/C/S), and barely accumulated in Russian. To non-Slavic speakers, all these are rustling leaves.

Chapter Takeaways

The sound profile of Slavic languages has been shaped by a series of various historical processes, which have made them distinct from other Indo-European families. What makes them different from English and other Germanic languages is that their systems of vowels are much simpler (among other things, diphthongs have been phased out) and that they shifted the pronunciation toward the front of the mouth cavity (which gives them a rustling quality). Despite the popular perception, there are numerous differences in the stress patterns and the sound systems of individual Slavic languages.

Recommended Chapter Readings

Carlton (1991) offers an introduction to the development of sound systems in Slavic languages. An accessible account can also be found in Towsend and Janda (1996). Lehmann (1952) discusses Indo-European phonology. Phonological developments and the characteristics of the sound systems in individual Slavic languages can be found in appropriate chapters in Comrie and Corbett (1993) and in Sussex and Cubberly (2006). Schenker (1995) offers an excellent review of the Proto-Slavic phonology. The NSA analysis of Marshal Tito's phonetics is available at https://www.nsa.gov/Portals/70/documents/news-features/declassified-documents /cryptologic-spectrum/is_yugoslav.pdf (accessed on September 11, 2022).

4 The Forms of Slavic Words: Bending and Gendering

The Shades of Bending

Slavs bend their words to mark who does what to whom in the sentence much, much more than do speakers of English. This bending is the most conspicuous feature of Slavic languages for English-language speakers. It is also the biggest hurdle in their learning Slavic languages. In linguistic terminology this is called *inflection*. This difference is caused by the fact that around the eleventh century CE, at the end of the Old English period (an earlier phase of English used from the fifth century CE to the twelfth), the speakers of English stopped inflecting their words, while Slavic languages continued this time-honored PIE practice. There are further prominent differences. The notion of gender sharply divides Slavic languages from English. Grammatical gender, understood very differently than in English, is the key feature of the inflections of the nouns and their modifiers. These two features are what bending and gendering mentioned in the title refer to. As was the case in the previous chapter, here too I will provide a very general introduction to some features that set apart Slavic languages from English. For full accounts of these extremely complex phenomena, look to the works mentioned in the selected readings.

The preservation, repurposing, and loss of certain grammatical categories are what has shaped historical developments of Slavic languages. Some grammatical categories have been lost almost universally (e.g., separate grammatical forms for two people or things), whereas others have been lost in some Slavic languages (e.g., nouns and adjectives are generally not bent for case in Macedonian and Bulgarian) but repurposed or preserved in others. Finally, the features of functional words such as pronouns (*me, him*, etc.) and auxiliary verbs (such as *was* in *She was working*, which helps build the grammatical form of the verb *to work* without having any meaning outside the grammar) are another differentiation factor. Notably, there are very particular rules for the placement of these small words in the sentence.

Enter Gender

When determining whether something is 'he,' 'she,' or 'it,' learners of Slavic languages are privileged over the students of German, another Indo-European language. In English, gender is sex. Males are 'he,' females are 'she,' and everything else is 'it,' with some minor exceptions—such as ships, engines, and countries—which can be 'she.' In Slavic languages and German alike, a noun's gender is purely mechanical. In German, determining gender is like a lottery, because there are only a limited number of situations in which gender assignment is predictable (e.g., if something ends in -*ung*, -*heit*, -*keit*, it is feminine, a 'she'). In Slavic languages, in contrast, the ending of the word pretty reliably predicts its gender. Following is the rule of thumb: If something ends in an -*a*, it is feminine. *Vodka* is consequently a 'she.' If something ends in a consonant (there is no vowel at the end), it is masculine. *Kefir* is thus a 'he.' Whatever ends in an -*o* or -*e* is neuter. *Sambo* 'a Russian martial art' is 'it,' and so is *gore* 'grief.' There are some exceptions to this pattern, but the gender assignment in Slavic languages is generally predictable, unlike in German. This association came about as a result of gradual development from PIE, via PSL, to present-day Slavic languages, where gender distribution has played a pivotal role, especially in the final phase of the process.

The starting point is the PIE system with three genders, but there are also three numbers and eight cases. In addition to singular (as in *hand*) and plural (as in *hands*), both PIE and PSL have had the dual number, which was used for two people or things (e.g., when referring to *two hands* of one's body). This distinction was preserved in some Slavic languages, such as Slovene, where 'hand' is *roka* (singular), 'two hands' is *roki* (dual), and three or more hands is *roke* (plural).

The Curious Case of Slavic Cases

The cases (the previously mentioned bending of words to show who does what to whom in the sentence) are a bit more complicated. Only most frequent uses of Slavic cases will be mentioned here. Each case has numerous other functions. Detailed information about them can be found in the selected readings sources. First, there was the default nominative case, literally naming case, aka the subject case, used mostly when just naming something or someone or when referring to the subject of the sentence. (This happens in English, when one uses *he* and *she*, rather than *him* and *her*.) Then, there is the accusative, literally accusation case, aka the object case. English still has it, in a drastically limited sphere. For example, in the sentence *He knows him, he* is the subject case, the nominative, and *him* is the object case, the accusative. There is also the genitive case, literally the birth case. In English, one talks about the Saxon genitive, as in *father's house*, where the addition of the *'s* ending signals the genitive case, and the Norman genitive, where the genitive relationship is signaled by the preposition 'of' (e.g., *a glass of water*). In general, the genitive is the case of the relationship, something belongs to something, as in the first example, or something is a part of something, as in the second. PIE also had the ablative case, literally separation case, aka the taking away case, which is generally expressed in English using the preposition *from* (e.g., *spiders from Mars*). In PSL, the ablative merged with the genitive. There is also the dative case, literally giving case, known as the case of the indirect object, typically expressed in English by the preposition *to* and a recipient of some kind. For example, in *Mark gave a book to Peter, Mark* is the subject and hence the nominative case. Then, the word *book* is the object and hence the accusative case, and *Peter* is the recipient and hence the dative case. Then, there is the vocative case, as if adding *hey* (or, in informal speaking, *yo, oi,* etc.) in front of somebody's name (e.g., *Hey, Mark!*). There is furthermore a location case, the locative, the main use of which is the location (hence the name), as in *in the house,* and topic of the conversation, as in *about the house.* In the tradition of teaching Russian, this case is known as the prepositional case, given that it always goes with a preposition. Finally, there is the instrument case, the instrumental, for the major functions of a tool or company (rendered in English mostly by using the preposition 'with,' as in *to cut with a knife* and *to travel with a friend*). Their order in grammatical tables and their abbreviations are as follows: N(ominative), G(enitive), D(ative), A(ccusative), V(ocative), I(nstrumental), L(ocative). In some Slavic traditions, the instrumental comes after the locative when lists and tables of cases and their endings in grammar are provided.

To exemplify all these most common uses of cases, let us consider the following sentence:

Hey, Peter (V), Mark (N) is serving a cup (A) of coffee (G) with milk (I) to Maria (D) in the bar (L).

In English, the vocative is signaled by intonation, adding an exclamation point, or adding an interjection such as *Hey*; nominative and accusative are signaled by the word order (what comes before the verb is the nominative, what comes after it is the accusative); and all other cases are signaled by their respective prepositions. In contrast, in most Slavic languages (and this was inherited from PIE and PSL) the relations are expressed either by bending words alone or by bending words and adding prepositions. For example, the aforementioned sentence reads as follows in Polish (with form modifications underlined and English glosses below):

Piot<u>rze</u> (V), Marek (N) serwuje filiżank<u>ę</u> (A) kaw<u>y</u> (G) z mlek<u>iem</u> (I) Mari<u>i</u> (D) w ba<u>rze</u> (L).
Hey, Peter (V), Mark (N) is serving a cup (A) of coffee (G) with milk (I) to Maria (D) in the bar (L).

Except for the nominative, the default naming case that remains unchanged, all other cases are signaled by "bending" the words (i.e., changing their endings), whereas I and L have a preposition in addition to having their forms bent. Not only nouns are bent; their respective modifiers, such as adjectives, possessive pronouns, and so forth, also must share their case, number, and gender with the noun to which they pertain. Thus, if Mark is serving a big cup of coffee, that would be *dużą szklankę* (the gender is feminine, the number is singular, the case is accusative, all this on both *big* and *coffee*). If he is serving big cups, that would be *duże szklanki* (feminine, plural, accusative). If he is serving a big mug, that would be *duży kubek* (masculine, singular, accusative), and big mugs would be *duże kubki* (masculine, plural, accusative).

Bending, Now and Then

Going from PIE via PSL, and then to the present-day Slavic languages, the way the words are bent (or inflected, to use a technical term) has generally been simplified, in that the dual has generally been lost and the number of inflection categories and inflected forms has decreased. Some languages took simplification to an extreme level. Macedonian and Bulgarian abandoned bending nouns altogether and evolved into the same system of using the preposition as the English language has. English itself went through the process of losing case inflection going from Proto-Germanic (an ancestral language of English, German, and many other northwestern European languages) via Old English, and by around the eleventh century CE, it had generally abandoned the inflection of nouns and their modifiers.

In nominal inflections, also called declensions, the most important process in Slavic languages was that the inflection type eventually became aligned with the gender. The changes that have shaped PSL inflections were mostly consequences of diverse phonological changes. Unlike in phonology, where the most profound changes occurred when Slavs left their Indo-European cousins, in inflections, the most far-reaching changes, the most prominent of which is the alignment of inflections with genders, occurred starting from PSL and moving into the present-day Slavic languages. It is those changes that lend an advantage to the learners of Slavic languages over their peers who are tackling German.

What exactly PIE inflections (the starting point of development for Slavic languages and English alike) looked like is the subject of various theories. Among the theories are stipulations that something akin to the classes one can find in the Bantu languages of today (inflections based on what the noun means) have existed in some areas. For example, kinship terms ended in *-ter* and they were inflected in a similar manner, as can be seen in today's English: *father, mother, brother,* and *sister*. Small living beings would end in *-ent*, as can be seen from today's Polish: *dziecię* 'child,' *kurczę* 'chicken,' *prosię* 'piglet,' *jagnię* 'lamb,' etc. (with that nasal *ę* stemming from the *-en-* sequence). It is known that some inflections were thematic—that they had a thematic vowel to which case endings were added. For example, the root that yielded the word *večer* 'evening' in several Slavic languages and the English word *west* (it makes perfect sense that these are connected: the sun sets in the west in the evening) was *ueksperǫs* in the nominative, *ueksperǫsjo* in the genitive, and so on (so the underlined thematic vowel *o* stayed in place). There were also athematic stems with no thematic vowel, some of which would have had alternations in the root: the word that yielded *med* 'honey' in some Slavic languages and *mead* in English had the following PIE forms: N *med^hu*, G *md^he^us*, and so forth. In any event, between the PIE and PSL periods phonological changes have destroyed the system of thematic vowels even in those cases where they can be reliably assumed to have existed in PIE. Take the word for *wolf,* which is *vuk, wilk, wolk,* and *vlk* in Slavic languages. The *o* sound has disappeared even in the naming case—what used to be *ulk^uos* became *$vъlkъ$*. The principle of open syllables (a syllable has to end in a vowel) has caused the final *s* to be dropped; consequently, the *o* sound has narrowed down to the short *u* sound, which has yielded the hard *yer* (*ъ*). In traditional Slavic historical linguistics, PSL inflections are named after that PIE thematic vowel or consonant ending. That is not always visible in PSL, as could be seen in the word for 'wolf.' Even though the phonology of the endings changed, the general types of inflections were retained.

The Variety of Slavic Bending

What has transpired going from PSL to the present-day Slavic languages is the simplification of inflectional types based on gender. Initially, the type of inflection was determined by the final vowel of the stem (which was inherited from PIE); hence the names *a*-type, *o*-type, and so forth. After the disintegration of PSL community, gender entered and stole the spotlight. By the principle of linguistic analogy, less-common inflection types have changed their endings to align with more common inflection types. This change in behavior is akin to a situation in which smaller immigrant groups assimilate their behavior and customs to match the majority ethnic group. Here, a less common way to inflect nouns assimilates to a more common one. The process was similar in all Slavic languages that have preserved declensions (i.e., all of them except Macedonian and Bulgarian).

Most inflectional types have assimilated to the most frequent type in each given gender. A majority of masculine nouns inflect in the same manner, which, as mentioned, are nouns ending in a consonant. Most feminine nouns are nouns ending in an -*a*. Finally, most neuter nouns belong to the type that ends in an -*o* or -*e*. There are still some declension types that cross gender boundaries, but their percentage is extremely low, both in the lexicon and in texts. The situation in most Slavic languages was similar, but two of them, Macedonian and Bulgarian, went a step further to join English and other languages that do not bend their words but rather use the word order and prepositions to tell who is doing what to whom in their sentences.

While reducing the number of inflection types, the speakers of Slavic languages have lost many declensions that they inherited from PSL. However, their endings have not been lost without a trace. In each daughter language, there are some remnants of the previous inflection types.

Bending Exemplified

In PSL, in the type that is known as masculine *u*-declension, nouns were inflected like this: N *synъ* 'son,' G *synu* 'of son,' D *synovi* 'to son,' etc. In present-day Slavic languages, this inflectional type assimilated to the more common type (known as *o*-type), which in PSL had the following inflection: N *rodъ* 'genus, kin,' G *roda* 'of genus, kin,' D *rodu* 'to genus, kin,' etc. If we look at Polish masculine endings, we note that animate nouns (referring to people and other animals) will generally have the -*a* ending in the genitive, e.g., *brata* 'of brother' and *przyjaciela* 'of friend,' which is the ending of the *-o* type (the dominant one). However, inanimate nouns (everything else) will have either *-a* (as in *od stycznia* 'from January'), from the *o*-type, or *-u* (as in *od poniedziałku* 'from Monday'), from the *u*-type that has disappeared. The ending that belonged to the *u* inflection type is even more prominent in the dative case. Most masculine nouns will have the *-owi* ending (as in *synowy* 'to [article or possessive pronoun here] son'), and only a small number of them will have the *-u* ending, which stems from the *o* inflection type, as in *bratu* 'to [article or possessive pronoun here] brother.' In S-Cr (B/C/S), the trace of the *u* inflectional type is much more subtle. Singular endings are all from the *o* inflection type: N *brat* 'brother,' G *brata* 'of [article or possessive pronoun here] brother,' D *bratu* 'to [article or possessive pronoun here] brother.' However, most one-syllable hard-stem nouns will have *-ovi* as their plural ending (as in *zid*—*zidovi* 'wall—walls,' *zet*—*zetovi* 'brother-in-law—brothers-in-law'), which derives from the *u* inflectional type.

An interesting development has happened with feminine nouns. PSL had two dominant inflection types: the *a*-type (i.e., hard feminine stems), which followed the pattern N **žena* 'woman,' G **ženy* 'of [article here] woman,' D **ženě* 'to [article here] woman,' etc., and the *ja*-type (i.e., soft feminine stems), which followed the pattern N **duša* 'soul,' G **dušę* 'of [article or possessive pronoun here] soul,' D **duši* 'to [article or possessive pronoun here] soul,' etc. These two types merged, but Russian and Polish went with the *a*-type and S-Cr (B/C/S) went with the *ja*-type. So, Russian has N *žena, duša*; G *ženy, duši*; and D *žene, duše*, whereas S-Cr (B/C/S) has N *žena, duša*; G *žene, duše*; and D *ženi, duši*.

Flexing the Verbs

A similar process happened with the verbal inflections (also called conjugations). However, the way the analogy worked was based on textual frequency in some languages and on lexical frequency in others.

Let us take the three largest languages of each branch—Russian, Polish, and S-Cr (B/C/S)—and their PSL verbal inheritance. The first-person present-tense form (the *I* form, as in *I am working*) in PSL was dependent on the verb category. The so-called thematic verbs (those with a vowel at the end of the stem and before the *-ti* infinitive ending) had the ending **-ǫ*, and the so-called athematic verbs (those without a vowel at the end of the stem) had the ending **-mь*, with some further differences in other forms. Most verbs were thematic. The athematic verbs formed a limited category, but they encompassed extremely common verbs. That is, they had a very high textual frequency (i.e., they were likely to be found in utterances people produced on a daily basis). Examples are *byti* 'to be,' *dati* 'to give,' *ěsti* 'to eat,' *jьměti* 'to have,' and *věděti* 'to know.' On the other hand, the lexical frequency of thematic verbs (how often we found those verbs in the vocabulary of PSL) was overwhelming because a vast majority of verbs were thematic.

The spread of one set of endings/variants or the other was based on either textual frequency, as in S-Cr (B/C/S) *govorim-govorimo* 'I am talking—we are talking,' where athematic endings prevailed, or on lexical frequency, as in Rus. *govorju-govorim* 'I am talking—we are talking,' where thematic endings prevailed. Polish is in between. Both thematic and athematic endings can be found in the four main inflection types: for example, *mogę* 'I can' (thematic), *lubię* 'I like' (thematic), *mam* 'I have' (athematic), and *wiem* 'I know' (athematic).

The Destitute Dual

Aside from marginal cases like Slovene and Sorbian, which have retained it, the dual number (used for two people or things) has merged with the plural, so what were initially three numbers (singular, plural, and dual) turned into two, just like in English. However, some traces of the categories that are lost always remain. Such is the paucal form of the Slavic nouns after numbers. The paucal form refers to quantities two through four (i.e., a paucity, a small number of something). So, for example, in S-Cr (B/C/S), it is *jedan dom* 'one home'; *dva, tri, četiri doma* 'two, three, four homes'; and *pet domova* 'five homes.' The form *doma* is the old dual form, which has spread from two (dual) to two through four (paucal), but only in combination with numbers. Similarly, while S-Cr (B/C/S) has a very predictable genitive plural, where the default ending is -*a*, as in *prozora* 'of windows' (with some minor exceptions), the words for body parts that go in pairs still have the old dual ending -*u*: *nogu* 'of legs/feet,' *ruku* 'of hands/arms,' *očiju* 'of eyes,' *ušiju* 'of ears,' etc. A similar remnant of the previous stages of development (that offers material for internal reconstruction) can also be found in the masculine *i*-type of inflection. Generally, it has merged with the *o*-type, as in N **gostь*, G **gosti* 'guest, of [article or possessive pronoun here] guest' changing into N *gost*, G *gosta* 'guest, of [article or possessive pronoun here] guest,' to use a S-Cr (B/C/S) example. However, in an isolated case, Russian *put'* has merged with the feminine *i*-type (e.g., nouns N *junost'*, G *junosti* 'youth, of [article or possessive pronoun here] youth'), but its adjectives are masculine, so 'safe travels' is *sčastlivogo puti*, literally '(have a) lucky trip'; here, the adjective 'lucky' is in the masculine form, and the noun inflects according to the feminine *i*-type.

As can be seen, the category of gender was a great organizer of the Slavic systems of noun inflections. The most frequent inflectional types have absorbed those that were less frequent. The same effect of frequency (lexical or textual) has also shaped portions of the verb system. The general tendency was toward simplification. What was simplified varies from language to language.

Should I Stay or Should I Go?

The inflections of the present-day Slavic languages are generally simpler compared to the Proto-Slavic period. However, languages differ in what their speakers retain and what they shed. In that, there is a general rule of thumb: a simpler system of noun inflections means a more elaborate system of verb inflections, and vice versa. This is evident when comparing Northern Slavic languages like Polish and Russian with their Southern Slavic counterparts like Bulgarian and Macedonian. Polish and Russian have an extremely simplified system of verb tenses (compared to Bulgarian and Macedonian), yet they have retained a robust system of case inflections. By contrast, Bulgarian and Macedonian have practically lost case inflections, but they retain a diversified system of tenses and moods. There are also other, not so neatly regular, differences between what remains and what gets lost in specific Slavic languages, which will be discussed later.

Some constants still exist, like the previously discussed gender-based inflections. One additional cohesive feature of Slavic languages that makes their profile distinctive from their neighboring language families is the category of verbal aspect, which is preserved and stable in all Slavic languages. In Slavic languages, one cannot simply say *to read, to drink,* or *to write.* In each of these instances, they have to choose between, what usually boils down to, 'to be doing' and 'completed doing.' For example, in Polish, *czytać* is 'to be reading,' and *przeczytać* is 'to finish reading'; *pić* is 'to be drinking,' and *wypić* is 'to drink up'; and *pisać* is 'to be writing,' and *napisać* is 'to write up, to finish writing.' What in most cases is the 'to be doing, to be unfolding' form of the verb is called its imperfective (literally noncompleted) aspect, and what most of the time boils down to the 'completed, finished, fully exhausted doing' is its perfective (literally completed) aspect. This is just the basic distinction within the category of aspects. Imperfective verbs can be durative, i.e., refer to an action that goes on without interruptions. For example, in Polish *iść* is 'to be in the process of going,' such as when going from home to work on foot in one single trip. They can also be iterative, i.e., refer to an action that repeats itself, lasting through these instances of repetition (e.g., Polish *chodzić* 'to go repeatedly,' as in saying that you go to work on foot every workday). This distinction can then be subdivided further. Perfective verbs also have a range of semantic nuances (completion of the initial phase of the process, completion in an instance, etc.). The category of aspect in Slavic languages is quite intricate; more information about all its peculiarities can be found in the works of literature recommended at the end of this chapter.

The category of verbal aspect is well preserved in all Slavic languages, and it impacts verbal inflections. For example, when referring to the events happening in the present time, one needs to use the imperfective (oversimplifying, the 'to be doing, to be unfolding') aspect. In many Slavic languages, using the perfective form in the present-tense form means future. Thus, in Russian, *pišu* means 'I am writing' (the verb is in its present-tense form and imperfective aspect), and *napišu* 'I will write' (with the verb in the same present-tense form but in its perfective aspect). In the past and future, perfective and imperfective are possible, depending on whether one focuses on the process itself or its completion. Thus, in Polish, *czytałem* means 'I was in the process of reading,' and *przeczytałem* means 'I finished reading.'

What Is Flexed in the North and in the South

As noted, Northern Slavic languages generally retain their case inflections quite well and simplify their verb tenses. The situation is very different in Eastern South Slavic languages, where there are practically no synthetic cases (i.e., cases marked by case endings) and the system of tenses is elaborate. For example, in the plural forms of the word for 'hand,' Russian has D *rukam* 'to hands,' I *rukami* 'with hands,' and L *o rukah* 'about hands,' i.e., three different forms. Macedonian, an Eastern South Slavic language, has D *na race* 'to hands,' I *so race* 'with hands,' and L *za race* 'about hands,' so the form 'hands' does not change at all, given that there is not synthetic declension in Macedonian. Even in S-Cr (B/C/S), a West-South Slavic language, the form does not change in D *rukama* 'to hands,' I *rukama* 'with hands,' or L *o rukama* 'about hands,' although this language features synthetic inflection.

The widespread case inflection is also seen in the so-called participles, which are common in languages like Polish and Russian but not used in the Slavic south.

For example, a woman who reads is *čitajuščaja ženščina*, and to say, 'I saw a reading woman,' one would need to put this phrase into the accusative case: *Ja videl čitajuščuju ženščinu*. Similarly, the book that is being read is *čitaemaja kniga*, and to say, 'I loved the book that is being read,' one would again have to put the 'book being read' into the accusative case: *Ja poljubil čitaemuju knigu*. Similarly, cardinal numbers five and up are inflected. For example, 'five' is *pjat*, but to say, 'of five' or 'to five' or 'about five,' one needs to change it into *pjati*, and to say, 'with five,' the form will be changed into *pjatju*. This does not happen in the Slavic south.

The situation with tenses (like past: *I worked*) and moods (like conditional: *I would work*) is the opposite. Languages in the Slavic north have an ideally simple system with one tense form each for the present, past, and future. In the Slavic south, many of the Proto-Slavic tenses have been preserved, with some of them acquiring new functions in some of the languages. Take the past-tense forms. To speak about one's own writing in the past, the Proto-Slavs could use four different forms of the verb *pъsati* (imperfective) and *napъsati* (perfective). There was the perfect, the baseline past tense—*(na)pъsalъ esmъ*; aorist, the completed past tense—*napъsahъ*; imperfect, the ongoing past tense—*pъsaahъ*; and pluperfect, the before-the-past tense—*běxъ *(na)pъsalъ*. Although some of them have a limited scope of use, all these forms were retained in S-Cr (B/C/S), as in perfect *(na)pisao sam*, aorist *napisah*, imperfect *pisah*, pluperfect *bijah (na)pisao*, or bio *sam (na)pisao*. In Macedonian, another South Slavic language, some of these forms were repurposed. Thus *(na)pisa* 'he/she wrote' (the aorist form) serves as the witness mode—it is used when I witnessed somebody's writing. On the other hand, perfect *(na)pisal* is the nonwitness mode, when we talk about learning about somebody's writing from another source, not having witnessed it ourselves.

The "The" at the End of Words

There are also processes of change that show more diversified patterns of differences across Slavic languages. Proto-Slavic had definite and indefinite forms of adjectives. For example, when saying, 'a clean house,' one would use *čistъ domъ*; when saying, 'the clean house,' that would be *čistyjь domъ*. So, what is expressed by using either the indefinite or the definite article in English was conveyed by the difference between the indefinite (short) and the definite (long) form of the adjectives. The definite form is created by adding a demonstrative pronoun at the end of the adjective, as if adding the "the" at the end of the adjective, like saying *clean-the house* instead of *the clean house*. Theoretically, S-Cr (B/C/S) still has this distinction: *čisti dom* is 'the clean home,' and *čist dom* is 'a clean home.' However, most speakers do not adhere to this distinction. In Russian, the long form grew to mean the permanent feature and the short form a temporary feature, as in *čistyj dom* 'a clean house,' that is, 'the house that is kept clean,' versus *dom čist* 'the house is clean,' that is, now being just cleaned but not likely to stay so permanently. In Polish, only the long form is used in all functions, with the short form appearing in a handful of individual words as in *Rad jestem* 'I am keen/ glad.' Macedonian and Bulgarian, on the other hand, have taken this feature a step further and developed the postpositive article *-t* that can be attached to adjectives but also to nouns, so *čistiot dom* is 'the clean home' as opposed to *čist dom* 'a clean house,' but there is also *domot* 'the home' versus *dom* 'a home.' Macedonian has even developed two additional postpositive articles, so it has *dom* 'a house,' *domov* 'the house next to the speaker,' *domot* 'the house, in general,' and *domon* 'the house over there, far from the speaker and listener.'

General lessons from the development of Slavic morphology is that of diversity in unity. Simplification is the general organizing principle. However, what gets simplified varies from one language to another. There are margins that resist innovation like Slovene and Sorbian, which still maintain the dual number. There are also margins of innovation like Macedonian and Bulgarian that have lost synthetic declensions and developed postpositive articles. Then, there are general tendencies such as simpler verbal and richer nominal inflection in the north versus richer verbal and simpler nominal inflection in the south.

Processions of Functional Words

Semantic words like nouns, adjectives, and verbs are only a part of the grammatical gear of Slavic languages. Equally interesting phenomena can be found in functional words like pronouns, prepositions, and particles (such words that establish relationships in the sentence, rather than referring to a segment of reality, like semantic words, such as nouns do).

In the sea of change, personal pronouns remain the rock of stability. English has lost synthetic inflections; however, the difference between *I* and *me* and *we* and *us* remains (pronouns defined by the subject vs. object position). One remarkable feature of PIE pronouns was that they used different stems for the singular and plural forms of the first-person pronoun. They also used different stems for the subject and object case. 'I' was **eǵ*, 'me' was **me*, 'we' was **uei*, and 'us' was **nōs*. There is a different stem when 'we' is the subject (e.g., when chasing a wild animal) and when 'we' is the object (as in being chased by that animal). Similarly, there is one stem when we are alone (singular) and when we are in a group. This usage has been retained in Slavic languages, e.g., in Polish: *ja* 'I,' *mnie* 'me,' *my* 'we,' and *nas* 'us.' This is also true for most other Indo-European languages, as the case of English clearly exemplifies.

Not everything is so universal. Another remarkable characteristic of Slavic languages is their word order. English religiously follows the SVO (subject, verb, object) word order. Thus, in *Peter is hitting Paul*, the subject (S, the hitter, Peter in this case) must come before the verb (V, the action, is hitting), and the object (O, the sufferer, Paul) needs to be behind that. SVO is the default in Slavic languages, but because sentence roles are marked with cases in most of them, they can change that word order to emphasize a point. Thus, in S-Cr (B/C/S), *Petar udara Pavla* is neutral, but, given that the lack of the ending clearly signals that Peter is the performer and the -*a* ending that Paul is the sufferer, one can render sentences like *Pavla udara Petar* (OVS), which roughly means, 'It is Paul whom Peter is hitting (and not somebody else)'; *Pavla Petar udara* (OSV), 'It is Paul who is being hit by Peter'; *Udara Petar Pavla* (VSO), 'Peter is hitting Paul (not doing something else to him),' and so forth.

However, in the field of enclitics (words without their own stress that come after stressed words), there are rather strict rules of how enclitics need to be ordered. First, there is Wackernagel's law, which applies to a range of Indo-European languages, including those from the Slavic branch, and states that enclitics tend to be in the second position in a clause. For example, 'I saw him yesterday' will have to be (1) *Widziałem* 'I saw' (2) **go** 'him' (3) *wczoraj* 'yesterday' or (3) *Wczoraj* (2) **go** (1) *widziałem* (the place of stress is underlined, and the enclitics are given in bold).

What is specific about Slavic languages, especially those in the south, are the rules of ordering within the cluster of enclitics (i.e., several enclitics right after one another). The cluster itself is in the second position, and the rules for the distribution within it are rather intricate. To use S-Cr (B/C/S) as an example, the position of enclitics in a cluster is regulated by the order of precedence presented in table 4.1. The rule is that a lower-order number should precede a higher-order number, as can be seen in table 4.2.

To make things complicated, there are exceptions to this rule, but we will let sleeping dogs lie. This suffices to explain how complex these language-specific rules of ordering may be, although they generally fall under Wackernagel's law for the entire cluster. Yet again, we can see rather intricate local developments under a neat global rule.

Table 4.1. The Order of the Enclitics

Order	Element
1	question tag *li*
2	auxiliary verb *sam* 'I am,' etc.
3	dative of a pronoun *mu* 'to him'
4	genitive of a pronoun *ih* 'of them'
5	accusative of a pronoun *me* 'me'
6	reflexive particle *se* 'oneself'

Table 4.2. Placement of the Enclitics

Ja	*sam*	*mu*	*ga*	*dao.*	'I have given it/him to him.'
I	have	to him	it/him	given	
1	2	2	2	3	cluster placement
	2	3	4		placement within the cluster
Ja	*sam*	*ga*	*se*	*sjetio.*	'I have remembered him.' (lit., 'I have remembered myself of him')
I	have	him	myself	remembered	
1	2	2	2	3	cluster placement
	2	4	6		placement within the cluster

Chapter Takeaways

One remarkable difference between the grammar of English and that of Slavic languages is the role of the gender in the inflection of Slavic nouns and adjectives and the need to match the gender of the nouns and their adjectives and other modifiers (which is also done in languages like Spanish or French). A further difference is that almost all Slavic languages need to inflect their nouns and adjectives to designate who does what to whom in the sentence. What is in English signaled by the use of a preposition, in Slavic languages is normally expressed with either just inflecting the end of the word or using a preposition and inflecting the end of the word. There are further specificities of Slavic inflections, most notably that typically a verb in English has two Slavic equivalents: the perfective and the imperfective. There is also a large degree in variation as to what is inflected in Slavic languages, with those in the north generally having more elaborate noun inflections, and those in the south having a more complex verb inflection.

Elaborate rules for ordering functional words in a sentence are a further idiosyncratic feature of Slavic languages.

Recommended Chapter Readings

Towsend and Janda (1996) provide an accessible introduction to the development of inflections. The developments from PIE via PSL to Slavic languages are also presented in Schenker (1995). Morphological and syntactic systems of individual Slavic languages are described in Comrie and Corbett (1993) and Sussex and Cubberly (2006). Browne (2014) provides an excellent review of the clitics in Slavic languages. Janda and Clacy (2002, 2006) discuss Slavic cases.

II Words, Words, Words

5　How Time and Space Split Slavic Roots

Slavic Words as Cleavers of Notions

Slavs do not have to differentiate between 'arm' and 'hand' (e.g., both are *ręka* in Polish), 'leg' and 'foot' (e.g., both are *noha* in Czech), or 'finger' and 'toe' (e.g., both are *prst* in Slovene). Russians do not even have to differentiate between 'brain' and 'spinal cord,' as both can be called *mozg*. The fact that a group of languages chops up its notions into more or less precise words gives them a certain profile compared to other language groups. Obviously, there are such features that differentiate one Slavic language from another. For example, Russian has one word for 'uncle,' *djadja*, whereas S-Cr (B/C/S) has three: *stric* 'one's father's brother,' *ujak* 'one's mother's brother,' and *tetak* 'husband of one's father's or mother's sister.'

The lexical profiles of individual Slavic languages and Slavic languages as a group are defined by a number of other features, such as common word associations (as in a draft of air considered a cause of all diseases), culture-bound words (e.g., Russian *toska*, the feeling of longing for something but not knowing what that is), idiosyncratic multiword units and proverbs (as in Russian: *gorlyško butylki* 'bottleneck,' literally 'little throat of the bottle' and *Ne v sile Bog a v pravde* 'God is not in force, but in justice'), and word-formation networks (as in a high number of words derived from *duša/dusza* 'soul' in many Slavic languages). These specific configurations result from the separate development of Slavic languages once they left the PIE ancestral homeland in the early first millennium BCE, and then the processes that have shaped each Slavic language after the dissolution of the PSL community that started around the third and fourth centuries CE.

The Fields of Chopping

To illustrate the differences in precision in subject-matter fields, I have analyzed the cases in which one S-Cr (B/C/S) word had multiple English equivalents in a well-known bilingual dictionary. It turns out that nearly 30 percent of these differences are found in words related to social interaction, including social roles (for example, *žena* is 'wife,' 'woman,' 'cleaning woman,' etc.). Very broadly understood measures amounted to over 25 percent of these cases (e.g., *visina* is 'height,' 'altitude,' 'elevation,' and 'pitch'). Over 10 percent of cases were words for institutions, for example, *pošta* is 'post office' and 'mail.' The remainder of the cases belonged to a range of narrower subject-matter fields. Some of them, like body parts, with over 4 percent (e.g., *noga* is 'foot' and 'leg'), are in some ways similar to the broader categories—naming body parts more or less precisely is similar to measuring the body. Operators, words that establish relations between other words, represent nearly 10 percent of cases (e.g., *a* is 'and,' 'but,' and 'while') and are like measuring in that some relationship is established.

One explanation that can be attached to these differences is that they are correlated with the cross-cultural differences discussed in chapter 1. Serving collectivistic polychronic cultures, S-Cr (B/C/S) is less precise (more holistic) in expressing the concepts related to social interactions and institutions, as well as broadly understood measuring concepts (and related logical operators and designations of body parts). English, on the other hand, serves individualist and monochronic cultures and is therefore more precise in expressing concepts in the fields of social interactions and measures. Similar results to the preceding example were found in Russian, another Slavic language, where in a Russian-English dictionary, which includes only those Russian words that have many English equivalents, nearly 40 percent were terms related to social interactions, and nearly 13 percent were measures, with additional terms that amounted to more than 6 percent, if logical operators and body parts are considered in this group. The category of institutions was considerably less present than in the case of S-Cr (B/C/S), but that is because the dictionary did not include those cases that have only two English equivalents, which is typical of institutions.

Calculations and Cultures

The extent of the differences in how concepts are chopped up into words in Slavic languages on the one hand and English on the other is seen very clearly in a word present in various Slavic languages that roughly means the action or the result of a calculation. The word is *ščot* in Russian, *rahunok* in Ukrainian, *rachunek* in Polish, *račun* in S-Cr (B/C/S) and Slovene, *smetka* in Bulgarian and Macedonian, and so forth. In English, these words can mean calculation, calculus, count, counting, bill, receipt, check (as in a restaurant), account, score, invoice, financial statement, profit, interest, and advantage. So, English is quite precise in stating what kind of calculation the word pertains to. For example, a bill that we get for electricity is something separate from the receipt we get in a store. A bank account is something different altogether.

The question then arises again whether these cross-linguistic differences have anything to do with the cross-cultural differences discussed in chapter 1. In particular, the dimension of collectivism versus individualism and the difference between polychronic and monochronic cultures come to mind. To repeat, Slavic cultures are collectivistic and polychronic, whereas mainstream North American cultures are individualistic and monochronic. Obviously, one example does not mean anything, but the fact is (as previously stated) that different types of measurement words and those relating to social interactions are more precisely carved out in English than in Slavic languages. These are whole areas of the vocabulary, not just individual examples. One can then ask if that has to do with the need to precisely determine interpersonal relations in individualistic cultures (what counts is primarily the individual) and the lack of such need in collectivistic cultures (what matters is the community, so it is not important to clearly define those relationships). Similarly, one can ask if this distinction has to do with more precise separation of personal and work spheres and higher punctuality in monochronic cultures as opposed to the overlapping of these spheres and a relaxed attitude toward appointment times in polychronic cultures. These are difficult questions to which there are no straightforward answers.

The Murderous Draft of Air

As previously noted, more may be connected to the predominant cultural patterns than just the way concepts are chopped into words. There are further linguistic data that might fit the pattern. There are also word associations. One such example is a draft of air. This word and concept in English are not really associated with the words for illness, disease, and the like. In Slavic cultures, there is a strong association between the words for a draft of air and the words for getting sick. The belief is that the draft of air is very dangerous and causes all kinds of diseases. Diseases like the flu, common cold, and pneumonia are often explained by the fact that the sick person was exposed to a draft of air. Needless to say, this word is not as ambiguous as it is in English. Words like the Russian *skvoznjak*, Polish *przeciąg*, S-Cr (B/C/S) and Macedonian *promaja*, and Slovene *prepih* all mean 'the draft of air' and nothing else.

In the 1970s, one could smoke freely on trains across Slavic countries, but it would be unimaginable to open the window while the train was in motion. One would be harshly admonished. The justification in S-Cr (B/C/S) would be *ubi pro-maja* 'the draft of air is going to kill you.' The actual form is the verb *ubiti* 'to kill' in the aorist tense (completed past tense). Using this past-tense form to mean future is emphasizing the inevitability of the event, something like saying, 'the draft of air will kill you for sure.' As we can see, there is not only a language-specific word association with illness but also an idiosyncratic collocation (a common combination of words) of the verb for 'to kill' and the word for a 'draft of air.' This example also shows something else. Not all culture-specific linguistic features can be connected to the predominant patterns in that culture. Many of them are a result of historical circumstances and often random events. This example might have been triggered by an observation of the homes of poor, and often sickly, people, which were shabbily built and featured ample drafts.

From *Arshin* to *Złoty*

A further piece of evidence in a cultural profile of Slavic languages is culture-bound words. These words range from the examples that simply label various culture-bound entities, to those more complex examples of possibly expressing a specific worldview by using the lexical item in question. Let us look at some examples. First, there are numerous words for food items, musical instruments and musical forms, garments, environment objects, flora and fauna, objects of daily life, historical institutions, and roles that are specific to the culture of the Slavic language in question. There is the East Slavic and Polish red beet soup called *boršč* in Russian and *barszcz* in Polish. There are stuffed fresh cabbage rolls called *golubcy* in Russian, *holubcy* in Ukrainian, and *gołąbki* in Polish. There are also pickled cabbage rolls in the Balkans that are called *sarma* in S-Cr (B/C/S), Macedonian, and Bulgarian. The list can go on forever, and it also includes spirits such as the North Slavic grain- or potato-based *vodka* and the South Slavic plum- or grape-based *rakia*. Most of these food items may have had their origins somewhere else, but their ubiquity in those Slavic countries and the level of familiarity and specific positive attitudes that speakers have toward these items make them inextricably connected with the cultural background of the Slavic languages in question.

Then there is *balalaika*, a Russian string instrument with a triangular body; *gusle*, a South Slavic single-stringed bowed instrument used in accompanying the narration of epic poetry; and many other similar instruments. Dances like the South Slavic *kolo* or the East Slavic *kozachok* are also culture-bound words. Furthermore, there are garments like the traditional Russian skewed-collared men's shirt called *rubashka* and traditional Serbian lambda-shaped (Λ) cap called *šajkača*.

Among culture-bound words, one can also find terms for environmental objects characteristic of some regions in Slavic countries, like the Russian *chernozem* (fertile black soil rich in humus) and *taiga* (coniferous forest in the northern latitudes). There are also names for various plants and animals characteristic of the typical biomes in Slavic countries, such as the Russian *beluga* (a type of sturgeon, known for caviar) and *kamyš* (club-rush, a tall grassy plant used to weave baskets, bags, etc.). Words for common characteristic artifacts also tend to be culture-bound words. The Russian word *dacha*, for a second home in the countryside, and *izba*, a typical Russian log hut, exemplify this group.

Some culture-bound words are clearly linked to the historical background of the language in question. There are old measures, such as the Russian *arshin* (2 1/3 feet) and *versta* (amounting to .6629 mile). There are currency units, such as the Russian *rouble* and Polish *złoty*, and names of parliaments, such as the Russian *Duma* or Macedonian *Sobranie*. There are furthermore titles and designations clearly stemming from distinct historical periods, such as *boyar*—an East Slavic, Bulgarian, and Serbian feudal title—or *apparatchik*, a member of the Communist establishment, primarily in the former Soviet Union.

All hitherto-presented examples are clear reflections of a historic, an ecological, or a cultural niche of a kind. The physical and intellectual landscape of each Slavic language is colored with entities from this niche, which give the language in question a certain cultural profile. Words are merely labels attached to these entities.

Words as Keys to Cultures

Aside from these, there are various culture-bound words that, according to some authors, offer a key to understanding the culture in question. These cultural keywords seem to encapsulate a culture-specific way of thinking. There are two famous literary examples of such words, one Russian and the other Czech.

The fifth part of the novel *The Book of Laughter and Forgetting* by the famous Czech writer Milan Kundera is titled "Lítost." The author presented his elaborate observations about this allegedly untranslatable Czech word most succinctly in the following segment of his extended discourse on the topic: "Lítost is a state of torment created by the sudden sight of one's own misery" (see suggested readings for this and the following quote). Although Kundera expressly claimed that the Czech word *lítost* is untranslatable, there are those who claim that it is akin to the English word *self-pity*.

In a similar example, Vladimir Nabokov wrote about the Russian culture-bound concept of *toska*:

> No single word in English renders all the shades of *toska*. At its deepest and most painful, it is a sensation of great spiritual anguish, often without any specific cause. At less morbid levels it is a dull ache of the soul, a longing with nothing to long for, a sick pining, a vague restlessness, mental throes, yearning. In particular cases it may be the desire for somebody of something specific, nostalgia, love-sickness. At the lowest level it grades into ennui, boredom.

I have also heard a more succinct definition of this term, which goes like this: I am longing for something, I do not know what it is, but I am very sad because I cannot have it.

Some of these cultural keywords are also found in other languages, but their prominence in Slavic languages makes them special. One such word is *duša* (rendered as *duše* in Czech and *dusza* in Polish), the word for 'soul.' The word is in frequent use even among those who are not religious, and there are also numerous idioms and derivatives involving this word. It is very common in Russian and other Slavic languages to describe somebody who is heartful using the word *duševnyj* 'soulful.' One can also say that somebody is doing something in a heartfelt manner: *duševno* 'soulfully.' It is also possible to praise somebody's heartfulness, i.e., *duševnost'* 'soulfulness.' In Poland, a priest taking care of a specific group of the faithful (e.g., a group of students or members of some profession) is called *duszpasterz* 'soul shepherd' and his work is *duszpasterstwo* 'soul shepherding.' It is also common to use *duša moja* (in Russian) and *dušo moja*, in S-Cr (B/C/S), both meaning 'my soul,' as a term of endearment for a beloved person.

Unlike the previous group of culture-bound words, which were quite straightforward in reflecting cultural entities, examples like *lítost*, *toska*, and *duša* are much more difficult to crack open. On the one hand, it is quite easy to point to possible connections between these words and the way of thinking prevalent in the Slavic culture in question. On the other hand, it is very difficult to provide consistent proof for such links.

The Mother Metaphor

One thing that seems to keep Slavic languages together is that they share metaphors connecting the meanings of their words. My analysis of multiple equivalence (single words that refer to two or more words in another language) in several Slavic-to-Slavic and Slavic-to-non-Slavic dictionaries has shown that there are two main types of generators of multiple equivalence: semantic differentiation and semantic transfer. Additionally, there are two other types that cover a very small number of cases and are of no relevance, so they will be not discussed here.

A classic example of semantic differentiation is body part names in Slavic languages versus English. For example, the Polish *ręka* is both *hand* and *arm* and *noga* is both *foot* and *leg*. In this case a conceptual sphere that is covered with one word in the source language is divided into two or more words in the target language. How this division is configured varies.

Semantic transfer is mostly metaphorical, as in the following Polish-English example: Polish *czoło* vs. English *forehead* (część *twarzy* 'part of the face') and *front* (*przód* 'front part'), where the concept of forehead is metaphorically transferred in Polish to mean 'front' (e.g., of a table), which is not the case in English.

I analyzed six dictionaries in my research on this topic (see the list of suggested readings for more information about this research): three Slavic-to-Slavic dictionaries (Russian-Polish, Polish-Russian, and Russian-Serbian) and three Slavic-to-non-Slavic dictionaries (Russian-English, Russian-German, and Polish-English). The most striking difference between Slavic-Slavic and Slavic–non-Slavic equivalence is that in the former case the dominant subtype of multiple equivalence is differentiation (58.2% on average across three dictionaries), and in the latter it is transfer (47.8% on average across three dictionaries). It seems that Slavic languages share a higher number of semantic transfers (mostly metaphors) with other Slavic languages than with non-Slavic languages. At the same time, inter-Slavic lexical divergence rests mostly on the need of each Slavic language to carve out more precise domains of meaning. In contrast, numerous semantic transfers in Slavic languages are not shared in non-Slavic languages. This can be explained by the common heritage of Slavic languages—semantic transfers were active in Proto-Slavic much later than in Proto-Indo-European, so their effects are likely to be stronger in the languages sharing a Proto-Slavic linguistic heritage.

War as a Measure of Time

Various idioms and proverbs may also be culture specific. In some cases, the links between language and culture are straightforward. For example, in all Slavic languages, it is common to refer to segments of time using expressions like S-Cr (B/C/S) *prije rata* 'before the war' and *poslije rata* 'after the war.' The instability of the region where this language is spoken has caused these expressions to become ambiguous because they can refer to World War II (as in other Slavic languages) or to the 1990s wars in the former Yugoslavia. Consequently, this time reference would commonly trigger the question *Kojeg?* 'Which one?' in S-Cr (B/C/S). There is also an idiom stating that some people suffered in the war and others profited from it: *Nekom rat, nekom brat* 'War to some, brother to some others.' Russian has an idiom that expresses the same idea, but its wording is a bit different: *Komu vojna, komu mat' rodnaja* 'War to some, dear/biological mother to some others.' The difference between the expressions in S-Cr (B/C/S) and Russian is caused by the fact that the word for war in Russian is feminine, so it needed to be connected to the feminine figure to create rhyme and reason. In S-Cr (B/C/S), the word for war is masculine and it rhymes with the word for 'brother.' This comparison clearly shows how structural linguistic elements (gender of the word, in this case) shape idioms in sync with historical circumstances.

A German with a Slavic Soul

How complicated things can be in establishing the links between predominant cultural patterns and linguistic elements should be obvious from the following example. In English-speaking cultures, especially those in North America, there is genuine optimism about people forging their own destiny. Stemming from the Protestant work ethic, the American Declaration of Independence mentions three birthrights God gave citizens that should be protected by the government: "Life, Liberty and the Pursuit of Happiness." Pursuit—i.e., a chance, an opportunity—is a key word here, indicating that it is up to each individual to forge their own destiny.

In Slavic cultures, on the other hand, there is a feeling that mysterious forces rule our lives and that we are but straws in the wind. The proverbs *Čelovek pred- polagaet a Bog raspolagaet* (literally 'Man assumes, God distributes') in Russian, *Człowiek strzela, Pan Bóg kulę nosi* (literally 'Man shoots, God carries the bullet') in Polish, and *Čovjek snuje, Bog određuje* (literally 'Man dreams, God determines') in S-Cr (B/C/S), which are well known in all these cultures, seem to encapsulate this attitude. The same feeling can be found in texts by numerous Slavic-language writers, Fyodor Dostoevsky the best known and most prototypical of this worldview. But the proverb is not restricted to Slavic languages. German has *Der Mensch denkt, Gott lenkt* (literally 'Man thinks, God turns'), and English has *Man proposes, but God disposes.* All of these expressions are translations of the Latin phrase *Homo proponit, sed Deus disponit* from bk. 1, chap. 19 of *The Imitation of Christ* by the fifteenth-century German cleric Thomas à Kempis—a German with a Slavic soul. So, something that perfectly fits the predominant cultural patterns of Slavic cultures does not really stem from those cultures. It is, rather, a borrowing from a single writer, coming from a completely different culture. What made this expression highly recognizable and frequently used in Slavic languages (unlike in German and English) is it encapsulates a worldview predominant in the cultures of these languages.

Making Sense of How Senses Change

As previously noted, Slavic languages developed from the same Proto-Slavic source. Among other things, this means that each Slavic language features words inherited from PSL that are also likely to be found in other Slavic languages, if not all of them. The meanings of these words are sometimes identical across several Slavic languages, but very commonly their meanings will be different in any two Slavic languages under comparison. These differences vary from those that are subtle to those that make the two meanings distant from each other. At the same time, some PSL words are retained in some Slavic languages and lost in others. Even if two Slavic languages have the same inherited word, its frequency may be very high in one of them and marginal in the other.

These divergent processes are a result of the separate development of each Slavic language since the dissolution of the PSL speech community. Another notable feature of idiosyncratic developments in each Slavic language is their interactions with other languages, from which they borrow words and to which they lend them. In addition to divergence (e.g., when one Slavic language borrows a word and another does not), there are also convergent processes. For example, most Slavic languages borrowed numerous scientific terms from German and French (and recently also from English). These three languages serve the cultures that have been economically and politically dominant in Europe, and these cultures are based on a Greek and Latin cultural heritage. Examples of borrowed words include scientific disciplines, such as biology or geography; various phenomena, such as electricity, atmosphere, and pollen; and assorted tools and techniques, such as computer, telescope, and titration.

The senses of inherited PSL roots could be retained or changed in several different ways. I will use examples from Rick Derksen (2008), a dictionary of the inherited PSL lexicon, to show how these inherited roots have changed in the three groups of Slavic languages. The following developments were possible:

- A sense that was in existence in PSL has been lost. For example, PSL *vol-sti 'rule' is not attested in South Slavic languages, and there is no new meaning that has developed from it.
- A PSL sense has been retained. For example, *vòńa or *vòńь 'smell' has been retained in West Slavic languages; it yields woń 'smell' in Polish.
- A PSL sense has been changed in a variety of configurations (examples will be provided further in the text).

Slavic Lexical Unity in Diversity

The statistics based on Derksen (2008) for the three groups of Slavic languages are shown in table 5.1. table 5.2 displays the ratio of loss, change, and preservation for each group.

As can be seen, there is a high degree of preservation, which testifies to the unity of the Slavic language branch, and a significant degree of variation, which indicates the diversity of the Slavic subgroups and their individual languages.

Similar results can be seen in the analysis of semantic words from Swadesh's list (a list of nearly two hundred very basic words, with functional words excluded) in the largest languages of the three Slavic branches: Russian, Polish, and S-Cr (B/C/S). In over one-half of the cases (55%) from this very basic vocabulary layer, Slavic languages share the inherited word in their basic meaning (e.g., S-Cr (B/C/S) ruka, Polish ręka, and Russian ruka 'hand/arm'). In nearly 30 percent of the cases, there is some differentiation in the meaning of an inherited word in one or more languages. The differentiation is most commonly semantic, as in S-Cr (B/C/S) zao ('evil, mean') and loš ('bad'), Polish zły and Russian zloj ('evil, mean') and plok-hoj ('bad/evil'). So in this example, the original PSL root *zъlъ ('bad, not good') has developed different meanings in individual Slavic languages. There are also cases of stylistic differentiation, as in S-Cr (B/C/S) kiša 'rain' (neutral) and dažd

Table 5.1. The Development of Inherited PSL Roots

Category	Number	Percent
Preservation in all three groups	471	27.7
Change in all three groups	436	25.6
Loss in all three groups	20	1.2
A combination of loss, change, and preservation	776	45.5
Total	1,703	100

Source: Author's analysis of data from Derksen (2008).

Table 5.2. Loss, Change, and Preservation in the Three Groups of Slavic Languages

	East Slavic		West Slavic		South Slavic	
	Number	Percent	Number	Percent	Number	Percent
Loss	175	10.3	204	12	168	9.9
Change	707	41.5	707	41.5	873	51.3
Preservation	821	48.2	792	46.5	662	38.9
Total	1,703	100	1,703	100	1,703	100

Source: Author's analysis of data from Derksen (2008).

'rain' (poetic), Polish *deszcz* 'rain' (neutral), and Russian *dožd* 'rain' (neutral). The number of cases in which at least one language has a different word is rather small—around 16 percent.

One consequence of all these processes is the so-called false cognates, discussed in chapter 6. Changes in inherited roots make the words with similar forms in two or more Slavic languages different in their meanings, just like in the example above in which the Polish *zły* can mean 'evil, mean' or 'bad, of inferior quality' whereas the Russian *zloj* is narrower, holding the first meaning but not the second.

Becoming Narrower, Wider, or Something Else

The most common of semantic processes that has differentiated the meaning of inherited Slavic roots in the three groups of Slavic languages is narrowing, followed closely by semantic transfer, whereas semantic widening has only played a minor role. The statistics for the Derksen (2008) data along with some examples of the three relevant semantic processes are provided in table 5.3.

Table 5.3. Semantic Narrowing, Transfer, and Widening in the Three Groups of Slavic Languages

	East		West		South	
	Number	**Percent**	**Number**	**Percent**	**Number**	**Percent**
Narrowing	357	52	367	50	478	47
Transfer	277	40	316	43	452	45
Widening	55	8	51	7	82	8
Total	689	100	734	100	1,012	100

Examples:
- Narrowing: Czech *jahoda* 'strawberry' from PSL **àgoda* 'berry'
- Transferring: S-Cr (B/C/S) *slatina* 'mineral spring' from PSL **soltina* 'salt marsh'
- Widening: Slovak *slatina* 'marsh' from PSL **soltina* 'salt marsh'

Source: Author's analysis of data from Derksen (2008).

A takeaway from all these data is that the areas of overlap between the meanings of Slavic words are substantial but that various semantic processes in the development of each Slavic language have led to formidable differences between them. These changes were happening in distinct subject-matter fields relevant when the PSL speech community disintegrated. Others were carried out by mechanisms such as word formation, semantic extension, and borrowing at a later point in time.

How Have Changes Reshaped Subject-Matter Fields?

Aside from what has been retained and what has not, another interesting question is what are the subject-matter fields of the words that Slavic languages have inherited from PSL. The scope of inherited PSL vocabulary was determined by the time in which this speech community existed. It encompasses the phenomena that were in existence before the second through the fourth centuries CE. The following five lexical fields can be established in the inherited PSL stock. First is the field that one can call *things* in a very broad sense of that word (a fancier word would be *entities*). This field can be broken down into seven categories, the first of which includes environment-related words, i.e., words related to the landscape, meteorological phenomena, etc., such as the PSL words **bagnò* 'marsh,' **padorga* 'bad weather,' and **golot* 'thin layer of ice.' The second of the seven categories is words related to plants, such as *bèrza* 'birch,' *àblo or *àblъ 'apple,' and *mъхъ 'moss.' Then there are words related to animals, e.g., *orьlъ 'eagle,' *pьsъ 'dog,' and *sòmъ 'sheatfish.' The fourth category includes words related to the human body, e.g., *golvà 'head,' *palьcъ 'finger,' and *môzgъ 'marrow, brain.' Then there were artifacts, words related to the household, farming, crafts, and so forth, such as *vьsь 'village,' *górdjь or *górdja 'fence,' and *lemexъ 'ploughshare, plough.' The next category involves beliefs and traditions, words related to spiritual life, and abstract concepts, e.g., *bôgъ 'god,' *čara 'magic, sorcery,' and *čùdo 'miracle.' The seventh and final category is social roles, including kinship and other social terms, e.g., *drûgъ 'companion, friend,' *nestera 'niece,' and *sestrà 'sister.'

The second PSL lexical field includes two types of features. One set within this field is physical and physiological features that describe appearance and body, e.g., *vôrnъ 'black,' *bridъkъ 'sharp,' and *bystrъ 'quick.' The other set involves affective and cognitive features, e.g., *dôrgъ 'dear,' *durъnъ 'stupid, crazy,' and *dьrzъ 'daring, bold.'

The third PSL lexical field contains two kinds of processes: physical-physiological and affective-cognitive. The set of physical and physiological processes includes words like *dъržati 'hold,' *ěxati 'go, ride,' and *ęti 'take.' The set of affective and cognitive processes is exemplified by words like *bojàti sę 'fear, be afraid,' *golgolati 'speak,' and *gādàti 'guess.'

Finally, in addition to all these content (or semantic) words, there are also two fields of so-called functional words. First (the fourth field), there are operators, that is, the words used to express logical, spatial, and other relations, such as *a* 'and, but,' *jьzъ 'from, out of,' and *nizъ 'down, below.' Second (the fifth field), there are measures—such as numbers, days, and seasons—e.g., *d(ъ)va 'two,' *lěto 'summer,' and *pętъ 'fifth.' Based on my analysis of the data from Derksen (2008), functional words show a considerably higher level of preservation in all three languages than content words (the meanings of 49% of the functional words were preserved in all three language groups without changes, compared to 24.1% of the content words). The same holds true in each of the three subgroups of Slavic languages. If we further break down content words into processes, states, and things, the differences between each of these sets are not dramatic (20.7% preserved without changes in processes, 24.4% in states, and 28.6% in things). If the set of things is further divided into human-related (like household) and non-human-related (like nature), the differences are again not especially pronounced: 27.3 percent of the human-related lexicon and 30.2 percent of the non-human-related lexicon were preserved without changes in all three language subgroups.

What Makes the Subject-Matter Fields Change

Given that loss is only marginal (it represents the cases where the sense is continued, changed, or unchanged in Church Slavonic only, so it is lost in present-day Slavic languages), the interesting issue is the ratio of preservation to change in various subject-matter fields. In addition to a higher preservation rate for functional words (with measures having a higher rate than operators), one can notice several trends that also hold true in each group of Slavic languages. Physical-physiological states and processes exhibit a higher preservation rate than affective-cognitive processes. Beliefs and environmental terms consistently show lower retention rates than other things. Fauna, flora, body parts, and social terms show the highest degree of preservation.

All of these findings offer a platform for speculation about underlying currents of preservation and change. For example, higher preservation in the field of physical and physiological processes and states compared to their affective and cognitive counterparts may lead to the conclusion that universal human cognitive faculties were behind this difference. The physical and physiological processes and states are more primary, more frequent, and more prominent because they are used about the living and nonliving world, about humans and nonhuman animals, and so forth.

On the other hand, the fact that flora, fauna, body parts, and social relationships show the highest degree of preservation may have something to do with the cultures in which Slavic languages are embedded. These terms may point to the conservativeness of the rural collectivist culture of the early Slavs, which continued to exist in individual Slavic cultures. Of course, there are no easy answers to all these questions, and they are destined to remain stimuli for further reflection on all the forces behind semantic preservation and change.

Chapter Takeaways

In the vocabularies of Slavic languages there are words, phrases, word associations, metaphors, and so on that connect them, but there are also those that give each Slavic language a specific profile. Starting with their ancestor language, Proto-Slavic, Slavic languages have changed their inherited vocabulary in several different ways. Some of the words have disappeared, but most of them are still there. In those that remain in use, some of their senses have been retained, and others have undergone semantic narrowing, widening, or transfer. These changes were more pronounced in some subject-matter fields than in others.

Recommended Chapter Readings

Traugott and Dasher (2001) discuss regularities in semantic change. Allan and Robinson (2012) address a methodology for studying semantic changes. Geeraerts (2009) provides further theoretical considerations about lexical semantics. Šipka (2019) analyzes the development of Proto-Slavic roots in the three groups of Slavic languages. That book also contains more information about the research on the six dictionaries mentioned in this chapter. The Kundera quote is in Kundera (1981:131). The Nabokov quote is in Puškin (1990:141, note to stanza xxxiv line 8). For cultural keywords, see Wierzbicka (1997). Kempis's proverb is in Kempis (1998).

6 How Well Do Slavs Understand Each Other?

Comprehension and Miscomprehension

There is a well-known statement by Vuk Stefanović Karadžić, a nineteenth-century Serbian philologist, that speakers of Slavic languages can understand each other out of necessity. The actual phrase for 'out of necessity' is *za nevolju*, literally 'for trouble,' that is, when hard-pressed, when in an emergency, when there is no alternative. This statement accurately captures the essence of lexical kinship between Slavic languages. There are wide areas of similarity between Slavic languages, which makes limited mutual intelligibility possible. However, this level of intelligibility is not something that enables normal communication. It is rather a means of last resort, something that should be used when everything else fails. There are some true Slavic friends of the translator (i.e., lexical cognates), those similar words that enable communication in a very basic manner. However, there are also the translator's *false friends* (i.e., false cognates), words with similar forms in Slavic languages but different meanings, which make direct communication between the speakers of Slavic languages difficult. So, shared vocabulary between Slavic languages gives its speakers a deceptive sense of security and confidence in their comprehension of other Slavic languages. That, in turn, takes them out onto the thin ice of false cognates and into the land of miscomprehension. A further complication arises from grammatical differences, whereby a speaker of one Slavic language may misinterpret a grammatical form or sentence construction in another. In this chapter I will only talk about how words affect understanding and misunderstanding. One should be aware that the issue of understanding or not is much more complex, but discussing the entire complexity of that kind would far exceed the limits of this book.

Harmful and Soiled People

There is a story, perhaps apocryphal, about a Yugoslav representative in Moscow, Soviet Union (today Russia), during the 1948 conflict between the two countries. He said the following in one meeting: *Znaete, my malenkij narod, no vrednyj i ponosnyj.* In his native S-Cr (B/C/S), this sentence would read: *Znate, mi smo malen narod, ali vredan i ponosan.* So, the words are all very similar in these two closely related Slavic languages, yet their meanings are completely different. In S-Cr (B/C/S), the meaning is 'You know, we are small people, but hardworking and proud.' This is what he intended to say. By contrast, the meaning in Russian is 'You know, we are small people, but harmful and covered with diarrhea.' That is what his Russian interlocutors heard.

Another example, again, possibly apocryphal, of S-Cr (B/C/S)–Russian false cognates was registered in the US military and its prime language-learning outlet, the Defense Language Institute. The increased need for S-Cr (B/C/S) linguists during the war in the former Yugoslavia in the 1990s was met by the course Turbo Serbo, in which Russian linguists were cross-trained in S-Cr (B/C/S). Russian linguists were selected because of the similarities between the two languages, which made the training much shorter than it would have been for speakers of unrelated languages. One of the commands that they used was *Stoj da pucam!* In Serbo-Croatian, this means 'Stop, so that I can shoot you.' The comic effect comes from the conjunction *da*, which in this context means 'so that' in S-Cr (B/C/S), but in Russian it means 'or else.'

Stories like these two point to a couple of important facts about the relationships between words in Slavic languages: First, there is a large degree of similarity between these languages, giving the impression that if one knows one Slavic language, another can be learned effortlessly. The second fact, which contradicts the first, is that there exist many dangerous false cognates that can cause misunderstanding between speakers.

Understanding Each Other out of Necessity

Let us start with the similarities. Slavic languages share vast areas of commonality in the core of their vocabularies, as can be seen from the statistical data presented in the previous chapter. These areas of commonality encompass broad areas of vocabulary in the following lexical fields. In each category, examples are provided from various Slavic languages. Their forms vary somewhat from language to language:

pronouns: *ja, jas, jaz, az* 'I'; *ty, ti* 'you, singular'; *my, mi, nie* 'we'

numbers: *dva, dwa* 'two'; *sem, siedem, sedm, sedam, sedum* 'seven'; *desjat', dziesięć, desat, deset* 'ten'

days of the week: *ponedjeljak, poniedziałek, ponedel'nik* 'Monday'; *sreda, środa, středa* 'Wednesday'; *petak, petok, pjatnica, piótek* 'Friday'

body parts: *nos* 'nose'; *noga, noha* 'foot/leg'; *ruka, ręka, roka, raka* 'hand/arm'

kinship terms: *brat, bratr* 'brother'; *sestra, siostra* 'sister'; *žena, żona, žona* 'wife'

flora and fauna: *trava, trawa* 'grass'; *lipa* 'linden tree'; *vuk, volk, vlk, wilk* 'wolf'

the environment: *solnce, słońce, slunce, sunce* 'sun'; *veter, wiatr, vetar, vítr* 'wind'; *voda, woda* 'water'

basic actions: *stajati, stać, stát, stojatъ, stoi* 'stand'; *sedeti, siedzieć, sedět, sidetъ, sedi* 'sit'; *jesti, jíst, jeść, jestъ, jade* 'eat'

basic features: *širok, široký, szeroki, širokij* 'wide'; *nov, nový, nowy, novyj* 'new'

These similarities are not restricted to lexical lists. They can also be seen if we compare versions of the same text in various Slavic languages. For example, the first article of the Universal Declaration of Human Rights in six Slavic languages (two from each of the three branches, with the English original provided first) reads like this:

English

All human beings are born free and equal in dignity and rights. They are endowed with reason and conscience and should act towards one another in a spirit of brotherhood.

Russian

Vse ljudi roždajutsja svobodnymi i ravnymi v svoem dostoinstve i pravakh. Oni nadeleny razumom i sovest'ju i dolžny postupat Oni nadeleny razumom i sovest' v otnošenii drug druga v dukhe bratstva (Original spelling: Все люди рождаются свободными и равными в своем достоинстве и правах. Они наделены разумом и совестью и должны поступать в отношении друг друга в духе братства.)

Ukrainian

Vsi ljudi narožḋajut'sja vilnimi i rivnimi u svoji gidnosti ta pravah. Voni nadileni rozumom i sovistju i povinni dijati u vidnošenii odin do odnogo v dusi braterstva. (Original spelling: Всі люди народжуються вільними і рівними у своїй гідності та правах. Вони наділені розумом і совістю і повинні діяти у відношенні один до одного в дусі братерства.)

Polish

Wszyscy ludzie rodzą się wolni i równi pod względem swej godności i swych praw. Są oni obdarzeni rozumem i sumieniem i powinni postępować wobec innych w duchu braterstwa.

Czech

Všichni lidé rodí se svobodní a sobě rovní co do důstojnosti a práv. Jsou nadáni rozumem a svědomím a mají spolu jednat v duchu bratrství.

Slovene

Vsi ljudje se rodijo svobodni ter imajo enako dostojanstvo in pravice. Dana sta jim razum in vest, in bi morali drug z drugim ravnati v duhu bratstva.

Bulgarian

Vsički hora se raždat svobodni i ravni po dostojnstvo i prava. Ta se nadareni s razum i sv'est i sledva da e otnasjat pomeždu si v duh na bratstvo. (Original spelling: Всички хора се раждат свободни и равни по достойнство и права. Те са надарени с разум и съвест и следва да се отнасят помежду си в дух на братство.)

As can be seen, most of the words in this short text are shared by these six languages. In some of these shared words, one can see the traces of various phonological and morphological developments particular to each individual language. They range from the very slight ones, as in the last word of the text, to more complex ones, as in its first word. In some cases, one or two languages break the mold, as in the Bulgarian *hora*, as opposed to the descendants of PSL *l'udьe* 'people' in all other languages. Another example is the Ukrainian *gidnosti* and Polish *godności* for 'dignity,' unlike all other Slavic languages, which have a descendant of PSL **dostoinъstvo*.

Obviously, in other parallel translations, there may be more differences because each translator will typically decide to follow their own strategy, not necessarily because there is a difference between the languages in question. The assessment of what Slavic languages have in common and where they differ is painstakingly intricate. In the lexicon, languages may have the same word, but its meaning may be broader in one language than in another, it may be more common in one language than another, and so forth. In textual corpora, words may be present or absent depending on a variety of factors, such as region, time, subject-matter area, intended readership, and personal style of the writer or translator.

Understanding Other Slavic Languages: From Almost Perfect to Not So Perfect

Golubović and Gooskens (2015) have measured the mutual intelligibility of the Slavic languages in the European Union (Bulgarian, Croatian, Slovene, Czech, Slovak, and Polish) using several tests. In all of them, the results varied significantly from language pair to language pair and then internally inside language pairs. For example, in a written translation test (the participants were asked to translate fifty words randomly selected out of one hundred), the speakers of Slovene scored 80.85 percent with Croatian words, 65 percent with Bulgarian, 56.42 percent with Czech, 56.78 percent with Slovak, and 43 percent with Polish. Croatians scored 74.31 percent with Slovene words, 64.07 percent with Bulgarian, 51.87 percent with Czech, 51.87 percent with Slovak, and 43.91 percent with Polish. The highest scores were with Czech speakers for Slovak words (96.52%) and Slovak speakers with Czech (94.26%). Other tasks that they deployed yielded much lower results. For example, when the participants were played spoken passages with twelve words replaced by a beep, and then asked to match the written words provided to them with the blanks in the transcripts of these passages, the highest score was 95.04 percent (Slovak speakers with Czech passages) and the lowest was 9.52 percent (Croatian speakers with Polish passages). While these numbers should be taken with a grain of salt because they may vary in part due to the participants and the experimental design, they certainly point to the following conclusions: First, some Slavic languages are in a much closer relationship than others. Second, there is no general inter-Slavic reliability. Third, mutual understanding is dependent on the concrete context of communication and the task at hand. In other words, it is indeed understanding "out of necessity."

Slavic Shortcut Dictionaries

In Slavic lexicography, there are so-called differential dictionaries that assume the areas of commonality and state only the differences between Slavic languages. For example, in 1937, a differential S-Cr (B/C/S)–Bulgarian dictionary was published in Sofia, Bulgaria (penned by Živko Gъlъbov), and in the same year, a Bulgarian–S-Cr (B/C/S) differential dictionary was published in Belgrade, Yugoslavia (compiled by Nikola Mirković). For these dictionary projects, it was possible to omit those words that are identical in the two languages in their form and basic meaning (such as *glava* 'head, chapter' or *kosa* 'hair, scythe'). They also did not include those words with roughly the same meaning and a predictable difference in form, as in S-Cr (B/C/S) *kuća* vs. Bulgarian *kъšta* 'house' and S-Cr (B/C/S) *ugao* vs. Bulgarian *ъgъl* 'corner, angle.' In these two examples, the differences are a consequence of the development of the nasals (PSL ϱ => *u* in S-Cr (B/C/S), and *ъ* in Bulgarian), semivowels (PSL *ъ* => *a* in S-Cr (B/C/S) and *ъ* in Bulgarian), the palatalization of the *t* sound (PSL *t'* => *ć* in S-Cr (B/C/S) and *št* in Bulgarian), and *l* at the end of the syllable (PSL *l* => *o* in S-Cr (B/C/S) and *l* in Bulgarian). These processes are discussed in chapter 3 of this book.

Assuming all these similarities, these dictionaries are very compact, focusing just on the differences. These include the words with completely different forms, as in S-Cr (B/C/S) *porodica* and Bulgarian *semejstvo* 'family' or S-Cr (B/C/S) *avion* and Bulgarian *samolet* 'airplane.' Then, there are also words with the same or similar form but different meanings, for example, S-Cr (B/C/S) *staja* 'stable' and Bulgarian *staja* 'room' and S-Cr (B/C/S) *armija* 'army' and Bulgarian *armeja* 'sauerkraut.' The latter examples are the so-called false cognates.

A Tapestry of Slavic Dialects

The situation with the dialects is much more diversified than that of the standard languages. Dialects often have words that are not used in the standard language variety that also may be spreading over a broader area. So, if we compare any two Slavic dialects rather than their standard language forms, we will find a much higher level of diversity. Linguists across the Slavic world have been involved in documenting the lexical and, more broadly, linguistic diversity of Slavic dialects in a project called the Slavic Linguistic Atlas (more information about the project is available in various languages at http://www.slavatlas.org). This project offers a wealth of information on lexical variation (along with data about dialectal variation in phonology, inflections, and other aspects of grammar).

The level of variation, continuation, and change in a narrow piece of land can be demonstrated using the data from the 2020 Linguistic Atlas of Macedonian Dialects (see suggested readings). Take the word for 'pupil (of the eye).' In the standard forms of Slavic languages, the words are as follows: Rus. *zračok*; Bel. *zrenka*; Ukr. *zinicja*, *čolovičok*; Pol. *źrenica*; Sorbian (Sor.) *zernička/pupila*; Slk. *zrenica*, *zrenička*; Cze. *zornice*, *panenka*; Slo. *zenica*; S-Cr (B/C/S) *zjenica*, *zenica*; Bul. *zenica*; and Mac. *zenica*. The PSL source is *zěnica*, and it is easy to see that this PSL word has been preserved in most languages with the usual phonetic changes. Macedonian (Mac.) dialects offer a much more colorful picture. Along with *zenica*, the word that some dialects share with the standard language, there are several additional roots. First, there are three specific Macedonian metaphors, linking the pupil with young humans: *čoveče*, literally 'small man'; *bebe*, literally 'baby'; and *detence*, literally 'small child.' Then, there is *crnka*, literally 'the black one'; *gletce*, literally 'small watching thing'; and finally *zrak*, literally 'ray of light.'

Even a more diversified pattern of naming can be seen in the words for slime. The word in standard Mac. is *gol polžav*, literally 'naked snail.' In addition to that, the dialects have *div polžav* 'wild snail,' *voden polžav* 'water snail,' *ciganski polžav* 'Gypsy snail,' *turski polžav* 'Turkish snail,' *ligavec* 'slithery one,' *golec* 'naked one,' *šulak* (which is borrowed from Greek *saligkaros* 'snail'), and *gol salmin* 'naked snail,' with the second word borrowed from the dialectal Turkish *sölümen* 'snail.' Dialectal diversity here is caused not only by various indigenous metaphors but also by borrowing, and, more generally, contact from neighboring languages.

All these Macedonian examples testify that lexical differentiation in the realm of dialects includes the same mechanisms one finds at the level of language at large. Continuation is present in some cases; various changes are to be found in others. Changes are shaped by a specific culture, in the case of the dialects of a given region. They include various semantic changes, often metaphorically motivated, along with the changes that result from contact with speakers of other languages or an authority of some kind that uses another language.

From Hard to Fresh and Stale

Sharing numerous inherited roots is also fraught with danger. As one could see in chapter 5, the roots inherited from Proto-Slavic underwent various transformations in each individual Slavic language. These processes have led to the emergence of the so-called false cognates—the words with a similar form but different meaning or usage characteristics in any given pair of Slavic languages.

Let us look at some examples. There are pairs like Rus. *von'* 'stench' and Pol. *woń* 'scent, fragrance'; the meaning of the first word has a negative connotation, whereas the other has a positive one. Both words come from the PSL *voňь* 'smell.' One can clearly see how this initial meaning, which was neutral, has acquired negative connotations in one language and positive in the other. Similar is the pair Pol. *czerstwy* 'stale' vs. Cze. *čerstvý* 'fresh.' Both come from PSL *čьrstvъ* 'hard, firm.' Some food items are firm when they are fresh, and others when they are stale, so there is some logic in the divergent development in the two languages.

Then, there are examples where the meanings of the two false cognates in the same lexical field are distinct but not opposite. Such is the pair of Rus. *grob* 'coffin' and Pol. *grób* 'grave.' Both words come from PSL *grobъ* 'grave.' Polish has retained the PLS meaning, and in Russian it has shifted to another new object in the same field, given that in Russian *mogila* (which comes from PSL *mogyla* 'sepulchral cairn') started to be used for 'grave.'

Sometimes the differences are subtle. Thus Rus. *kreslo* means 'armchair' and Pol. *krzesło* means 'chair.' Polish has retained the wide meaning of the PSL word *krěslo*, whereas Russian narrowed its meaning, given that the word *stul* (borrowed from Germanic languages, which ultimately comes from the same Germanic root *stōlaz*, as does the English *stool*) has come to mean 'chair.' A very common situation is that the two languages share one or more meanings but differ in others. For example, *listopad* means 'the falling of leaves' in Russian and Polish alike. However, in Polish it has an additional meaning of 'November,' which is not present in Russian (Old Russian had the month of *listopadъ*, from mid-September to mid-October, but this disappeared with the reforms of Peter the Great in the early eighteenth century, as he strove for Westernization and the use of international month names). This additional meaning of the month in Polish is because Polish, just like some other Slavic languages, uses month names based on the natural and agricultural annual cycles, while present-day Russian uses words borrowed from Latin, the same ones found in English.

From Delusion to Debauchery

The cases of false cognates offer excellent examples of the changes in meanings discussed in chapter 5. One can see different paths of development of the languages involved, leading to pairs of false cognates. At the same time, false cognates clearly point to the mechanism that has led to language-specific semantic developments (e.g., semantic narrowing caused by the adoption of a new word). One can also see how these extensions interact with the process of lexical borrowing, which will be discussed in chapter 7.

Semantic narrowing in some Slavic languages and widening in others can be seen in the PSL root *blǫdъ, which meant 'delusion' and 'debauchery.' In Russian, Macedonian, and S-Cr (B/C/S), the meaning was narrowed to just 'debauchery.' The other meaning, 'delusion,' is covered by another noun derived from this root: *zabluždenie* in Russian and *zabluda* in S-Cr (B/C/S) and Macedonian. Czech also features semantic narrowing, but the meaning of the Czech word *blud* that is retained is 'delusion.' Polish, on the other hand, has the word *bląd* as the continuation of this PSL root, and its meaning is widened to 'error, mistake,' so from a particular mistake and moral conduct, the meaning expands into any kind of mistake.

The PSL root *doba* is equally interesting. Its PSL meaning was very broad; it meant 'time.' With some minor exceptions, the meaning of this root narrows in individual Slavic languages, but the way it is done varies. In addition to retaining the original meaning of 'time'—although it is used rarely and in very limited contexts because there is another word with that meaning—S-Cr (B/C/S) has developed a narrower meaning for it of 'age, period.' The latter meaning is the only one to be found in Czech, Slovene, and Macedonian. Bulgarian has retained the original sense of the root without developing additional meanings, but the word is becoming obsolete. Then, there is Polish, where the narrowing of the sense pertains to a much shorter period of time than in other languages. The Polish word *doba* means 'twenty-four hours.'

The PSL root *okъno* offers a story of continuation and limited narrowing. In most languages—including Russian, Polish, Czech, Slovak, and Slovene—the word *okno* continues the original PSL meaning of 'window.' Colloquial Czech also adds a new meaning of 'blackout.' Then, there is a very limited narrowing to 'windowpane' in S-Cr (B/C/S) and Macedonian, which creates very subtle false cognates between these two and the five aforementioned Slavic languages. S-Cr (B/C/S) and Macedonian have also developed the meaning of 'mining shaft.' The original PSL root with its original meaning has also been borrowed by non-Slavic languages such as Finnish *ikkuna* and Estonian *aken*, both of which mean 'window.'

A King Who Became the Moon

Borrowed words also undergo similar processes. Such is an early PSL borrowing from Proto-Germanic *kuningaz 'king.' In PSL, this Proto-Germanic word was adapted as *kъnędzъ to mean 'leader' and then 'prince (as in the ruler of a principate).' The initial Slavic meaning is largely preserved in the Slavic east and south, as in the Russian, Belarusian, and Ukrainian *knjaz'*, as well as the Slovene, S-Cr (B/C/S), Macedonian, and Bulgarian *knez*, all of which mean 'prince (as in the ruler of a principate).' In contrast to this rather monotonous continuation, in the West Slavic branch, semantic changes were happening and thus creating false cognates. The Pol. *ksiądz* and Cze. and Slk. *kněz* all mean 'priest.' So, there was a semantic transfer from ruling an earthly realm to ruling a spiritual lot. In Lower Sor., *kněz* broadened its meaning into 'lord' and then into the title and prefix 'mister' and 'Mr.' It is interesting that the meaning of 'prince (the ruler of a principate and a crown prince)' has been retained in Polish and Czech through the PSL root **kъnęžę*, which was derived from **kъędzь* by the suffix *-'ę*, used to refer to young beings. Thus, **kъnęžę* would be 'young prince,' which yielded Pol. *książę* and Cze. *kníže*, both of which mean 'prince.' In an interesting turn of events, the word for the 'Moon' in Pol. is derived from the same root. The word for the Moon is *księżyc and* the suffix is *-yc*, again referring to someone junior. In this case, the name arose from the construction of the Moon as the Sun's prince.

Later borrowings in each individual Slavic language are also a source of false cognates as a result of peculiar semantic developments in each of them. For example, many Slavic languages have borrowed the Latin word *pēnsiō*, which had the basic meaning of 'payment' and then also 'pension' (as in the retirement benefit), as one of its more specialized senses. In most Slavic languages, the word retained this specialized meaning of 'pension': in Russian, Ukrainian, Belarusian, and Bulgarian *pensija*; in S-Cr (B/C/S) and Macedonian *penzija*; in Czech *penze*; and in Slovak *penzia*. However, in Polish, the word *pensja* means 'salary' rather than 'retirement (money),' which then creates a very subtle difference from all the other languages.

Old Slavs versus Greeks and Romans

Inter-Slavic false cognates are very different from false cognates between Slavic and non-Slavic languages. In general, there needs to exist some connection between two languages to consider their words false cognates. For example, the word *kita* exists in many languages. However, one would not consider that word in any of the Slavic languages, like Slovene, where it means 'braid, plait,' or Polish, where the meaning is 'fluffy tail (e.g., of a horse),' to be a false cognate with the Japanese word, which means 'north'; Indonesian, where it means 'we'; or Swahili, where it means 'war.' There is simply no connection between the languages in question, and a similar form is considered just a random coincidence.

There are generally two possible connections that permit considering two words in two different languages to be false cognates. I will demonstrate this with data from two dictionaries of false cognates that I have compiled. The first one involved Polish and S-Cr (B/C/S), two Slavic languages that have developed from the same source, the Proto-Slavic language. The other involves English and S-Cr (B/C/S), where the two languages are not directly related (although they have a common Indo-European heritage) but share the Greco-Roman cultural sphere. The data from these two projects show that in more closely related languages, the main generator of false cognates is the split of the root from the ancestor language. In less-related languages, they are mostly generated by new meanings of the words borrowed from the classical Greco-Roman stock. Between Polish and S-Cr (B/C/S), 91 percent of the cases were caused by the Slavic root split (see suggested readings for the source of these data). For example, *jutro* is 'morning' in S-Cr (B/C/S) and 'tomorrow' in Polish. The link is obvious—tomorrow starts in the morning, the next morning. Between English and S-Cr (B/C/S), Latin roots are responsible for 51 percent of the cases (e.g., *honoraran* 'part-time' vs. *honorary*). The other major factors include splits in the borrowings from other languages (24% of all cases of false cognates) as in S-Cr (B/C/S) *akademija* 'academy, college, commemoration' vs. English *academia*, both borrowed from Greek), and the development of new meanings in the English words borrowed in S-Cr (B/C/S) (22% of false cognates) as in S-Cr (B/C/S) *spiker*, which means 'announcer' and the English *speaker*).

Among other things, this unequal distribution of the underlying causes for the emergence of false cognates determines approaches to language teaching and learning. Inter-Slavic language learning at the novice and intermediate levels has been greatly facilitated by the substantial lexical similarities illustrated in the first part of this chapter. However, given that false cognates happen most frequently in that very same basic vocabulary inherited from PSL, the difficulties in the early phases of the acquisition of another Slavic language largely stem from false cognates. On the other hand, when English speakers learn Slavic languages and vice versa, this process does not come with a springboard of lexical similarities. However, false cognates appear much later, mainly at the advanced or superior level of instruction, because they mostly belong to complex abstract concepts.

Chapter Takeaways

There are significant areas of overlap between the vocabularies of Slavic languages. These similarities enable a very imperfect, limited level of understanding from one Slavic language to another. However, the quality of understanding is seriously compromised by grammatical differences and the so-called false cognates, such words that have a similar form but different meaning. These false cognates result from various diverging processes in semantic development of individual Slavic languages. Many of them are found in core vocabulary areas, which is a serious obstacle even in initial learning of another Slavic language.

Recommended Chapter Readings

Šipka (2015a) discusses general patterns of lexical differences across the world's languages. Šipka (2019) addresses the cultural profiles of the vocabularies in Slavic languages. Šipka (2015b) discusses Slavic false cognates, including the data from the two dictionaries mentioned in this chapter. Soglasnova (2018) outlines strategies for dealing with false cognates. Golubović and Gooskens (2015) present the results of their tests of intelligibility in several Slavic languages. Developments in the vocabularies of individual Slavic languages are sketched in the work by Comrie and Corbett (1993) and Sussex and Cubberly (2006). Markoviḱ (2020) offers interesting lexical variation data in Macedonian dialects.

7 | How Slavic Languages Lend and Borrow Words

Language as a Trading Post

Words wander from language to language, and Slavic languages are no exception. From the earliest times, Slavs have been exchanging words with neighboring languages, most prominently with those from the Germanic branch (e.g., they have borrowed words for 'bread,' 'onion,' 'bowl,' 'taste,' 'buy,' etc., from Germanic languages) but also from Iranian and Italic languages as well as from Greek and possibly Celtic. Lexical transfer also has gone in the opposite direction. For example, the German words for 'border' (*Grenze*), 'whip' (*Peitsche*), and 'curd cheese' (*Quark*) are of Slavic origin, as is the name of the German capital Berlin, which comes from the Slavic root *berl-* meaning 'swamp'—in this case, the meaning is literal, unlike the much later metaphorical use in reference to Washington, DC. However, the bear on the coat of arms of the city established the so-called folk etymology by erroneously connecting the name of the city Berlin to the German word for bear, that is, *Bär*.

With advancements in communication—most notably, the printing press in the mid-fifteenth century; the spread of newspapers in the nineteenth century; and then radio, television, and the internet in the twentieth century—regional and global sources of cultural influence were added to neighboring languages as sources of lexical influence. In this recent word trade, Slavic languages have been primarily importers and much less so exporters. There are voluminous lexical imports in Slavic languages (like the words for 'pension' mentioned in the previous chapter) and much less-pronounced exports from them (including the old ones, like the word for 'window' mentioned in the previous chapter, and those relatively new ones pertaining to the Communist experiment, such as *perestroika*).

Lexical transfer is a part of intercultural communication. Words are lent and borrowed on the waves of cultural influences. The dynamics happened with writing systems, the so-called epilinguistic elements (i.e., not strictly linguistic but based on linguistic facts) that are also tied to intercultural communication.

From Slavic to English and Back

There are well over six hundred Slavic words in English—642 in the *Oxford English Dictionary* (OED), to be precise—and they encompass .28 percent of all entries in that dictionary. Alas, aside from *vampire, robot, vodka,* and *paprika,* most of them are unknown to most speakers of English. Entities related to Slavic environments and cultures have been borrowed by English in various areas. Most of these are in history: words like *hussar, szlachta, boyar, heyduk,* and *tsarevich* (from older historical periods) or *Bolshevik, commissar, Gosplan, kolkhoz, sovkhoz, subbotnik,* and *udarnik* (from newer history). But there are also numerous other fields, such as geography and geology (*steppe* and *taiga*), food (*borsch, kielbasa, pierogi[e], shaslik,* and *stroganoff*), politics (*duma, Sejm, Sobranie, Skupština,* and *oblast*), and garments (*rubashka, shapka, shuba,* and *parka*). If you are not familiar with these words attested in the OED, do not worry—you are not alone; even the spell checker tool for the most used word-processing software does not recognize more than three-fourths of these words. Of course, some words of Slavic origin, such as *vampire, vodka, paprika,* and *robot,* will sound familiar to you.

The number of English borrowings that have made their way into Slavic languages is considerably higher; it is measured in the thousands rather than the hundreds. More importantly, most of them are known to the speakers of Slavic languages because these words signify well-known concepts, such as *marketing, computer, dock, football,* and so forth. The difference between lending and borrowing is even more drastic with the traditional languages of cultural influence— German and French. In general, Slavic languages have a word trade deficit—they import many more words than they export. The deficit is not equally distributed across all Slavic languages—it is of considerably lower magnitude in Russian than it is in languages with fewer speakers, such as Slovene or Slovak. One can see this disproportion in the previously discussed Slavic borrowings in the OED. Russian (serving the most prominent Slavic culture) accounts for three-quarters of the borrowings, whereas Slovene and Slovak do not even reach 1 percent.

In both directions of word trade, the volume of words lent and borrowed is directly proportionate to the level of cultural influence behind the lending language. Cultural influence, in turn, hinges upon economic and political might. It is then no wonder that traditional sources of lexical influence on Slavic languages are German and French (languages of major European powers) and, more recently, English, first by the power of the British Empire, then by the global clout of the United States. By the same token, it is no wonder that Russian is the most prominent lender among Slavic languages, to English and otherwise. The "great and mighty Russian language," as they call it over there, rests on the culture of globally known writers (e.g., Leo Tolstoy and Anton Chekhov) and composers (e.g., Tchaikovsky and Stravinsky). This great and mighty culture behind a great and mighty language—just like in the German, French, and English cases— is driven by economic and political power.

Slavic Lexical Imports

Let us talk about lexical imports first. On the one hand, lexical borrowings in Slavic languages stand in relation to the lexicon inherited from Proto-Slavic. First, the ratio of inherited and borrowed words is different in various Slavic languages. Second, borrowings are spread in different subject-matter areas, with core vocabulary items (like the one from the Swadesh list mentioned in chapter 5) generally retaining a much higher percentage of inherited vocabulary items than other areas. Third, the cultural traditions of various Slavic languages have established different attitudes toward borrowed words. In some traditions, borrowed words are used in both formal and informal communication. In others, borrowings tend to be confined to informal discourse.

On the other hand, borrowed lexical strata are a result of either cultural influences or geographical contact. These two sources are not always clearly distinguishable. For example, for some South Slavic languages, Turkish used to be a language of both geographical contact and cultural influence. With the demise of the Ottoman Turkish Empire, cultural influence weakened, and languages like Macedonian and S-Cr (B/C/S) have lost geographical contact with Turkish. Similarly, German lost geographical contact with S-Cr (B/C/S) with the downfall of the Austro-Hungarian Empire, yet it remained a language of cultural influence. All this notwithstanding, in each Slavic language, one can identify large areas of vocabulary borrowed from languages of cultural influence, such as German, French, and, most recently, English, words that in many cases ultimately come from the Greco-Latin lexical fund. Then, there are borrowings from neighboring languages that are not languages of cultural influence, for example, Hungarian borrowings in S-Cr (B/C/S). These borrowings are a very small fraction compared to those from the languages of cultural influence.

Neighborly Borrowing

Contact borrowing can take different shapes. First, there is a kind of horizontal geographical contact (i.e., lexical exchange with neighboring languages, e.g., between Hungarian and any neighboring Slavic language, like Slovak, Ukrainian, or S-Cr (B/C/S)). Horizontal here means that the two languages are equal, that neither of them is dominant. Some of these horizonal geographical contacts were present as early as in the PSL times. PSL consequently featured various early borrowings from Iranian, Germanic, Greek, and Turkic languages, possibly even Celtic. Second, there is also a concurrent vertical geographical contact of a dominant national language with a local language, for instance, between Turkish and any of the Slavic languages spoken in the Ottoman Turkish Empire, including Bulgarian, Macedonian, and S-Cr (B/C/S). Concurrent here means that the two languages that participate in word trade continue to be spoken throughout their word trade. The concept of a dominant language here refers to a more influential language, a language of state administration, and so on. This word trade is called vertical in the sense of the dominant language being metaphorically above the other one. Finally, it is possible to distinguish the subsequent vertical geographical contact of a dominant language with a substrate language, for example, S-Cr (B/C/S) with its substrate language Illyrian. Subsequent means that one of the two languages ceased to be used. In this case, Illyrian was spoken in the Balkans before the Slavs came to that part of the world. It gradually became extinct in that region, but some of its words have been incorporated into S-Cr (B/C/S). Substrate or substratum languages are indigenous languages that contribute features, most commonly words, to the languages of the invaders.

The heritage of substrate languages is important in light of Slavic migrations starting from the fourth through sixth centuries, as mentioned in chapter 2. While who will eventually become Southern Slavs migrated toward the Balkans in Southern Europe, various pre-Slavic ethnic groups—including the Illyrians, the Thracians, and the Celts—occupied the regions in the Balkans, where the Slavs would eventually settle. When Southern Slavs settled in the Balkans through the sixth and seventh centuries, these languages either gradually became extinct altogether or their speakers eventually moved to a different territory. Borrowed words from these languages, including some place-names, are important indicators of the previous presence of all these languages and their speakers in the territory that is now occupied by the Slavs. Most of these words borrowed by Southern Slavs were pertinent to shepherding terminology and the configuration of geographical terrains.

Domestic versus Imported

The proportion of inherited versus borrowed vocabulary in Slavic languages is difficult to assess because it varies across several parameters. First, the register, especially in some languages, influences whether informal language forms are more likely to have more borrowings than their formal counterparts. Second, core vocabulary areas, those that refer to most basic concepts, feature considerably fewer borrowings. Third, some Slavic languages (such as Slovene or Czech) are less prone to borrowings in their neutral and formal registers than other Slavic languages (such as Russian or Polish).

The sources of borrowing are somewhat less difficult to assess. A vast majority (well over 90%) of borrowings in Slavic languages come from western European languages. Approximately a bit less than one-third are Greek-Latin internationalisms, mostly terms found in sciences and other scholarship. Somewhat less than one-third comes from Germanic languages, mostly German (somewhat less than two-thirds of the borrowings from the Germanic branch) but increasingly so from English (somewhat less than one-third of Germanic loanwords). Finally, somewhat less than one-third comes from Italic languages, mostly French (French amounts to between 65% and 85% within the Italic borrowings, depending on the language) and then Italian (between 10% and 30%). Many of the borrowings from Germanic and Italic languages ultimately come from the Greek-Latin lexical stock.

This picture is somewhat different in languages such as Bulgarian, Macedonian, and S-Cr (B/C/S), which are spoken in the territories that were a part of the Ottoman Turkish Empire for extended periods of time. They feature some 10 percent of borrowings from Turkish (which may ultimately be Arabic or Persian words that Turkish has borrowed). The borrowings from the western European languages amount to less than 90 percent, and each of these groups have been proportionately smaller than in the case of other Slavic languages. However, the borrowings from Turkish are becoming increasingly obsolete. They are usually a part of restricted registers, and in the general lexicon most vocabulary items have been replaced, typically by Slavic words or, less commonly, borrowings from other languages. I have analyzed the current usage of the borrowings from Turkish from the most reputable dictionary of these words in S-Cr (B/C/S). A combined analysis of the usage in texts and native speaker judgments has shown that over 60 percent of these words have been replaced, most commonly with a word of Slavic origin that coexisted with the Turkish loanword. For example, the Turkish borrowing *deniz* 'sea' was fully replaced by the inherited Slavic *more*. An additional

20 percent of Turkish loanwords refer to items that are not in use anymore, for instance, *džilit* 'thin and long spear.' Out of the surviving loanwords, less than 20 percent of this vocabulary borrowed from Turkish, one-fourth (5% of the total of the Turkish loanwords) are in general use, either without a synonym (as in *džep* 'pocket') or with a synonym that is not borrowed from Turkish (e.g., the Turkish borrowing *dželat* 'executioner' has a synonym *krvnik* that was inherited from PSL). The remaining three-fourths of these survivors (nearly 14% of the entire borrowings from Turkish) are found in only restricted usage spheres, most commonly the field of Islam (e.g., *dženet* 'Jannah, the Islamic concept of paradise,' *dova* 'Dawah, Islamic prayer'). The data about the current status of Turkish loanwords are similar in other South Slavic languages, and this statistic only emphasizes the primacy of western European borrowings, even in those Slavic languages with a substantial layer of Turkish loanwords. Although the borrowings from western European languages remain in frequent general use and in various terminologies, most of those from Turkish are either obsolete or in a restricted sphere of usage.

Futile Attempts at Purity

Even in those Slavic languages that feature a strong tradition of purism—in other words, the tendency to replace borrowings with the words coined from inherited Slavic stems—the languages of cultural influence are still indirectly present. As a rule, the replacements are the so-called calques—more or less literal translations of the words in the sources of cultural influence, most commonly German words. An example of a literal translation is the word for a periodical in Slovene: *časnik* (*čas* 'time' and suffix -*nik*), which is calqued from German *Zeitung* (*Zeit* 'time' and suffix -*ung*). Similarly, Slovene has *pravopis* 'orthography': *pravo* 'correctly,' *pis(ati)* 'write'; it also has the so-called zero suffix: -0. This word was modeled after the German *Rechtsschreibung* 'orthography': *recht* 'correctly,' *schreib(en)* 'write,' and suffix -*ung* (replaced by -0 in Slovene). In some cases, the word was based on German, but the calque is less literal. For example, the word for 'high-rise building' in Slovene is *nebotičnik*: *nebo* 'sky,' *tik(ati)* 'touch,' and suffix -*nik*, which is loosely based on the English *skyscraper*, where the second part of the compound is somewhat different. It is also partially based on the German *Voklenkratzer* 'skyscraper, literally cloud scratcher,' where the concept is similar but both parts are different. Similarly, *železnica* 'railway'—*želez(e)n* 'iron' and suffix -*ica*—is partially based on the German *Eisenbahn* 'railroad'—*Eisen* 'iron,' *Bahn* 'route, trail' (unlike, e.g., the Italian *ferrovia*, which is a full calque: *ferro* 'iron' and *via* 'route').

The German language has a special role in Slavic word trade given that cultural centers and entire or substantial areas of territories of Sorbians, Czechs, Slovaks, Slovenes, Croats, and Serbs were part of German-speaking empires for long periods of time, and the same is true of some Polish and Ukrainian regions, and for Bosnia for a short period of time around the turn of the nineteenth and twentieth centuries. German thus occupied a special place as the main non-Slavic contact language, the language of imperial overlords and their administration. German was also the language of progress and technology at the time of industrialization in the nineteenth century, when many technical and scientific terminologies were developed. At the time when most modern Slavic standard languages underwent formation, German exerted strong lexical influence and provoked even stronger negative attitudes, which has led to the purist tendency to replace German words with their Slavic equivalents.

Emigrants, Expats, Guest Workers

While German contact lexical influence today pertains mostly to languages like Upper and Lower Sorbian and Burgenland Croatian, which are still spoken in predominantly German-speaking territories, German still strongly shaped various Slavic heritage-language forms (i.e., the forms of second-generation emigrant speakers). For example, German-speaking Vienna, Austria, is de facto the second-largest Serbian city, right after Belgrade, the capital of Serbia. Over a quarter of a million Serbs reside in Vienna, and, aside from Belgrade no other Serbian city has as many people in it (although Niš and Novi Sad come close). English is similar in its influence on Slavic heritage-language forms on the British Isles, as well as in North America and Australasia. Well-known examples of such heritage communities are the so-called Polish patches in Chicago and Russian-speaking heritage communities in Brighton Beach, New York, and Sunny Isles, Florida.

These heritage-language communities (also called expats, emigrants, or guest workers, depending on the perspective one takes) represent microcosms of lexical borrowing. An interesting question is: Which lexical fields are more prone to lexical hybridization (mixing the words from the dominant language in the environment into the language inherited from one's parents)? As a first step in answering that question, I have analyzed data relating to heritage S-Cr (B/C/S) in English-speaking parts of Canada, which were collected by Milan Surdučki in the 1970s.

This list of 3,805 words borrowed from English in heritage S-Cr (B/C/S) shows that more than half of the cases (54%) consist of concepts that were new to the immigrants. A further 21 percent are concepts from the spheres of labor and legal relations, and 4 percent are common English phrases, which were also new to the immigrants. The remaining 22 percent of these words do not seem to have a single common denominator. Obviously, the concepts from the spheres of labor and legal relations are to be found among the new concepts, too. If we add those to the 21 percent of the concepts previously known to the immigrants, the total number of the concepts from the spheres of labor and legal relations is 39 percent of all loanwords. This is logical given that it is precisely in those spheres where the immigrants had the most intensive contacts with their English-speaking environment.

Unknown concepts include those that are generally unknown in the areas where S-Cr (B/C/S) is spoken, such as *auns* 'ounce,' *paun* 'pound,' *kornid bif* 'corned beef,' and *sandvič men* 'sandwich man.' Then, there are concepts likely to be unknown to many speakers given their rural backgrounds and low educational standing, such as *Čajnaman* 'Chinaman,' *Đapan* 'Japan,' and *eringa* 'herring,' or, because of the new context of a different system of institutions and lifestyles, *bečelor digri* 'bachelor's degree,' *hajskul tičer* 'high school teacher,' *trafika* 'traffic,' etc. Some of these new concepts are from the spheres of work and legal relations, e.g., *tu baj fors* 'two-by-four,' *tredunija* 'trade union,' *bed rekord* 'bad record,' and *lenč* 'lunch.' Known concepts from work and legal spheres are exemplified by *pentati* 'paint,' *sendati* 'sand,' etc. In the category of borrowed phrases, one can find examples like *goš* 'gosh,' *acet* 'that is it,' and *orajt* 'all right.'

Examples that belong to various fields (also found in David Andrews's analysis of Russian immigrants in the United States) include words relating to motorization: *autokara* 'auto, car' and *gasolin* 'gasoline'; households: *kičen* 'kitchen,' *furničer* 'furniture,' and *čimni* 'chimney'; clothing: *slekse* 'slacks' and *šuza* 'shoe'; food: *brekfest* 'breakfast' and *čiken* 'chicken'; measures and landmarks: *đulaj* 'July,' *saturdej* 'Saturday,' *nort* 'North,' and *forti* 'forty'; basic actions: *muvati* 'move,' *roniti* 'run,' and *tačati* 'touch'; and basic features: *dori* 'dirty' and *loki* 'lucky.' All these diverse examples belong to situations of direct contact with the environment—filling up a gas tank, dining in a restaurant, needing a repairman for one's home, and the like. By the same token, many of these examples are related to the sphere of work, too—one normally commutes to work in a car, work environments typically have dress codes, some meals are eaten at work, schedules are planned at work, and so on.

Obviously, this is just one case of immigrant lexical borrowing and further research is needed, but it seems that more intensive contact with the environment, both at work and when dealing with administration outside it, and the fact that the concepts remain unknown to the speaker, represent good predictors of lexical borrowing. This process is not very different from the borrowing across the territories where Slavic languages are spoken. Over here, too, words for new concepts are typically borrowed (e.g., when new technology of some kind is introduced), and there is always a contact of some kind, either geographical or via cultural influence.

World Trade as an Identity Builder

The distinction between the inherited Slavic lexicon on the one hand and the borrowed lexical items on the other is the primary feature that contributes to the cultural identity profile. In some Slavic languages, like Slovene and Czech, it is very prominent. In others, like Russian and Polish, it is more subdued yet still present. Speakers make lexical choices partially based on this distinction. They also have opinions and attach value judgments to either side of this distinction. At a lower level, the cultural circle of the source language of cultural or contact exchange represents an important cultural profile builder. Again, speakers are aware of these cultural circles (e.g., western European vs. Near Eastern, classical vs. living western European languages) and potentially attach value judgments to the words from these circles. Finally, the subject matter is an additional profiling element, for example, operatic terminology in many languages features noticeable Italian lexical influences, automotive terminology is German, computing terminology is English, and the like. The speakers are aware of this distribution in subject-matter fields and find certain lexical influences natural and normal in certain fields. How the fields are matched with source languages for borrowing is either common for all Slavic languages (just like in the case of operatic, automotive, and computing terms in general usage) or else specific to one language or group of Slavic languages (e.g., administrative terms in Polish with strong German influences—*ratusz* <= *Rathaus* 'city hall,' and *burmistrz* <= *Bürgermeister* 'mayor'—or tools of Turkish provenance in S-Cr (B/C/S)—*čekić* <= *çekiç* 'hammer' and *turpija* <= *törpü* 'file'). The features that profile lexical cultural identity in this layer are thus thematically organized, first in the general thematic categories of the donor languages (e.g., western European, Middle Eastern, etc.) and then in the subject-matter fields such as technology and the arts. While cross-language lexical exchange happens as a consequence of broader sociohistorical and technological processes, speakers can potentially modify the exchange by accepting or rejecting inbound lexical transfer. However, this interference is rare given that most of the exchange happens spontaneously, and speakers tend to use borrowed words, most of which cannot be replaced. The change in the balance between inherited and borrowed words or between any categories of borrowings is generally a consequence of slow spontaneous processes. For example, this is evident when one looks at the lexemes from some cultural circles, say Near Eastern, and one can clearly see that they are becoming obsolete and others are becoming more common, say those from English. There may be situations in which a single loanword or cohorts of them are accepted abruptly, but generally it takes a considerable amount of time to shape the general features of this lexical layer.

Scripts as Flags of Religions

Similar mechanisms of power, influence, and identity were involved in the borrowing of the writing systems that Slavic languages use today and those that they have used in the past. Moreover, even particular solutions within the chosen scripts have been subject to these mechanisms. One distinct factor that remains closely correlated with the choice of script is religion. However, there are also other factors at play. The first Slavic script was the Glagolitic alphabet. It was a native script of unclear origin, but more than one half of it was derived from the Greek alphabet. For example, the letter L looks like this in the Glagolitic script—ꙉ—and its Greek equivalent is Λ. The letter D looks like this in the Glagolitic script—ꙋ—and its Greek equivalent is Δ. As one can see, there is a faint similarity in the top-pointed shape and the fact that the letters represent roughly the same sounds. However, the similarity is not pronounced enough to prove the origin of the Glagolitic letters beyond reasonable doubt.

The geopolitical background of the Glagolitic script was the desire of the Moravian prince Rastislav to Christianize the Slavs. He was a Slav and the ruler of Great Moravia, his principate, which stretched across wide areas of central Europe. His aim in the campaign of Christianization was to counter the influences of East Frankish priests (who belonged to Germanic tribes). Two South Slavic brothers, Cyril and Methodius, were sent to Great Moravia in 862 by the Byzantine emperor upon Rastislav's request. Their principal motivation was the spread of Christianity. Their inventions: the Glagolitic script and the Old Church Slavonic language for which the script was intended, which were then tools of Slavic emancipation and Christianization. The Glagolitic script was eventually displaced by the Cyrillic and Latin scripts that are still in use. The latter two scripts along with all others that were used at any point in time were correlated with religious affiliations. Italian Slavist Ricardo Picchio has introduced the concepts of *Slavia Orthodoxa* and *Slavia Latina*, representing Eastern and Western Christian cultural spheres in the Slavic world. Today, those in the sphere of Eastern Christianity use the Cyrillic script and those in the sphere of Western Christianity use the Latin script. This split started very early, after the East-West Chism of 1054, and the Glagolitic script was gradually replaced with the Latin script in Slavia Latina and by the Cyrillic script in *Slavia Orthodoxa*. Some exceptions were present, but they were eventually phased out. For example, the members of the Catholic order of Franciscans (i.e., Western Christians) in Bosnia have used the *Bosanchica*, a version of the Cyrillic script that was associated with Eastern Christians.

Japanese Slavist Motoki Nomachi and American Slavist Roberg Greenberg have also pointed to *Slavia Islamica*, the Slavs belonging to the Islamic cultural sphere, such as Bosniaks, that is, Bosnian Muslims who used a modified Arabic script. Historically, one could also mention *Slavia Iudaica*, Slavic-speaking Jews, who used the Hebrew Script. Within Slavia Latina one can also note various Protestant traditions (e.g., *Slavia Lutherana*), some of which used the Gothic version of the Latin script during certain periods of time. Finally, within *Slavia Orthodoxa*, there was a tradition of *Slavia Graeca*, with the use of the Greek script among Aegean Slavic Macedonians.

The Swords Behind the Pens

The introductions of all the scripts used in Slavia were based on religions, supported by the economic and geopolitical powers in their arsenal. The processes that led to the reduction of Slavic scripts to the two used today were primarily ideological. Bosniaks abandoned their version of the Arabic script and replaced it with the Latin script in the process of Westernization in the late nineteenth century, when Bosnia was annexed by the Austro-Hungarian Empire. The Gothic script was eventually replaced with the common Latin script in the Sorbian lands after World War II as a distancing maneuver from the National Socialist regime, which preferred the Gothic script. *Slavia Iudaica* and *Slavia Graeca* were marginal episodes that seem to have "died a natural death."

The use of scripts was a function of regional economic and geopolitical power, as well as ideological orientations. The same development is true for concrete orthographic solutions within each script. We will see in the next chapter that the Soviet reform of the Cyrillic script was motivated by ideological distancing from the previous imperial regime. Similarly, in early modern Croatian dictionaries, there were two ways of rendering specific characters not found in the basic Latin script. One was based on Hungarian, and it was used in the north of today's Croatia because this was a zone of Hungarian cultural influence. The other was based on Venetian spelling traditions, and it was used in the south of today's Croatia because this was a zone of Venetian influence. Even individual letters within Slavic alphabets were a function of geopolitical and ideological struggles. We will see in the next chapter that Vuk Stefanović Karadžić reformed the Serbian Cyrillic script in the early nineteenth century as part of the maneuver of displacing Russian with Austrian influence among Serbs. One solution he deployed was to introduce the letter *j* from the Latin script rather than generalizing the use of the Cyrillic *ŭ*. This was an ideological maneuver that was met with a strong ideological rebuke.

It should be clear by now that imports of words and scripts alike happen in certain spheres of cultural influence. Cultural influences, in turn, are a result of economic and geopolitical power. Cultural influences combined with ideological orientations form the various configurations of borrowings the Slavic world over.

Russian Word-Lending Champions

Not only do Slavic languages borrow words and scripts but they also lend them to other languages. Among Slavic languages, Russian is a well-known example of a donor language for the languages of Russia and the Russian "near abroad," in other words, for the Russophone cultural sphere (those nations that at some point had or still have Russian as their official language). The lexical influences of the indigenous languages of Russia on the Russian language remain marginal (with Tatar the only noticeable source of influence). In sharp contrast, the lexical influence of the Russian language on all these languages is overwhelming. This power was well documented in a series of publications about the languages of the peoples of Russia from the Russian Academy of Sciences' Institute of the Russian Language. For example, a dictionary of Russian borrowings in the Tabasaran language (spoken in the Caucasus region of the Russian Federation) includes 62 common words for professions, 79 words for sociopolitical phenomena, 130 words for scientific and technological terminology, and 116 words used in daily life. Most words are very common, such as 'author,' 'student,' 'army,' 'organization,' 'motor,' 'radio,' 'necktie,' and 'coffee.' Similar data is attested from numerous other languages of the Russophone sphere. A clear picture of an extreme imbalance in the lexical transfer of these languages emerges with Russian's dominance in this relationship. Speakers of both languages in any given pair of indigenous languages of Russia on one side and Russian on the other are acutely aware of the status of their respective languages, which in turn is a part of their linguistic identity.

Similar is the situation in what Russians call "the near abroad," that is, post-Soviet countries, especially those in central Asia. If one explores the list of Russian borrowings in central Asian languages, it becomes clear that most of the words that Russian loaned to these languages were previously borrowed by Russian from western European languages, most notably French and German, of which the eventual origin is Greek-Latin. They are the so-called internationalisms, which spread first through Europe and then the world over wherever European imperial conquests (in this case Russian) took place. Let us look at two of these languages, Uzbek, a Turkic language, and Tajik, an Iranian language, with both these languages situated in the Russian "near abroad." On the one hand, Uzbek features borrowings that are originally Russian words, such as *moroženoe* 'ice cream,' *noski* 'socks,' *stol* 'table,' *samoljot* 'airplane,' and *vertoljot* 'helicopter.' That last word was very popular across the Soviet realm, and it is used in Belarusian, Ukrainian, Azerbaijani, Kyrgyz, Turkmen, Uyghur, and many other languages. Some of these words are calques from western European languages, such as *det-sad* 'kindergarten,' a calque of the German word *Kindergarten*: *det(skij)* is translated from *Kinder-* 'children's,' and *sad* is translated from *Garten* 'garden.'

However, for most borrowings, Russian was just an intermediary language, because these words either come from a western European language or, most commonly, from the Greco-Latin stock through a western European language. The first group includes examples like *botinok* 'high shoe' from the French *bottine* 'small boot' or *flag* 'flag' from the Dutch *vlag* 'flag.' In some cases, Russian borrowed the word loaned to Uzbek directly from classical languages, as in *tetrad'* 'notebook,' from the Greek *tetraidon* 'quaternion of parchment.' Most commonly, however, a word from the Greco-Latin stock has entered a western European language. It was then borrowed by Russian and loaned to Uzbek. The word *cirk* 'circus' was borrowed from the Latin *circus* via the German *Zirkus*. The word *komp-juter* was borrowed from the English *computer*, which contains the verb *to compute*, borrowed from the Latin *computō* via the French *computer*. In some cases, the chains of borrowing are quite intricate. The Russian word *gazeta* 'newspaper,' which was borrowed by Uzbek, comes from the French *gazette*, which in turn comes from the Italian *gazzetta*, which in turn comes from the word *gazeta* in the Venetian dialect, all of which mean 'newspaper.' The Venetian word comes from the name of a coin, *gazeta*, which was the cost of that newspaper. A further etymology is disputed, and there are also theories of an origin either from Greek or from Persian via Greek and Latin. This convoluted origin of the word did not prevent its widespread use in the Russian near abroad. Russian also loaned this word to Bashkir, Georgian, Kazakh, Kyrgyz, Tajik, Tatar, Turkmen, and Uyghur, among others.

The situation with the Russian loanwords in Tajik is identical. There are some words that are originally Russian, such as *budil'nik* 'alarm clock,' *stol* 'table,' and *vypusknik* 'graduate.' However, most other borrowings are either from western European languages or from Greek and Latin via western European languages, and they can also be found in English. They include words like *albatros* 'albatross,' *alpinist* 'mountain climber,' *artist* 'artist,' *bank* 'bank,' *mašina* 'machine, car,' *radio* 'radio,' and *televizor* 'television.'

Beyond Russians

Lending and borrowing can also happen between standard Slavic languages and nonstandard non-Slavic forms, as demonstrated by the case of Romani in many Slavic countries. In all these contexts, Slavic languages are dominant. While a part of the lexical transfer from Slavic languages into Romani comes from the dialects, general media and the school systems also cause transfer from the standard-language lexical stock. Thus, for example, a Gurbet dialect of the Romani language includes very common lexical items such as *bolnica* 'hospital,' *koža* 'skin, leather,' *sijalica* 'lightbulb,' *reka* 'river,' *okruglo* 'round,' *dugo* 'long,' *isplatil* 'pay off,' *osetil* 'feel,' *učil* 'learn,' and *pušil* 'smoke'—all borrowed from S-Cr (B/C/S).

Romanian and Hungarian alike are often cited as featuring a sizeable number of Slavic borrowings in their lexicons. Obviously, S-Cr (B/C/S) (which has geographical contact with both these languages) is prominently represented in this material, with other sources being Old Church Slavonic, Russian, Ukrainian, and Slovak. However, even if we make a very conservative estimate of the number of S-Cr (B/C/S) words in the mass of Slavic borrowings in these two languages, there is no doubt that for both these languages, and especially with Romanian, the balance is shifted heavily to the S-Cr (B/C/S) side. Only fifteen Romanian loanwords have been documented in S-Cr (B/C/S). The situation with Slavic borrowings in Romanian is drastically different, with some dictionaries attesting nine thousand borrowings from S-Cr (B/C/S) alone. The imbalance is somewhat less drastic with Hungarian. Relevant studies attest some eight hundred Hungarian loanwords in S-Cr (B/C/S) and some two thousand S-Cr (B/C/S) loanwords in Hungarian.

Russian is the uncontested lender in the lexical transfer between Slavic languages. There are a handful of loanwords from other Slavic languages; only Polish breaks the mold, with some one hundred words loaned to Russian. By contrast, a dictionary of Russian loanwords in other Slavic languages notes 1,225 Serbian, 496 Croatian, 437 Slovenian, 1,415 Macedonian, 3,802 Bulgarian, 504 Czech, 513 Slovak, and 505 Polish borrowings from Russian. It is noteworthy that the language varieties serving the Orthodox Christian culture (Serbian, Macedonian, and especially Bulgarian)—the mainstream culture of the Russian language—feature considerably more Russian loanwords. This fact shows that lexical transfer is primarily a function of cultural transfer.

Exporting the Cyrillic Script

Russian is also a major exporter of the Cyrillic script. In the business cycle of that exporting product, since the 1990s, we have been witnessing a bit of a downturn, which came after the growth of the early Soviet era. The period after 1917 saw an enormous expansion of the Russian Cyrillic script, mutatis mutandis, into numerous languages at the time of the Soviet Union, and some neighboring languages. After the dissolution of the Soviet Union in 1991, the use of the Cyrillic script continued in those non-Slavic languages spoken across Russia. Outside of Russia, a general trend was the gradual displacement of the Cyrillic script, mostly with the Latin script. Some exceptions in which the Cyrillic script was preserved outside of Russia without plans to replace it mostly occurred in the countries and territories closely aligned with Russia.

In Russia, the Cyrillic script has been used in a range of indigenous languages such as the Uralic languages, for example, Mari, Mordvin, and Enets; the Turkic languages, for example, Bashkir and Chuvash; the Mongolian languages, for example, Buryat and Kalmyk; and various other languages, for example, Chukchi, Koryak, Aleut, Yupik, Evenk, Nanai, and many others. The design of the new Latin alphabet for Tatar, a Turkic language spoken in Russia, is an exception from the general trend of the preservation of the Cyrillic script. However, this new Latin alphabet is mostly restricted to use on the internet.

In the post-Soviet realm outside of Russia, most Turkic languages are in the process of replacing the Cyrillic script with the Latin script, which is used in Turkey, where Turkish, the most populous of these languages, is spoken. These Turkic languages include Azerbaijani, Kazakh, Kyrgyz, Turkmen, and Uzbek. These languages are in different stages of that process, anywhere from being completed in Azerbaijani to being announced but not really happening yet in Uzbek. The Cyrillic script has been used in Mongolian since 1940, but it has been announced that by 2025 the traditional Mongolian script will be used alongside it in official documents.

The exceptions in which non-Slavic Cyrillic scripts still stand strong outside of Russia include Tajik, with Tajikistan strongly allied with Russia, as well as Moldovan (in the disputed territory of Transnistria), Ossetian (in the disputed territory of South Ossetia), and Abkhaz (in the disputed territory of Abkhazia), all of which are allied with Russia, so that this could be seen as a case of soft political influence of Russia.

The use of the Cyrillic script was not restricted to the Soviet and post-Soviet realm. Romanian, an Italic language, was written in the Cyrillic script until the nineteenth century. Bulgarian Sephardic Jews have used it to write in Ladino, an Italic language. Romani, an Indo-Aryan language, had been written in the Cyrillic script not only in the Soviet Union but also in Bulgaria. Even some of the Aleut dialects in Alaska, while that area was still a part of the Russian territory, were written in the Cyrillic script, which was introduced in the first half of the nineteenth century by a Russian missionary named Saint Innocent of Alaska.

Just like lending words, lending the Cyrillic script to non-Slavic languages has been closely correlated with the spheres of cultural influence. These spheres, in turn, are defined by sources of economic and political power. This influence shows that interlanguage trade (in linguistic material and epilinguistic elements like writing systems) is a form of cross-cultural communication. This kind of cross-cultural communication is best described by the wise words of Thucydides: the strong do what they can and the weak suffer what they must.

Slavs Stick Together in Word Borrowing

We have seen in the previous two chapters that the disintegration of the initial PSL language community was characterized by various semantic processes that caused the divergent development of the roots of inherited words in each Slavic language from PSL. Despite all these changes, substantial areas of meaning in these roots are still shared by various Slavic languages. The preservation of the original roots and their meanings is what enables cross-Slavic communication at some basic level. The divergent semantic development in these roots is what makes that communication a minefield. A further convergence in wide areas of the vocabulary of Slavic languages has been caused by lexical borrowing.

An overwhelming majority of Slavic words have been borrowed from western European languages: Greek, Latin, German, and French. The process of lexical borrowing and the attitudes toward that process are at the same time what has diversified Slavic languages. Some sources of borrowing, such as Turkish and Hungarian, are more prominent in some Slavic languages than in others. Additionally, the cultures of some Slavic languages are less tolerant toward lexical borrowing. Instead, in the standard language variety, they are likely to replace borrowed words with those based on the inherited Slavic stock, mostly calques of the borrowings. Some Slavic languages, most notably Russian, are not only high-volume importers but also powerful exporters of linguistic material and of epilinguistic elements.

Chapter Takeaways

Slavic languages borrow many more words than they lend. The exchange of words is a function of economic, technological, political, religious, and cultural influences. Similar forces are also behind the borrowing of scripts. Most word borrowings in Slavic languages come from western European languages as a part of cultural transfer. Borrowing also happens in the communities of Slavic emigrants, who hybridize their language by combining it with lexical items borrowed from the language of their new surrounding (most commonly English or German speaking). The only Slavic language with a strong record of lending words (and in some cases also the Cyrillic script) to non-Slavic languages is Russian.

Recommended Chapter Readings

General regularities in lexical borrowing are discussed in works by Grant (2015) and Haspelmath and Tadmor (2009). Šipka (2019) discusses Slavic borrowings into English and international borrowings in Slavic languages. Andrews (1999) addresses heritage Russian in the United States, and Surdučki (1978) discusses heritage S-Cr (B/C/S) in Canada. Proshina (2016) talks about Russian in central Asia. Kempgen (2015–16) offers a variety of illustrations with Slavic alphabets. Theoretical insights about scripts, both Slavic and non-Slavic, can be found in Bunčić, Lippert, and Rabus's work (2016). Picchio, Goldblatt, and Susanne Fusso (1984) discuss the notion of Slavia Orthodoxa and Slavia Latina. Greenberg and Nomachi (2012) address Slavia Islamica.

III Languages as Tools of Cultures

8 Pens and Peasants: How Slavic Literacies Have Emerged

What Does It Mean to Be *Kulturny* and *Nekulturny?*

"Bond laughed. 'Nobody's kulturny enough for you,'" reads a line from Ian Fleming's novel *From Russia with Love*. The word *kulturny* is defined in the *Oxford English Dictionary* as follows: "in the Soviet Union: cultured, civilized." For the adjective *cultured*, the same dictionary lists several meanings related to soil, plants, and so on, before it comes to the one related to *kulturny*, which is "esp. of a person—improved by education and training; possessed of or characterized by culture, esp. with reference to the arts and intellectual pursuits; refined, cultivated." While this concept and the use of the word remain rather marginal in English, in Slavic languages, they are central. It is not only that Google NGram Viewer (a webpage that measures the frequency of words in a body of literature for each given language) shows a multifold higher usage of the same word in Russian compared to the English word, but it is also how people perceive the word. In Slavic languages, it is as common to characterize someone as cultured as it is to portray them as kind or pleasant. It is also as common to call someone uncultured as it is to call them rude or unpleasant. A person can also be linguistically cultured or noncultured. There is a concept of the so-called linguistic culture in all Slavic languages. It entails proper and appropriate use of the standard language form. The standard language form is the formal language variety, which is used in contexts like legal proceedings, news reporting, and formal lectures, in other words, all those situations that require a certain level of formality. In the history of Slavic languages, these standard language forms have emerged from literary language forms, that is, the language of fine literature, which was the primary place for formal writing throughout centuries.

While the role of rockstar linguists and other authorities, which entails cultivating linguistic culture, will be discussed in the next chapter, it is important to note at the very outset that there is a strong link between the notion of being

cultured and the use of the standard language form, along with strong value judgments on this score. This state of affairs has emerged in the historical processes
that will be elucidated in the remaining sections of this chapter. As noted, in all
Slavic languages, these processes involved the creation of the so-called literary
language. The term itself is indicative—there is a strong connection between
the belles lettres and the standard language. Despite the differences between the
present-day standard languages and literary languages of the past, in Slavic cultures, the term *literary language* is used equally in reference to the present-day
standard languages and various prestandard forms used in high-shelf fiction.

Nations and Their Linguistic Authorities

The emergence of literary languages was a result of a gradual spread of authority
over an ethnic or national group. What typically starts as an endeavor of an individual, a group, or dispersed groups and individuals working independently from
one another eventually leads to the formation of one or more central authorities
that function at an all-ethnic or all-national level.

Authority has been a focus of social sciences ever since Max Weber ground-
breakingly established its three main types: traditional (e.g., in religious contexts),
charismatic (e.g., of a populist politician), and rational-legal (e.g., of legal authority). In a recent book, Michael Huemer reviewed the notion of authority (primarily
political) by citing various authors and intellectual traditions, most of them based
on Weber's seminal essay. The picture that emerges is that of a multitude of justifications that have been used and a variety of sources that have been introduced.
In the context of this discussion, it is important to realize that the establishment
of a normative linguistic authority can take various forms and resort to various
justifications. Linguistic authority is based on the fact that the source of authority
(including linguists, writers, journalists, and educators) establishes a model that
the general body of speakers is expected to follow (e.g., that certain words or
grammatical forms are "correct" or "incorrect"). Obviously, normative linguists
and other sources of authority make claims that the source of their authority
is rational, but in truth the decisions may have various other motivating factors
behind them (e.g., the charisma of writers or traditional authority of cultural
institutions). This idea of a normative linguistic authority is widespread in all
Slavic cultures and is considerably more prominent in Slavic cultures than in
many non-Slavic cultures, where normative linguists have a very limited impact,

as demonstrated by James Milroy and Lesley Milroy, who explored the idea of authority in the English language.

When ethnicity is mentioned here, the line of research begins with Ernest Gellner, who emphasized a constructivist nature of nationalism (his adage was that nationalists create nations, not the other way around). Rogers Brubaker has developed this concept further, understanding ethnicity not as a state but rather as a process. He advocated "thinking of ethnicity, race and nation not in terms of substantial groups or entities but in terms of *practical categories, cultural idioms, cognitive schemas, discursive frames, organizational routines, institutional forms, political projects* and *contingent events.*" The creation and maintenance of Slavic literary languages and linguistic culture are thus a part of these constructivist mechanisms in creating and maintaining ethnic or national unity. This system will become obvious from the ensuing review of the history of literacy in Slavic nations.

It is always some authority, which can be represented by various institutions, individuals, and so forth, that sifts apart speakers who are *kulturny* and those who are *nekulturny*. In doing so, it also draws borders between different language forms.

Dialectal, Vernacular, and then Literary in the Lofty Heights above Them

For many years, the way people (Slavic peoples, among others) used language was spontaneous and local. As time went on, in areas of intense communication, such as broader or narrower regions where people traded and engaged in myriad social interactions, people would develop their own linguistic peculiarities and diverge from other similar areas. Each of these areas represented a separate dialect. Most of the world's seven thousand languages still function in this same manner. Some languages will gradually develop a vernacular form spoken in a broader area (e.g., covering several dialects) but still not subject to normative interventions. A minority of the world's languages, including Slavic languages, have developed another linguistic form, known today as a standard language. In the case of Slavic languages, a standard typically involves the emergence from the literary form, hence the term *literary language*, commonly used in Slavic languages. The *standard variety* would be a better term than the *standard language*, because several standard varieties may coexist within one language, for example, British, American, and other standard varieties of the English language.

The emergence of literacy and the writing system is a related phenomenon, but only some of the languages with literacy develop a standard variety. Out of the world's more than seven thousand languages, fewer than four thousand have developed writing systems, and the majority of them are not really used (e.g., a writing system created by a visiting missionary or linguist might exist in only a handful of books). Even among those languages that use their writing systems, only a small number have a standard variety. The notion of what makes a standard language variety differs from culture to culture, but it entails the function of unifying a group of speakers beyond regional varieties (it is therefore inclusive) and separates the standard variety usage from the nonstandard one (in this function, it is exclusive).

The standardization of Slavic languages is a relatively new phenomenon. While some paths of standardization can be traced back to an earlier time, the impulse to standardize has caused the gradual loss of the dominant position of the literacy of another language (Latin and German for Slavs who were Western Christians, Church Slavonic for Eastern Christians, and Turkish for Muslims). Throughout the years, the linguistic situation of the Slavic-speaking populations was diglossic: one language form was in everyday use—the so-called L, or low level, in diglossia—and the other language form was prestigious, meaning it was used in the so-called H, or high level, of diglossia. For example, on many Croatian islands today, the H form is standard Croatian and the L form is a local Chakavian dialect (to name one of many examples, the H word for one thousand is *tisuća*, and the L word is *mijor* or *mijur*). Diglossia is hence when the same language-speaking community uses several different language forms together, either different languages or dialects. Historically, in the Slavic-speaking areas, living and local languages were used informally and colloquially while Latin, German, Church Slavonic, and Turkish were the prestigious language forms in use as well. Ideological movements such as the Renaissance, the Reformation and the Counter-Reformation, and Romanticism all paved the road for national revivals, which then required a standardized unifying language form for the imagined community of a particular ethnic group (while rejecting non-Slavic languages and Church Slavonic in that role). Various processes in national emancipation and the establishment of standard varieties for Slavic people happened at different moments in time, spanning the early sixteenth century to the late twentieth century, with most enlivened standardization processes solidifying in the nineteenth century. The belles lettres have played a special role in the process of literary language standardization. Even in those cases when the standard variety was based on a dialect, the process occurred with some mediation from the belles lettres.

The Life of a Standard Language

The theorists of language standardization differentiate various stages of the process (and language standardization is always an ongoing process). A standard language's life includes several stages (and they are also present in the emergence of literary languages). First, the selection of a variety that will eventually serve as the standard language form has to take place. Upon acceptance by those who propose it, this form undergoes diffusion in society (use in various fields of life and by a variety of speakers). The next step is codification by means of normative activities (e.g., publishing grammars, dictionaries, etc.). The standard variety then goes through elaboration, in which the norms of use in various social contexts are established. Following that step, a constant need for maintenance of the standard language variety is present, whereby it is cultivated, modernized, and developed. All these processes are visible in the development of Slavic literary languages, which undergo discussion in the following sections of this chapter and in the next chapter. This review of historical developments in Slavic literary languages and of ongoing efforts in the maintenance of their standard varieties is skeletal and simplified. It only includes the main points and broadly accepted claims. The situation of each literary language discussed here was much more complex, and each situation lends itself to contending interpretations. Therefore, the following review represents merely a teaser, rather than a full account, of complex developments. Readings recommended at the end of the chapter should be consulted for more thorough insight into these complex issues. Readers should also note that the descriptions of various Slavic literary traditions do not follow a unified template. Each research tradition is different. For example, for some languages, it is customary to differentiate and name periods (e.g., old, middle, modern, just like in English), which is not as common in other languages.

Of Gospels and Chants

Among living Slavic languages, Church Slavonic features the most narrowly restricted field of usage. It only lives on in the Orthodox Christian church rites. Church Slavonic is the later stage of Old Church Slavonic, created in the late ninth century, with its classical period ending in the eleventh century. After that period, the role of Church Slavonic morphed in different directions under the vicissitudes of history. Church Slavonic has had an important role, serving as the language of high culture in various Slavic environments across long periods of time.

The establishment of Old Church Slavonic was a part of the ninth-century Christianization effort in Great Moravia (a large medieval state in central Europe with today's eastern Czech Republic at its center). Cyril and Methodius, Slavic theologian brothers from Thessaloniki, were invited by Prince Rastislav of Great Moravia to spread Christianity. Their creation of the Glagolitic script and the establishment of Old Church Slavonic as an all-Slavic literary language were tools of that trade. This relatively short mission to Great Moravia was followed by the establishment of two important schools of the Bulgarian Empire—in Preslav, with Naum of Preslav as its most prominent representative, and in Ohrid, with Kliment of Ohrid as its founding father. The Preslav school is credited with the establishment of the Cyrillic script.

The texts that are consistent with the features of the original Old Church Slavonic, as established by Cyril and Methodius, belong to the canonical period of this language, and they fall under the category of classical Old Church Slavonic, which stretches from the ninth through the eleventh century CE. There are Glagolitic texts in the canon, such as Codex Marianus, Codex Zographensis, Codex Assemainus, and Kiev Missal; Cyrillic texts; and others, such as Codex Suprasliensis, Hilandar Folios, and Sava's Book. The versions in which the texts are interspersed with some local linguistic features are called redactions (sometimes recensions). Since the twelfth century, after the classical Moravian, Ohrid (the Western and Macedonian sides equally), and Preslav Schools (Eastern or Bulgarian), the following major recensions have been distinguished: Russian, Middle Bulgarian, Croatian, Serbian, and Bosnian.

The further life of Church Slavonic—from the gospels translated during the Moravian mission of Christianization, to today's rather narrow field of usage in the Eastern Orthodox Christian chants, icons, and frescos—will be further described in the overview of the development of Slavic literary languages, starting from the East Slavic branch in the next section. The role Church Slavonic has played in many of them was exceptionally important. Today's use of so-called New Church Slavonic is marked by some degree of variation. The most used recension is the Moscow (Synodal) Recension, generally used in Eastern Orthodox churches. There is also an Old Moscow Recension used by the Old Believers (those who maintain religious practices before the fifteenth- and sixteenth-century changes in the Russian Orthodox Church), and there was also limited use of the Croatian and the Czech redactions among the Catholics. What has started as Old Church Slavonic in gospels still lives in a very limited field of Church Slavonic chants.

From Kievan Rus' to Cursed Orthography

East Slavic people (Russians, Ukrainians, and Belarusians) share the initial stage of their literary language development. The common East Slavic period, which lasted until the late thirteenth century CE, is traditionally called Old Russian (recently also Old East Slavic, to emphasize the fact that the heritage is not exclusively Russian). This entire period, situated in the common East Slavic land of Kievan Rus', is characterized by Church Slavonic as the language of literacy and high culture and by local Southern East Slavic dialects as the language variety used colloquially. However, these two spheres of usage are not completely separated. While sacral literature remains firmly grounded in the Church Slavonic rendering, some secular high-culture texts are gradually interspersed with dialectal features. In the period between the eleventh century and thirteenth century CE, numerous important literary works were produced in Kievan Rus', most notably the chronicle "Tale of Bygone Years" and the poem "Tale of Igor's Campaign." These and many other works were written in Church Slavonic but with some dialectal influences, as evidenced especially by the latter of the two texts. The role of Church Slavonic in the formation of the Russian literary standards of this period is called the first South Slavic influence.

In the next stage of development, which historians of the Russian literary standard call the Middle Russian period, from the late thirteenth to the sixteenth century, the East Slavic languages gradually grew apart. The Russian literary standard developed within the Grand Duchy of Moscow, between the thirteenth and fifteenth centuries. The spoken language was formed around the Moscow medley of dialects, while the literary Church Slavonic language underwent archaization, known as the second South Slavic influence. In the Tsardom of Russia (between the sixteenth century and the eighteenth), the road toward democratization of the literary language was paved by a series of works in the seventeenth century, most notably by *The Life of the Archpriest Avvakum by Himself*, in which the author used the vernacular to write his autobiography.

The era of Peter the Great, in the late seventeenth and early eighteenth centuries, brought a dynamic kind of development in linguistic and epilinguistic phenomena relevant to the literary language. Peter the Great introduced the *Grazhdanka* (the civil script), modifying the Church Slavic script to make it more consistent with the specifically Russian needs of the time. At the same time, numerous borrowings from western European languages contributed to shaping the Russian literary language. What is noticeable in this period is a high degree of variation and the absence of generally binding rules.

The most important contribution to the development of the Russian literary language in the eighteenth century was the grammar by the Russian polymath Mikhail Vasilyevich Lomonosov. In addition to contributing the first normative grammar to the development of the literary language, his work also led to the differentiation of a three-tier system of low, middle, and high styles of writing. At the turn from the eighteenth century to the nineteenth, a prolific writer named Nikolay Mikhailovich Karamzin created a "new style," enriching the Russian language with various calques, that is, loan translations, based primarily on French (e.g., he coined the Russian word for 'brilliant' *blistatel'nyj*, after the French word *brilliant*, derived from the verb meaning 'to shine' *briller* in French and correspondingly *blistat'* in Russian). He also established stylistic norms of the Russian language, departing from Lomonosov.

The processes in the formation of the Modern Russian literary language culminated in the work of the national poet Alexander Sergeyevich Pushkin, who was influential in the first half of the nineteenth century. Pushkin is considered the founder of contemporary standard Russian, based on the mix of influences from the Church Slavonic tradition, dialects, and foreign languages (most notably German, French, and Dutch). A further contribution to modern Russian was the *Explanatory Dictionary of the Live Great Russian Language* published by Vladimir Ivanovich Dal in the 1860s. The nineteenth century was also marked by the cultural wars between the so-called Westernizers and Slavophiles. The former strove to bring Russian culture closer to the west, whereas the latter sought a return to the Slavic roots. These battles were mirrored in the attitudes toward the west's lexical influence.

The Russian language has further evolved, and many lexical innovations have happened during the Soviet Era. As a matter of fact, many Russian borrowings in English stem from this period—from *kolkhoz* and *sputnik* to *glasnost* and *perestroika*. The most recent modification to the orthography was completed right after the Soviet revolution in the early twentieth century, which commanded attention and strong attitudes. For example, Ivan Alekseyevich Bunin, a Nobel Prize–winning writer and a royalist, wrote the following about a major Soviet newspaper: "Izvestia—oh, the cursed orthography it uses!"

As can be seen from this concise account, the development of standard Russian was an intricate process that mostly went through the literary tradition but was constantly enriched with dialectal and other sources. It started with the common East Slavic period in Kievan Rus', and the last major reform of the writing system in early twentieth century resulted in something that its enemies called cursed orthography.

From Kievan Rus' via Little Russia to Ukraine

Ukrainian shares the Kievan Rus' period with Russian. In the so-called Middle Ukrainian period from the fourteenth to the eighteenth century, the spoken language underwent various changes under the influence of Polish and western European languages and even of the Tatar language from the Turkic languages branch. The earliest works of Modern Ukrainian were recorded in the late eighteenth century in the opus of Ivan Petryovich Kotliarevsky, who based his writings on the Southeastern Ukrainian dialects. This tradition was continued by the most notable Ukrainian writers of the nineteenth century: Taras Hryhorovych Shevchenko, Ivan Yakovych Franko, and Lesya Ukrainka.

In addition to these writers, an important role in the formation of the Ukrainian national identity and its language was played by national institutions such as the Kyiv-Mohyla Academy (established, under a different name in 1615), an institution of higher learning. Equally important were grammars, beginning with the one published in 1818 by Oleksy Pavlovich Pavlovsky. The Ukrainian nation and its language alike went through a period of negation of denial in imperial Russia, where they were considered the Lesser Russian part of the All-Russian Nation. In the second half of the nineteenth century, most publications in Ukrainian appeared in Austrian Galicia (the western part of today's Ukraine), which led to a new wave of German language influences because German was the language of the Austrian crown.

During the Soviet times, there were years of Ukrainization in the 1920s, when the Ukrainian language was actively promoted, but then these promotional activities were abandoned during Stalin's reign. In the Soviet period, the spelling system was finally shaped in a series of reforms and conversion with the help of the Russian system, starting with a great degree of variation between the eastern and western parts of the Ukrainian-speaking territories. The affirmation of the Ukrainian language has been unfolding again since the country gained its independence in 1991, and it has been accelerating in recent times. So, the Ukrainian language has developed from the common East Slavic period in the Kievan Rus'; gone through a period of negation in imperial Russia, where it was considered the Little Russian variant of the Russian language; and finally reached its full emancipation in the Soviet Union and especially in independent Ukraine.

The Third Cousin

The third cousin is Belarusian. It is the third East Slavic language that shares the Old East Slavic tradition. The period between the fourteenth century and the eighteenth, in which East Slavic dialects diverged and the Belarusian literary tradition emerged, is called the Old Belarusian Literary Language. That form of Belarusian was the official language in the Grand Duchy of Lithuania until the seventeenth century, and it was gradually replaced by the Polish language in that function. A great number of documents (statutes and various other legal documents), as well as some literary works, were written during this period of the Belarusian language.

The modern Belarusian literary tradition was formed in the nineteenth century in the works of writers like Vikenty Pavlovich Rovinsky and Konstantin Vasil'evich Verencyn. This new period constituted a break from the Old Belarusian tradition because these works were based on spoken dialects rather than on the old tradition of literacy.

An important step in the development of Modern Belarusian was the grammar published by Branislaw Adamovich Tarashkievich in 1918. In addition to codifying the language, he also reformed the orthography, and this orthographic convention was named after him: *tarashkievitsa*. This type of orthography was reformed in the Soviet Union in 1933 in the wake of Belarusization (i.e., the effort to promote the Belarusian language), but *tarashkievitsa* continued to be used in the Belarusian diaspora. The reformed version, still in use in Belarus, is called *narkomovka* (named after *Narodnyj komissariat prosveščenija* 'National Commissariat of Education,' shortened to *Narkom*, a Soviet government authority that introduced the reformed version of the orthography).

Although Ukrainian and Belarusian parted ways with Russian after the fall of the Kievan Rus', they stayed in a loose symbiotic relationship with the Russian language in two important ways. First, both countries feature a high level of Russian-Ukrainian and Russian-Belarusian bilingualism, respectively. Secondly, there exist hybrid, colloquial language forms combining Ukrainian or Belarussian on one side and Russian on the other. These hybrid forms include the Ukrainian-Russian Surzhyk in Ukraine and the Belarusian-Russian Trasianka in Belarus.

Steady Pace of Polish

The history of literary Polish is marked by steady and gradual changes in a continuous line of development. The first stage of development, in the ninth through the mid-twelfth centuries CE, called the preliteracy phase, shows some Polish place-names, preserved in Latin documents (most notably in the 1136 "Bull of Gniezno"). Polish literacy started in the Old Polish period from the mid-twelfth century to the end of the fifteenth. Texts fully written in Polish emerged in this period, the most notable being the hymn "Mother of God," "Holy Cross Sermons," "Gniezno Sermons," the "Bible of Queen Sophia," and several psalters (books of biblical Psalms). Initially, Polish was influenced by the Czech literary tradition. At the end of the fourteenth century, it was decided that Polish would be used in schools along with Latin, which gave another boost to the development of Polish literacy. Equally important were the Latin-Polish dictionaries that began to appear in the fifteenth century. The oldest Polish university founded in this period, in 1364, Jagiellonian University of Kraków is among the oldest institutions of higher learning in the world.

The Middle Polish period lasted from the turn of the fifteenth to the sixteenth century to the end of the eighteenth. It was imbued with the spirit of the Renaissance, and other colleges and universities followed in the footsteps of Jagiellonian University: Lubrański Academy (1519), Collegium Hosianum (1565), Akademia Zamojska (1594), and the like. Printing flourished in this period, and numerous dictionaries and grammars were published. Many important authors contributed to the language, including Jan Kochanowski, Mikołaj Rej, and Piotr Skarga.

The next period in the development of literary Polish, known as the New Polish period, lasted from the end of the eighteenth century to 1939. Its main characteristics were the unification of regional literary traditions and democratization. An important impulse for literary Polish's further development was the creation of the Commission of National Education during the rule of Stanislaw II Augustus in the late eighteenth century. The commission promoted the Polish language in schools and contributed to the appearance of various school grammars and primers. All this change was quite in the spirit of the Enlightenment that flourished in Poland at that time. Further development of literary Polish continued even after the First Polish Republic was partitioned among Prussia, Russia, and Austria in 1772. Most notably, a monolingual Polish language dictionary was written by Samuil Bogumił Linde in the early nineteenth century. This period of partitioning was marked by a struggle to maintain the use of the Polish language. As usually happens, major authors, such as Adam Mickiewicz and Juliusz Słowacki, also contributed to the maintenance and development of the Polish language. The resurrection of the so-called Second Polish Republic in 1918 reinstituted an unimpeded use of Polish in all spheres of life. A notable event was the establishment of the Polish Academy of Literature, which included prominent writers and was meant to be an authority on issues of language and literature. The Modern Polish period has been unfolding since 1939. In that period, the norms of Polish have been maintained by various normative grammars, dictionaries, manuals, and the work of many prominent linguists.

An interesting phenomenon was caused by the Polish population movements in the aftermath of World War II from what is now western Ukraine, western Belarus, western Lithuania, and central and eastern Poland into the areas of today's western Poland. The speakers of various Polish dialects gradually converged into what came to be known as the Polish linguistic crucible, and their colloquial language today is the closest to standard Polish now. As can be seen, the story of the literary and later the standard Polish language is one of continuity, in which various factors contributed to their development (ideological movements, historical events, literature, linguistic works, etc.).

The epilinguistic issue of representing Polish sounds not found in Latin was a constant ingredient of the development of literary Polish. The Old Polish period began when people started using only the Latin letters, which created ample ambiguity. For example, the letter c stood for the sounds k (as in kilo), ch (as in chat; it is cz in today's Polish), and ts (as in blitz; it is c in today's Polish). Next, letter combinations were used but rather inconsistently, so, for example, the ch sound was written as either a c, ch, or che. During the Middle Polish period, the use of combined letters was more consistently introduced, from which diacritics started to emerge. Thus, the distinction that exists in Polish between s (as in set), the soft sh (as in sheet), and the hard sh (as in shoot) was represented in Polish with s, ś, and sz, respectively. Current Polish spelling was eventually shaped by a series of orthographic reforms, most notably those in the late eighteenth century and then in 1936, which were mostly about orthographic conventions rather than the letters themselves.

High and Low Czech

The dawn of Czech and Slovak alike is marked by the use of other languages in prestigious functions. Likewise, their history has a similar rhythm of abandonment ebbs and revival flows. For Czech, Preliteracy Czech, during the tenth century through twelfth century CE, was the initial period of development, when Latin and Old Church Slavonic were the languages of literacy. At the beginning of Old Czech (between the thirteenth and fifteenth centuries), the first written traces of Czech appear in the forms of Czech names and glosses in Latin documents.

The early thirteenth-century Czech reverse of the "Foundation Charter of the Litomer Chapter" was considered the first recorded text in Czech. Just like in Polish, throughout the thirteenth century, Latin letters were used ambiguously to represent various sounds of the Czech language. In the fourteenth century, letter combinations emerged as a way to record specific Czech sounds. For example, *ch* as in the English word *charm* (which is *č* in today's Czech) was recorded at that time as *chz*. A variety of efforts were recorded in Czech in the fourteenth century. Most notably, the Chronicle of Dalimil along with some prayers and legal documents were recorded in Czech. A major boost in the development of Czech was noted during the Hussite Era, a fifteenth-century period in which Jan Hus and several other authors contributed to the development of literary Czech. The spelling system switched from combined letters to a diacritical system in which specific soft sounds were noted with a dot above them and the length of the vowels was marked by the acute sign (e.g., *a* and *á*).

Middle Czech, which lasted from the sixteenth to the seventeenth century, brought about the first full Czech translation of the Holy Scripture, the so-called Bible of Kralice. Its language served as an example of good writing for other writers. This period also featured the first grammar, introducing a modified diacritic orthography, in which the dot was replaced with the caron, for instance, *ch* (as in chat) was recorded as *č*, and this same letter is still used today. Czech literature flourished on the wave of Protestant Humanism. These trends were brought to their abrupt end at the Battle of White Mountain in 1620 (in which Protestant Czechs were defeated by the Catholic alliance of the Habsburg Empire, Spanish Empire, and Catholic League) and its aftermath. The peak and at the same time the end of the rich Protestant literary tradition came with the Baroque writer John Amos Comenius, who served as the last bishop of the Unity of the Brethren, a Protestant movement, which had an enormous role in shaping literary Czech.

The stagnation in the development of literary Czech lasted until the late eighteenth century, when Revival Czech began. It lasted until the mid-nineteenth century, at which time the Modern Czech era was ushered in. At the time of Revival Czech, Humanist philosophy was underpinning a resurrection of literary Czech and its codification by Josef Dobrovský. At the same time, mostly successful attempts by the Purists to replace foreign borrowings with those of Slavic origin were underway. Most notably, the de-Germanization of the literary language was at stake, and that practice continued well into the twentieth century, most notably after Czechoslovakia gained independence in 1918. To unite Czechoslovakia, the Constitution of 1920 promoted the Czechoslovak language, establishing it as the official language of the Czechoslovak Republic following an early nineteenth-century revival initiative to merge Czech with Slovak. However, this effort had no real effect in practice because most official documents were in Czech, and the two languages remain separate to this day.

As a consequence of the wave of purism, Standard Czech bears significant differences from so-called Common Czech. The latter is a nonstandard and noncodified interdialect, based on the Prague dialect, which then spread as a vernacular for informal communication across the country. It features differences in phonology and inflections in relation to Standard Czech. It also contains a substantial share of foreign and dialectal words, whereas Standard Czech remains purist. So, there is a different Czech when you speak low and a different one when you speak high. The so-called Colloquial Czech, the spoken form of the Standard Czech, increasingly became a form of compromise between the common and the standard varieties.

The Slovak Saga

The initial period of the development of the Slovak language was identical to that of its Czech counterpart, but that is not where the intertwining of these two languages end. They share the role of Old Church Slavonic as the literary language that appeared in Great Moravia in the ninth and early tenth centuries. After the fall of Great Moravia, Slovaks became a part of the Hungarian state. From the eleventh to the eighteenth century, a preliteracy period reigned over the Slovak language. In the initial phase of that period, Slovak appeared in Latin documents, containing names and some notes. The first texts in languages other than Latin and Church Slavonic in Slovakia appeared in the fourteenth and fifteenth centuries—in this case, written in Czech. Needless to say, these documents coexisted with the ubiquitous Latin language. The Czech language has become increasingly important since the fifteenth century under the influence of the Czech Protestant movement. Some of the Czech texts of that time, such as a law book from Zhilina, were interspersed with Slovak linguistic elements. In the latter part of the preliteracy period (the sixteenth through the eighteenth centuries), further Slovakization of Czech texts ensued in so-called cultural Western Slovak, cultural Central Slovak, and Jesuit Slovak. The first two were hybrid forms used mostly in administration (Western and Central refer to the parts of the Slovak lands where they were used, whereas cultural means that it was formal, i.e., not colloquial); the latter was a result of the Counter-Reformation efforts of the Catholic Church.

The ground for the literacy period of Slovak was paved by the Enlightenment, which emancipated local languages throughout Europe. The first attempt at codifying Slovak was undertaken by Anton Bernolák around the turn of the nineteenth century. This Catholic priest built upon the West Slovak tradition, but being from central Slovakia, he incorporated elements from there, too, making the literary Slovak of his proposal more distinct from Czech. His language form was accepted by Catholic priests, while the Lutherans continued to use the Czech language, based on the Bible of Kralice. Bernolák's codification proposal was eventually abandoned.

A consequent boost in the codification of Slovak was provided by the Romanticist movement. In that period, which started in the early nineteenth century, the poet Ján Kollár published a collection of Slovak folk songs, making Slovak dialectal forms prominent. A major further contribution to the establishment of literary Slovak in this period was the work of Ľudevít Štúr. He was a trained philologist who codified literary Slovak based on cultural Central Slovak. Philology is the study of mainly the historical development of a language but also its structure and relationships to other languages. Following some modifications in the form of the so-called Hoža-Hattala reform, Štúr's codification was accepted, and in 1852, he published a book whose title in translation would be 'A short Slovak grammar.' This book was signed by three Lutheran and three Catholic leaders. This grammar also encouraged a codified orthography based on diacritics, which have largely been preserved to this day. Later in the century, the most prestigious literary-language form thrived in the city of Martin in northern Slovakia, which made the so-called Martin usage the paragon of "good Slovak." In the interwar Czechoslovak Republic (1918–39), the role of the guardian of good Slovak was taken over by the *Matica slovenská* (literally 'Slovak queen bee'), a major Slovak cultural organization. Somewhat overshadowed by the Czech of the interwar period, the Slovak language saw its full affirmation in socialist Czechoslovakia after 1945, and this flourishment ensued in independent Slovakia after 1993.

The histories of literary Czech and Slovak were intertwined from the very beginning. They were also marked by pronounced differences in language registers. For many years on the Slovak side, Czech was used as a tool of high culture alongside Slovak's dialects in daily communication. This contradiction was eventually resolved with a wave of national revival. On the Czech side, this high-low cultural linguistic rift still exists in the (recently somewhat moderated) dichotomy between standard and Common Czech.

Sorbians: Twin Survival Islands

The two Sorbian languages are even more intertwined than Czech and Slovak. Their common history was marked by foreign control: initially Polish, later Czech, and, to this day, German. Much of the history of the Upper and Lower Sorbian areas alike includes struggles for ethnic and linguistic survival, and Sorbian territories have remained like islands in the German-speaking body of water. As in the case of other West Slavic languages, the earliest traces of Sorbian languages can be found in place-names mentioned in Latin and German documents. The first written Sorbian text, "Bautzen Burgher's Oath," is from 1532. The first literary text in Lower Sorbian, Mikławš Jakubica's translation of the New Testament, followed shortly after in 1548. The earliest printed books in both Lower and Upper Sorbian emerged in the final three decades of the sixteenth century.

The seventeenth century brought about Sorbian grammars and dictionaries. The earliest Lower Sorbian grammar appeared in 1650. The first Upper Sorbian grammar followed in 1679. An important development occurred during the late seventeenth and early eighteenth centuries, when the commission charged with standardizing Protestant writings established the Upper Sorbian norm of using the dialects of the Bautzen region. Similarly, an early eighteenth-century Protestant translation of the New Testament established the Lower Serbian standard based on the dialect of Cottbus. In the eighteenth century, in addition to the two major standards that the Protestants followed, there was a standard used by the Upper Sorbian Catholics. One prominent difference was in the spelling. The Protestants based theirs on German conventions, whereas the Catholics adopted Czech principles.

The nineteenth century brought about the convergence of these traditions. Handrij Zejler, a poet and author of a Sorbian grammar, should be credited along with other secular writers for further developing the Sorbian standards. Zejler was also the cofounder of the *Maćica serbska* (literally 'Sorbian queen bee'), which was the Central Sorbian cultural and scholarly society and had an important role in maintaining language norms. Two other prominent figures of the time are Jan Pětr Jordan, the author of an Upper Sorbian grammar, and Jan Arnošt Smoler, a leader of the Sorbian national movement. They created the spelling system based on the Latin alphabet (rather than the Gothic script, then in wide use among the Protestants), which, in a somewhat modified form, was promoted by the Maćica serbska to enter general use after World War II. The authors of this period had strong purist views. Around the turn of the nineteenth century to the twentieth, the Young Sorbian Movement, headed by the poet Jakub Bart-Ćišinski and linguist Arnošt Muka, introduced a more lax attitude toward foreign words, criticizing the purism of their predecessors.

During the first half of the twentieth century, Sorbians were exposed to Germanization and repression. They resisted these various attempts, most notably through their national organizations *Domowina*, meaning homeland; *Sokoł*, meaning falcon; and the aforementioned Maćica serbska. These organizations were suppressed during the Nazi regime, so they were not allowed to continue their work toward further affirmation of the two Sorbian standards until the fall of Nazism in 1945. While very close and mutually intelligible, the two standards exhibit differences in their phonology, inflections, and vocabulary. Their struggle for survival continues, with the outcome still to be seen.

Are Serbs Russians or Austrians?

Serbs are neither Russians nor Austrians, but in the course of their history they have built strong ties to the Russian and Austrian Empires. S-Cr (B/C/S) standards stem from a conversion of Serbian and Croatian literary traditions in the nineteenth century. Both Serbian and Croatian literary traditions began with some local linguistic features within Old Church Slavonic texts, as is even evident in the classical Old Church Slavonic corpus of the ninth through eleventh centuries, and then from the twelfth century, in the Serbian and Croatian recensions. The dominance of the Cyrillic script was swiftly established in the Serbian documents. Various schools of writing have been established throughout Serbia. Written Croatian is mostly Glagolitic, rendered in the specific Croatian angular version of the script (as opposed to the classical round script). There are also some Cyrillic Croatian manuscripts. In the mid-fourteenth century, the first texts started to appear in the Latin script, which eventually became dominant.

On the Serbian side, the Church Slavonic of the Serbian redaction continued to be the literary language until the eighteenth century. The time during which Serbian medieval states flourished, the twelfth through fourteenth centuries, brought about a rich corpus of sacral and secular texts. There are legal and administrative documents, such as the Codex of Czar Dushan and the Hilandar Statute (rules for monastic life in a Serbian monastery in today's Greece); various city statutes; and religious texts, say, the Hagiography of St. Sava. This tradition continued in the fifteenth century during the decline of Serbian statehood, of which the prime poetic examples are what would be translated as 'The eulogy to Count Lazar' by

Jefimija, considered to be the first female Serbian poet of the mediaeval times, and 'The word of love' by Stefan Lazarevich, who was one of Serbia's finest knights and military leaders. Following a period of decline under Ottoman Turkish rule, new circumstances formed in the late seventeenth and early eighteenth centuries with the Great Migrations of Serbs from the Ottoman Turkish Empire to southern Hungary (today's northern Serbia). In southern Hungary, the Serbian redaction of Church Slavonic (with Gavril Stefanović Venclović as its most prominent writer) was gradually replaced with the Russian redaction, as the Russians, fellow Ortho-dox Christians, sent their teachers to the new Serbian settlements. This develop-ment, largely in consequence of Russian geopolitical influences, resulted in a rich eighteenth-century literary tradition (in high culture) that continued in the first half of the nineteenth century. Most prominent authors of this tradition were Zaharija Orfelin and Hristifor Žefarović. The Russian redaction was then replaced by the Slavonic-Serbian, which incorporated the features of the Russian redac-tion of Church Slavonic, the Russian language, and local Serbian dialects. Major authors of this tradition were Milovan Vidaković, Jovan Hadžić, and Sima Miluti-nović Sarajlija. This Slavonic-Serbian tradition was hybrid in its nature because it included elements of Serbian Slavic and Russian Slavic traditions. However, given that this language functioned in the sphere of high culture, it is typically not discussed in the same context as other hybrid Slavic languages, like Surzhyk and Trasianka, which function in a colloquial sphere.

Are Croats Illyrians?

No, they are not, but that is the name they used in the Croatian National Revival in the nineteenth century. The Croatian literary tradition was much more diverse due to a considerably fragmented dialectal base and owing to the absence of one dominant language of the high culture. The Renaissance period occurring from the fifteenth to the sixteenth century saw two strong centers of literary life. One was in Dalmatia, based on the Chakavian dialect. The language spoken at this center was very different from the present-day standard language. Authors such as Marko Marulić, Petar Zoranić, and Petar Hektorović were influential, and important dictionaries were among the notable texts of that time. Another center of strong literary life was based in the city-state of Dubrovnik, based on the Shto-kavian dialect, which was close to the present-day standard language. Prominent authors included Đore Držić and Marin Držić, continuing into the seventeenth century with Ivan Gundulić and even into the early eighteenth century with the lexicographer Ardelio Della Bella. (Some Serbian scholars link this Dubrovnik center with the Serbian literary tradition.) Further Croatian sixteenth-to-eighteenth-century literary traditions include the Kajkavian tradition (another dialect very different from the present-day standard language), with prominent authors such as Pavao Ritter Vitezović and lexicographer Juraj Habdelić. There was also Istrian Protestant literature, which remained a marginal phenomenon, and the Dalmatian Counter-Reformation, with the first Croatian grammar by Bartol Kašić in the early seventeenth century. There was furthermore the Shtokavian Bosnian Franciscan tradition, with prominent authors such as Matija Divković and Andrija Kačić Miošić, and the Shtokavian Slavonian Enlightenment tradition, represented by Antun Matija Reljković and others.

The Serbian and Croatian literary traditions converged in the mid-nineteenth century into the BCS (Serbo-Croatian) literary and then standard languages. This convergence was the result of reforms conducted by the Serbian Romanticist philologist Vuk Stefanović Karadžić, on the one hand, and the reforms of the Illyrian movement in Croatia, on the other. At that time, Southern Slavs were thought to be the descendants of Illyrians, who were an ancient tribe that used to occupy the Balkans. Today, Illyrians are believed to be the ancestors of Albanians.

Karadžić elevated the East Herzegovinian dialect to the rank of a standard language and reformed the script by introducing a full correspondence between the sounds and the characters. His most prominent works include a Serbian dictionary (first published in 1818), and his translation of the *New Testament*. Karadžić's reforms—that is, his breakup with the Slavonic-Serbian tradition—were deeply influenced, if not engineered, by the Slovenian philologist and Austrian state censor Jernej Kopitar. The idea of separating Serbian literacy from Slavonic-Serbian (influenced by the Russian-backed program of Pan-Slavism) was part of an ideological maneuver of Austroslavism, which advocated for the loyalty of Slavic nations to Austria.

In Croatia, Karadžić's reforms were paralleled by those of the Illyrian movement, with Ljudevit Gaj as the most prominent author. Just as Karadžić reformed the Serbian Cyrillic script to be more in line with the phonology of the spoken language, Gaj reformed the Croatian Latin script in a similar manner. A formal political event confirming the convergence of the Serbian and Croatian standards was the Vienna Linguistic Agreement of 1850, signed by several prominent Serbian and Croatian philologists. Leading to that agreement and following decades of disputes between different philological schools (in Rijeka, Zagreb, and Zadar), Karadžić's ideas were adopted in Croatia and vigorously spread by his Croatian followers. Karadžić was in part influenced by older Croatian dictionaries, so some of the previous Croatian tradition was incorporated into his work. Another similar Serbian-Croatian agreement was signed in 1954 in Novi Sad, which resulted in the common Serbo-Croatian manual of orthography. It was used until the 1990s when Yugoslavia, a common home to Serbs and Croats, disintegrated. An important role in the maintenance of the Serbian and Croatian standards was played by the cultural institutions of *Matica srpska* (literally 'Serbian queen bee') and *Matica hrvatska* (literally 'Croatian queen bee'), as well as by the Serbian and Yugoslav (since the 1990s, it was Croatian and no longer Yugoslav) academies of arts and sciences.

Beyond Serbs and Croats

The later development of the S-Cr (B/C/S) language saw the official establishment of the Montenegrin ethnic group in 1945 and Bosniak nation in the 1970s. Bosniak literary traditions have been in existence for much longer, most notably in the so-called Alhamiado texts (written in the Shtokavian dialect in the Arabic script, including a rhymed Turkish-Bosnian dictionary) during the Ottoman Turkish times. There were also prominent nineteenth- and twentieth-century writers such as poets Safvet-beg Bašagić, Musa Ćazim Ćatić, Hamza Humo, and Mak Dizdar. The pre-1945 Montenegrin literary tradition was a part of Serbian literature.

Although there were constant tensions between Serbo-Croatian unitarists and ethnic separatists, and because there had been earlier attempts to have a separate Croatian standard (most notably during World War II), the common language form was in use until the end of the 1980s. The three ethnic standards—Serbian, Croatian, and Bosnian (the standard of the ethnic group of Bosniaks rather than of all inhabitants of Bosnia)—were established for official use in the 1990s. Recently, there have been attempts to establish the Montenegrin standard. These intricate political issues will be discussed in chapter 10. In the Slavic world, the Serbo-Croatian (Bosnian/Croatian/Serbian) situation is perhaps the most illustrative, having the various ideological, political, and geostrategic factors at play in the development of the literary traditions.

Slovene Protestants and the Alphabet Wars

The earliest, mostly preliteracy, period of the Slovene language stretches from the tenth to the mid-sixteenth century. A notable written work at the very beginning of this period (from the late tenth and early eleventh centuries) is titled Freising

Manuscripts (Freising was the town in Bavaria where they were discovered). They are the oldest written texts of the Slovene language, and of any other living Slavic language. During the rest of the period, there were only marginal fragments of short Slovene texts.

The Slovene literary language was formed during the second half of the sixteenth century as part of an effort by the Slovene Protestant Church. This language form was based on the city speech of Ljubljana, which is now the capital of Slovenia. The first books printed in this tradition were a catechism and an abecedarium, published in 1550 by Primož Trubar. Trubar has been credited as the founding father of the Slovene literary language. Additionally, important publications of the second half of the seventeenth century include a translation of the Bible by Juraj Dalmatin, a grammar by Adam Bohorič, and a multilingual dictionary by Hieronymus Megiser. These traditions used a modified German orthography, based on the combinations of letters that represented specific Slovene sounds, known as *bohorčica* (after the name of its inventor).

At the time of the Counter-Reformation, which occurred during the seventeenth and eighteenth centuries, centrifugal tendencies were at work—there were regional centers of literacy in Carniola, Styria, and Carinthia (various regions of the Slovene language) along with a rather distinct variety of a literary language in the isolated Prekmurje region of the Slovenian language. Following this rather chaotic period marked by resistance against Germanization, the modern variety of the Slovenian literary language was formed in the nineteenth century.

There were two pivotal events in 1809 that have shaped further developments in literary Slovene. First, the Napoleonic Conquest of the region and the formation of the Illyrian provinces significantly improved the status of the Slovene language, which began to be used in schools, newspapers, and administration. These developments were celebrated in the poetry of Valentin Vodnik. Second, Kopitar published a grammar of Slovene, contributing further to the codification of the language. The period of Slovenian national revival was marked by the competing regional norms and competing proposals for orthographic conventions (i.e., the alphabet wars). Examples of this include *dajnčica*, a convention of writing created by the Styrian (a person from the north-northeast of today's Slovenia) Peter Dajnko, and *metelčica*, proposed by the Lower Carniolan (a person from the east of today's Slovenia) Franc Metelko. At the same time, the Slovene national poet France Prešern and the philologist Matija Čop contributed to the refinement of the literary language in various stylistic functions. There was also a vivid intellectual exchange with the Illyrian movement in neighboring Croatia, which led to the adoption of the so-called *gajica*, based on a system of diacritics, which is still used in Slovene to this day. Eventually, the standard contemporary Slovene was shaped in the 1850s as a compromised, supradialectal form of the language, with mostly Upper Carniolan (a region in the north-northwest of today's Slovenia) phonetics, and inflections from other dialectal zones, mostly Styrian (a region in the north-northeast of today's Slovenia). Purism, the desire to remove the Germanisms from literary Slovene, was a prominent ingredient of the Slovene national revival. This then made the standard form different from the colloquial forms, in which words of German origin were used more freely. Another important boost to the development of standard Slovene was the formation of the Kingdom of Serbs, Croats, and Slovenes in 1918. In this kingdom the University of Ljubljana was established in 1919, and the Slovenian Academy of Sciences and Arts was founded in 1938. These two remain the foremost authorities on issues of standardization.

From Literary Schools to Bulgarian Linguistic Chaos

In the history of the Bulgarian language, the period between the seventh century and the second half of the ninth century, when Bulgarians moved into the eastern part of the Balkan Peninsula, is known as the preliterary phase. In it, worth noting are the occasional instances of Bulgarian names in other languages. The first literary phase is called Old Bulgarian. A bit of a controversy in relation to this phase of literary Bulgarian is whether Old Bulgarian was synonymous with Old Church Slavonic or was a separate literary tradition.

The literacy of the First Bulgarian Empire in the tenth and eleventh centuries was concentrated in two major literary schools: the Ohrid Literary School and the Preslav Literary School. The texts produced in the scriptoria of these two schools were in Old Church Slavonic. Controversial today is whether they (at that time) also represented the state of Old Bulgarian. Scholars have diverged in their opinions about how much similarity there was between Old Church Slavonic and the spoken Bulgarian dialects back then, and the jury is still out.

The Middle Bulgarian period stretches from the twelfth to the sixteenth century. It was during this period that profound changes happened, such as the loss of inflections on nouns (resulting in sentence relationships expressed using prepositions, just like in English); the development of the postpositive article, which is placed after the noun it modifies (as if saying *tablethe* instead of *the table*); and so on, making Bulgarian structurally distinct from its Slavic cousins. The most important center of cultural life was the Tarnovo Literary School in the late four-teenth and the fifteenth centuries. This school produced notable works of sacral literature—epistles, hymns, and others—and it also left a rich tradition of secu-lar works, including stories and chronicles. Prominent representatives of this school include Saint Efthymius of Tarnovo, Dionisiy Divniy, Grigoriy Tsamblak, and Vladislav Gramatik. The literacy of this period included Church Slavonic-based manuscripts. Bulgarian dialects were at the same time used in the spoken language.

The formation of Modern Bulgarian was a gradual process that began in the sixteenth century. An important first step in its development was the literary tradition of the so-called *damaskini*. Initially, they included translations from Modern Greek of the thesaurus by Damaskinos Stouditis (hence the name), a col-lection of sermons. Damaskini gradually evolved in a rich literary tradition of short texts—sermons, biographies about the lives of saints, theological teachings, and so on—which were in circulation until the nineteenth century. Notably, this literary tradition used simple everyday language, in other words, the dialects of the time, bringing the literary tradition closer to the spoken language. Another important step toward the standardization of Modern Bulgarian was the pub-lication of its first grammar in 1835 by Neofit Rilski, a prominent figure in the Bulgarian National Revival.

The linguistic chaos, mentioned in the name of this section, ensued from 1836 to 1880, when numerous contending proposals for the development of the standard were advanced and passionately debated. The key issues in the debate were the relationship of the dialects and Church Slavonic, the role of the Eastern and Western Bulgarian dialects, and the orthography (phonological, faithfully reflecting the sounds; or etymological, trying to preserve the link between the word and the root in its stem). In addition to Rilski, who was previously men-tioned, additional and prominent figures in this debate were Ivan Bogorov, Jurij Venelin, Xristaki Pavlovič, Vasil Beron, and many others. An important step in the development of Modern Bulgarian was the purist movement, which was poised to replace the words of Turkish and Greek origin with Slavicisms, in many cases borrowing from the Russian language. Eventually, Modern Bulgarian became based primarily on the dialects rather than Church Slavonic. It is based mostly on the Eastern Bulgarian dialect, with some compromises between the Eastern and Western dialects in terms of the phonology. After a prolonged period of debates, a modified phonetic principle has been adopted in the orthography.

The Poet and the Party

While various literary traditions were used in Macedonia for a long period of time, with some of them, like a part of the damaskini firmly rooted in Macedonian dialects, the codification of Modern Standard Macedonian was a unique endeavor of language planning at the end of the Second World War. The pivotal event in the codification of Macedonian was a 1944 decision by the Anti-fascist Assembly for the National Liberation of Macedonia (a local branch of the Yugoslav Communist Party that emerged victorious from World War II) to establish Macedonian as the official language of the newly formed Yugoslav Republic of Macedonia. The lion's share of work for the codification of the language was entrusted to Blaže Koneski, the most esteemed Macedonian poet and a true philological polymath. So, the party charged the poet with establishing the standard variety of the Macedonian language. The previously established tradition of that time (and for other Slavs) was a codification that relied on the following books: a grammar, a monolingual dictionary, and a manual of orthography. Koneski was involved in all three of these resources. The manual of orthography came first in 1945. Koneski's grammar was published next in 1952 (preceded by another grammar as part of the same effort, penned by Krume Kepeski in 1946). Finally, the three-volume tome of what would translate to 'Dictionary of the Macedonian language with Serbo-Croatian explanations' was published between 1961 and 1966, with Koneski as one of its general editors. The establishment of the Macedonian language was part of a broader effort of the emancipation of the Macedonian nation and the creation of a Macedonian statehood within socialist Yugoslavia. It is significant that the dictionary of the Macedonian language has explanations in Serbo-Croatian, the dominant language in Yugoslavia at the time, which clearly reflects the geostrategic orientation of Macedonians.

While part of a planned effort, the codification of the modern standard Macedonian was not a deus ex machina event. The political and cultural circumstances of previous periods shaped political decision-making at the end of World War II. On the one hand, the codification was foreshadowed in various literary traditions of the previous centuries; on the other hand, it was advanced in previous political agendas.

The ethnic Macedonian movement started shaping up in the second half of the nineteenth century, culminating in the 1903 Ilinden Uprising (named after the Macedonian name for Saint Elija's Day, observed on August 2) against the crumbling Ottoman Turkish administration. After the fall of the short-lived

Krushevo Republic, established during the uprising, the Macedonian language was the subject of contending Bulgarian and Serbian claims attempting to include the Macedonian people in their respective ethnic groups. These political circumstances influenced Koneski to select Central Macedonian dialects, with a generous inclusion of a mix of other dialectal features, in order to emphasize a separate Macedonian identity and create an equidistance from the Bulgarians and Serbs.

As noted, Macedonian literary and philological tradition does not begin with Koneski. There was a Macedonian grammar published in 1880 by Georgi Pulevski and a 1903 book by Krste Misirkov that advocated in favor of a separate Macedonian language. Then, there is an important line of literature that stretches from the Macedonian damaskini and includes prominent Macedonian authors such as Joakim Krčovski, Kirli Peyčinović, the Miladinov brothers, Grigor Prličev, and others. While these authors are also considered to be a part of the Bulgarian National Revival, one can trace local Macedonian language features in their work that have eventually, even if peripatetically, found their way into the post–World War II language-planning project. The contentious issues around the Macedonian language, most notably the Bulgarian perspective on it, will be discussed in chapter 10.

The Others: A Thin Line between Triumph and Demise

In addition to the previously discussed standard languages, there have been numerous attempts at codification or at least the establishment of a literary tradition for many other Slavic language forms. These projects have exhibited a vast variation in the degree of their success, the range of the fields in which the literary form is used, and the extent of their codification. Perhaps the most vital and the best known among these so-called Slavic microlanguages is Kashubian. Its establishment was a story of success culminating in a 2005 legal act in the Republic of Poland that gave it the status of a regional language. This act symbolically ended some long years of debate as to whether Kashubian is an external dialect of Polish or a separate language, notwithstanding the fact that opinions on that matter are still divided (at least in Poland). While there are some texts with clear Kashubian features, spanning from as early as the fifteenth century (a court oath) and lasting through the sixteenth century (some religious texts), the real impulse for the codification of the Kashubian language came in the nineteenth-century work of Florian Ceynowa, who was the author of the first Kashubian grammar and a publisher of Kashubian folklore. The Kashubian literary tradition continued in the early twentieth century with the Young Kashubian movement and its most prominent representative, Aleksander Majkowski. The tradition was continued by the authors of the Kashubian Regional Association in the interbellum (including Aleksander Labuda and Jan Trepczyk). Finally, a number of others, like authors from the People's Republic of Poland (1945–89) and the Republic of Poland thereafter (including Jan Piepka, Alojzy Nagel, Stefan Fikus, Marian Majkowski, and many others), continued this same tradition. In many respects, Kashubian is a story of success, yet it remains severely endangered, according to UNESCO.

There is thus a thin line between triumph and demise here and with many other Slavic microlanguages. Although there was definite success in establishing the use of these microlanguages in some spheres (e.g., Burgenland Croatian publishing and media programming in Austria and similar outlets for Rusyn in Serbia), they are now all listed on the UNESCO scale of language endangerment, which includes vulnerable, definitely endangered, severely endangered, critically endangered, and extinct. There are vulnerable microlanguages, including Polessian and Northern Rusyn, and there are those that are definitely endangered, including Burgenland Croatian, Resian, and Vojvodina Rusyn. Then, there are those that are severely endangered, such as Molise Croatian. It remains to be seen if these languages will join their extinct kin, such as Polabian and Slovincian. The same is true about Belarusian and the two Sorbian languages that were previously described here, which are also on this list and are listed as vulnerable and definitely endangered, respectively. It comes as no surprise that some projects that involved the establishment of literary languages never took off. A case in point is Lachian, which remained confined to the opus of one poet, Óndra Łysohorsky. The attempts to codify new Slavic standards are far from over, as demonstrated by the project that attempted to elevate the Silesian dialect to the level of a standard language.

Mighty Pens and Mightier Swords

The ebbs and flows of establishing various Slavic standard languages have shown notable similarities. First, ideology and politics have been a constant ingredient in the rise of Slavic literary standards. The first such standard, Old Church Slavonic, was an ideological tool of Christianization. Centuries later, Macedonian, a relatively recent addition to standard Slavic languages, was a tool of the emancipation of the Macedonian nation. Between these two projects, it is evident that there were a variety of ideological, political, and geopolitical factors present, from vibrant Protestant philology in various Central European Slavic nations to geopolitical games between the Russian and Austrian Empires, as seen in the case of Serbian. The ideologies were also responsible for the repression of Slavic languages, as demonstrated by the campaigns of Germanization of the Slavic people under the Austrian and Prussian Empires, as well as in the Third Reich. Mighty pens were hard at work in establishing literary and then standard language forms of various Slavic languages. In a typical case, behind these mighty pens were even mightier swards of ideological and political influence.

Chapter Takeaways

A prominent similarity in the development of the Slavic literary languages and the ensuing establishment of the standard language varieties discussed in this chapter is their dual origin. All of them emerged at the confluence of literary traditions with living dialects. The degree to which each of those influenced the eventually selected standard differs from one Slavic language to another. Yet these two factors are always present, with the writers and other philologists often serving as the ones who elevate the dialects to the literary level. It is then no surprise that the term *literary language* has been used to denote the standard language variety in Slavic languages.

Most Slavic literary traditions are also similar in the pivotal importance of the nineteenth century. The period of both Romanticism and the National Revival movements represents the epicenter of the establishment of modern standards. In some Slavic languages, development was more gradual. In others, the nineteenth century was the movement of a precipitous breakup with the previous tradition. In all of them, this period and its ideology were invariably of critical importance.

Finally, the paths of codified Slavic languages are similar in respect to the critical books that must be published in this process. The modern-era normative "Holy Trinity" includes a normative grammar, a general monolingual dictionary, and a manual of orthography, as could be seen from the case of the previously discussed Macedonian. Historically, translations of the Bible or its fragments also served in that role. Slavic cultures are furthermore similar in the way they maintain their standard language varieties, which will be the topic of the next chapter, "Standards and Authorities."

Recommended Chapter Readings

Various forms of authority are elucidated by Huemer (2013). Milroy and Milroy (2012) explore the concept of authority in language using the example of standard English. The nature of nationalism is discussed by Anderson (1991) and Brubaker (2004).

Concepts related to standard language variety and linguistic forms are explored in various chapters edited by Ammon, Dittmar, and Mattheier (2004). A further exploration of topics in the overarching field of sociolinguistics can be found in Holmes and Wilson's text (2014). Smakman (2012) offers an excellent review of the variation in definitions of standard languages in different cultures. The notion of purism, very prominent in most Slavic languages, is addressed by Thomas (1991).

The most comprehensive review of the development of Slavic literary languages is offered by Schenker and Stankiewicz (1980). The topic is further explored by Hill and Lehmann (1988). Minority Slavic languages are addressed by Gustavsson (1998). UNESCO (2019) offers the data about language endangerment.

The Bond reference is in Fleming (1957:32). The OED reference is in OED Online (2023:s.v.). Weber's seminal essay can be found in Weber (1946). Huemer (2013) discusses political authority. Nationalism is discussed in Gellner (1983) and Brubaker (2004). The Bunin reference is in Bunin (1998).

9   Slavic Rock Star Linguists

Who's in Charge of Language?

Linguists are rock stars in some Slavic countries. In all of them, educated speakers take a keen interest in the issue of language standardization, and they have strong opinions about the proposed solutions. The standard language variety is always shaped in negotiation between linguistic authorities and the body of speakers. In all Slavic languages there exists the concept of linguistic culture, a notion rather unknown to speakers of English, that addresses the efforts of linguistic authorities and the general body of speakers in maintaining the norms of a standard language. Polish even has an adjective, *poprawnościowy*, which roughly means 'pertaining to the norms of standard language correctness.' The fact that this convoluted concept deserves a word in Polish testifies to its speakers' heightened interest in linguistic issues. In general, the standard language variety and the issues around it have been prominent in the public discourse of all Slavic cultures, much more so than in the case of English-speaking cultures.

As can be seen from the previous chapter, the present forms of Slavic languages, primarily their standard language varieties, have emerged from literary traditions and their dialectal bases, something that was promoted by philologists. Initially, these initiatives came from some emerging authorities within a relatively thin layer of literate speakers. Those literate speakers eventually accepted the initiatives of emerging linguistic authorities and recognized the status of these authorities. With the democratization of literacy and urbanization in the nineteenth and twentieth centuries, the layer of those speakers who used the standard language variety grew exponentially. This brought us to the current states of affairs, in which the standard language variety has been shaped by the dynamics of the negotiations between linguistic authorities and educated speakers of Slavic languages.

Asserting Linguistic Authority: Declarations and Corrections

A typical development across Slavic languages starts with the activities of linguistic authorities (who these authorities were and are will be discussed further in this chapter). The ultimate measure of the success of these initiatives is their level of public acceptance. Generally, there are two levels of activities in which linguistic authorities engage: the macrolevel and the microlevel. At the macrolevel, various public announcements and other appearances, general policies, desirables, and undesirables in the field of language planning for the standard form of the language in question are proclaimed. Concurrently, major reference works are published (the Holy Trinity of a normative grammar, a dictionary, and a manual of orthography, with a translation of the Bible having additionally played a similar role in the earlier stages of development). At the microlevel, concrete interventions concerning certain words and forms are performed. These encompass dictionary labels such as colloquial and incorrect; edits made by copy editors in books and media; and corrections that teachers of the language in question would make. A common maneuver at the microlevel is refereeing, that is, declaring one word or form more desirable than another. This intervention may be supported by a purist narrative at the macrolevel or by some other general principle. In Slavic languages, a common action is also lexical introduction in response to a word declared undesirable in lexical refereeing, which is rather uncommon in English. To exemplify lexical refereeing, when referring to a cemetery, the norm of the standard Slovene prefers the word *pokopališče*, a word from the Slavic stock, to *britof*, borrowed from the German *Friedhof* (both words mean 'cemetery'). Lexical introduction can be seen in the action of replacing the loanword *tekst* 'text' (from the German *Text*, with the same meaning, ultimately from the Latin *textus* 'fiber, literary style') with the new coinage, *besedilo* (domestic word, coming from *beseda* 'word' and the suffix *-ilo* to create the meaning: collection of words), in standard Slovene. The examples of refereeing and introduction alike are related to a purist narrative at the macrolevel.

The main difference from the English-speaking cultures, most notably the ones in North America, is the ratio of the macro- and microlevel activities. The former activities are virtually absent in the English-speaking cultures, and the standard language variety maintenance is performed almost exclusively at the microlevel by copy editors, teachers, lexicographers, and so on. Responding to calls in the United States to abandon language planning altogether, the famous Czech-American linguist Ladislav Zgusta once said (in private communication) that those who believe there is no need for the standard language variety should write an article about that in bad English and try to publish it in a prestigious linguistic journal. Indeed, standard language planning and maintenance are always present, but cultures differ in the manner in which they perform the maintenance.

Ultimately, educated speakers—those who typically use the standard language variety—will either follow the suggestions or there will be significant deviation among them, which will then prompt corrections on the part of authorities by allowing exceptions, and so forth. The whole process flowed top-down throughout the twentieth century, when Slavic countries were, with some minor exceptions, under authoritarian regimes—royalist and right-wing first, Communist next. Linguistic elites have enforced solutions, and the body of standard language users have mostly followed—or, alternatively, tacitly exhibited their lack of approval for these solutions by not implementing them. On a wave of democratization that started with the fall of Communism in the late 1980s and early 1990s, things have begun to change. The general public takes a more active role in addressing issues related to the standard language variety. At the same time, linguists are gradually accepting this increased role of society in shaping the standard language form, seeing their relations with the public increasingly more like a partnership rather than a hierarchy.

Successful and Not-So-Successful Linguistic Engineering

Let us look at some examples. During the nineteenth century, German loanwords were common in Slavic languages across central Europe. On a wave of national renewal of Slavic peoples and other nations in the Austro-Hungarian Empire, linguistic and cultural elites proposed to replace words borrowed from German with those from the Slavic stock. Czechs, Slovenes, and Croats are particularly known for these purist tendencies. One of the national-revival streams was a mid-nineteenth-century Illyrian movement in Croatia, which strove to emancipate Southern Slavs. As a part of their general tendencies, the followers of this movement were fighting the Germanization of Southern Slavs. One of their tools was to propose South Slavic replacements for German loanwords. George Thomas, a scholar of purism, has analyzed 155 words proposed by the Illyrians. Out of these proposals, 87 (56%) are still in use, and 18 of them (12%) were eventually replaced by internationalisms (foreign words—so, these proposals were not embraced by the speakers). The remaining 50 words (32%) have been replaced by new Slavic coinages or competing Illyrian terms. It is easy to see that this de-Germanization campaign was very successful and widely accepted by the speakers. Around the same time, there was an equally successful purist campaign among Serbs, who are not exactly known for their purism. An anonymous 1863 newspaper article proposed replacing loanwords in Serbian, most of them borrowed from German but a substantial additional part from Turkish. Out of the 245 proposals for replacement, 152 (62%) were successful and 31 (12.7%) were partially successful (in that both the loanword and its proposed replacement are in use today.) In 34 cases (13.9%), the loanword has been replaced with a word different from the proposed replacement. Only 28 existing words (11.4%) were not replaced.

Later successful interventions of this type also occurred in the twentieth century. For example, when the Czech Republic was formed in 1918 on the ruins of the Austro-Hungarian monarchy, military terminology, which was entirely in German, the official language of the empire, was replaced by Czech terms. There were also not-so-successful attempts to maintain the norms. In Russia, ever since the second half of the twentieth century, there has been the following saying: *devjanosto prócentov dócentov govorjat pórtfel' i tol'ko desjat' procéntov docéntov govorjat portfél'*, which means '90 percent of assistant professors say wallet, and only 10 percent of assistant professors say wallet.' In the first part of the sentence, the words for percent, assistant professor, and wallet have the stress on the first syllable, the way '90 percent of assistant professors pronounce these words. In the second part of the sentence, the stress is on the second syllable, the way 10 percent pronounce them. The norm of standard Russian mandates the second option, which is, as apparent from the saying, followed by 10 percent of educated speakers. This quip is akin to the jokes that were circulating in the Soviet Union (1917–91) about popular insubordination against the government (e.g., the official slogan 'Lenin has died, but his cause lives on!' was told in a joke followed by the punchline: 'I would prefer it the other way around'). In this attempt to enforce a linguistic solution, the authorities have proposed one solution, but a vast majority of the population does not follow it (they wish it was the other way around). A similar development has happened in the Croatian and Bosnian variants of S-Cr (B/C/S). Politically motivated linguistic elites have introduced numerous words to emphasize the ethnic identity of the speakers of these two variants, respectively. Eventually, it turned out that the interventions have had rather limited success, with only nationalistically minded media embracing the new introductions.

The interventions and their acceptance or refusal happen in a concrete sociocultural setting. As was apparent in chapter 8, the lines of development of the literary forms of numerous Slavic languages were part of a political struggle, sometimes involving geopolitical cleavages, as in the case of Vuk Stefanović Karadžić, a linguist who was a tool of the Austrian Empire in its rivalry with the Russian Empire. Language at large and its standard language forms in particular remain embedded in the social fiber of the various speech communities it serves. All phenomena discussed in this chapter clearly belong to the scope of external language history, because it is impossible to separate linguistic from nonlinguistic issues.

Linguistic Authority: Professors and Academicians

As noted in the previous chapter, Max Weber differentiated between three main types of authority: traditional (as, e.g., in religious contexts), charismatic (e.g., that of a populist politician), and rational-legal (e.g., the kind of authority the law has). While the third type of authority, and to a degree the first type, too, has been present in almost any attempt at maintaining a standard language variety, the charismatic authority is equally present, if not more prominent, in Slavic cultures. The sources of the charismatic type of authority are prominent individuals (linguists, writers, etc.) and institutions (academies of science, various cultural societies, etc.). The emergence of the standard language varieties outlined in chapter 8 explains how these authorities came to claim their place in society. While the role of prominent individuals varies from one Slavic culture to another, the charismatic authority of the institutions is present across the board.

Universally, university departments of the country's main language (e.g., Russian in Russia, and Polish in Poland), along with academies of sciences and arts (and their institutes that focus on linguistic issues), are the most respected sources of authority. Major monolingual dictionaries and grammars are typically published by the academies, and their authors, just like the authors of the manuals of orthography, come from university language departments. Additionally, there are cultural societies, like the *Maticas*, mentioned in the previous chapter, that publish dictionaries and manuals in some countries. Finally, there are language councils and boards, again composed mostly of university professors and members of language institutes in academies, that issue their opinions about linguistic issues, mainly those pertinent to the maintenance of the standard language variety.

Celebrity Writers and Rock Star Linguists

In all Slavic cultures, writers are regarded as additional authorities on proper language use. Not only are their books seen as paragons of good writing but they are often asked for opinions about linguistic issues revolving around the standard language variety. They readily respond, offering their opinions on this score, often passionately so. This role of writers within a society is a natural development of the evolution of standard language varieties from literary traditions and dialects. Philologists, many of whom were also writers, were those who brought attention to literary traditions and dialects.

Additionally, in many Slavic cultures, linguists are rock stars. They are household names; their columns in newspapers and shows on radio and television have a large and extremely devoted following. In some countries, there are several such professors, each working in a separate niche. For example, in Poland, from the latter half of the previous century to the time when this book was written, there have been three major linguists very much in the public eye. Jan Miodek, probably the best known of the three, started with his newspaper column on language back in the late 1960s, but he became famous through his weekly TV shows *Ojcyzna polszczyzna* 'Polish language fatherland' (1987–2007) and *Słownik polsko@polski* 'Polish@Polish Dictionary' (2009–). In these shows, Miodek responds to numerous questions from the viewers, sent in by e-mail in the latter show, hence the @ sign. Although known for his various radio and TV appearances, Andrzej Markowski is most famous for his popular linguistic books and his many years of service on the Polish Language Council, an influential normative linguistic body (although his reputation has been blemished by some completely nonlinguistic issues). Finally, Jerzy Bralczyk is known primarily for his blogs on Polish linguistic topics. This Miodek-Markowski-Bralczyk trio has even published two books about Polish linguistic topics together, which shows that the market for their products is large enough to accommodate all three of them. It is also worth noting that in the scholarly community, each of them is known for various scholarly papers and monographs. This interest in issues around the standard language variety is similarly held in many other Slavic countries—Ivan Klajn has been a household name in Serbia for many years due to his magazine columns that discuss linguistic issues. We can also see the emergence of new authorities. For example, in Slovenia in 2017, linguist Kozma Ahačič was voted the person of the year in a survey conducted by the most influential Slovene daily *Delo*. He was also put on the list of twenty-five of the most influential Slovenes in a survey by influential magazine *Večer*. American culture has seen some prominent language columnists like William Safire, but the name recognition of the Slavic rock star linguists goes beyond a thin layer of intellectuals. It reaches deep into all segments of their respective societies. In addition, the texts by Slavic rock star linguists are first and foremost about the language, rather than politics by the means of language, as was the case with Safire.

This public prominence of linguists, which would be quite unusual in many other parts of the world, is a part of the general prominence of philologists in Slavic countries. It is common to see writers and literary critics offer political commentaries in the main media outlets. As we know, in English-speaking countries, the people belonging to these professions remain obscure figures unknown to most people and practically without any broad media attention. This is also true for most other cultures with this type of literacy around the world. The Slavic situation seems to be at least partially caused by the identity-based development of the standard language forms via the literary language traditions described in chapter 8. Politics in many Slavic countries remains based on ethnic identity, which then puts language and literary forms at a prominent place in the public discourse.

Multitasking Mother Tongues

The eventual outcome of the negotiation between linguistic elites and the general body of speakers is a specific form of the standard language variety, especially as it relates to other forms of the same language. Let us look at some examples. In chapter 1, I mentioned the situation of diglossia on Croatian islands between standard Croatian and the local Chakavian dialect. If you take a closer look, the situation is a bit more complicated. In my formative years, I spent summers in the village of Vrboska on the Croatian island of Hvar. Over there, when two villagers speak to each other, they use the local variety of the Chakavian dialect, a dialect that is spoken on most Croatian islands, as well as in some places on the central and northwestern coast and its hinterland. The pronounced presence of Italian loanwords (these islands were a part of the Venetian Empire for centuries), coupled with some phonological peculiarities, makes this dialect mostly incomprehensible to mainland Croats and other speakers of S-Cr (B/C/S). So, when engaging in informal communication with speakers from the mainland, the villagers use something akin to the urban dialect of Split, the main center of the region, which represents a mixture of the Chakavian and Shtokavian dialects, the latter the basis for the standard varieties of S-Cr (B/C/S). They also tend to replace some Italian loanwords with the words used in standard Croatian. That way, they can communicate while still marking their regional linguistic identity. Finally, when in school and when they need to communicate formally, for example, with authorities of some kind, they use standard Croatian. The distance between the form of language used between two villagers and the form of language used between a villager and the country's authorities is colossal. The same is true of the Kajkavian dialect in northwest Croatia (studded with German and Hungarian loanwords), which is more akin to neighboring Slovene dialects (and even standard Slovene, in its grammatical features) than to standard Croatian. On the other hand, the third main Croatian dialect, Shtokavian, is much closer to standard Croatian, given that the standard language variety is based on varieties of the Shtokavian dialect.

Although Chakavian, with some minor exceptions of dialectal literature, remains confined to informal colloquial use in Croatia, in nearby Austria it was used to form Burgenland Croatian, one of many Slavic microlanguages. The Burgenland Croatian literary language is based on the local Chakavian dialect with some influences from the local Kajkavian and Shtokavian dialects. The Austrian state-owned national radio and TV broadcaster has regular programming in Burgenland Croatian as part of its minority language broadcasts. Burgenland Croatian is also taught in schools in regions with a sizeable Burgenland Croatian minority. The distance that these speakers of a Chakavian dialect have from their respective standard language variety (i.e., standard Burgenland Croatian) is considerably smaller than the difference the Chakavian speakers have in Croatia from standard Croatian. This example shows not only that there is a varied distance of dialects from their standard language variety but also that in different circumstances the same dialect may or may not be elevated at the level of standard variety (as one could see from the Chakavian dialect in Croatia and in Austria).

Homely and Highbrowed Language

In some Slavic languages the relationship between the standard language variety and other language varieties is even more complicated. First, in some languages, there is a distinct all-national informal colloquial variety in addition to the dialects and the standard language variety. Second, there are languages with hybrid colloquial forms, including other Slavic languages. Czech and, to some degree, Slovene are examples of the first situation, whereas Ukrainian and Belarusian exemplify the second.

The prestigious formal variety of the Czech language is Standard Czech (called *spisovná čeština* in Czech), which also has a (bit more relaxed) spoken variety, called Spoken Czech (*hovorová čeština*). There are also dialects. Additionally, there is the form called Common Czech (*obecná čeština*), which is the informal all-Czech colloquial language form. It is different from the standard language form on several levels. To name several examples, there are phonetic phenomena characteristic of Common Czech, for example, inserting the prosthetic *v-*, as in *vokno* versus Standard Czech *okno* 'window.' Then, there are different case endings; for example, 'a small house' is *malej dům* in Common Czech, but *malý dům* in Standard Czech. Finally, there is a more relaxed attitude toward loanwords, as in the word for a 'trade deal,' which is *kšeft* (from the German *Geschäft*) in Standard Czech, as opposed to *obchod* (a word from the Slavic stock).

Slovene is similar to Czech in the distribution of loanwords, in particular those from German. In many places where the standard language variety uses words of Slavic origin, the vernacular resorts to German loanwords. For example, 'soap' is *milo* in Standard Slovene, a Slavic word, but the vernacular uses *žajfa* (from the German *Seife*); 'cemetery' is *pokopališče* in Standard Slovene, another Slavic word, but the vernacular uses *britof*, from the German *Friedhof*.

Slavic Hybrids: Wheat and Chaff

There are also hybrid forms in which the words and forms of two Slavic languages merge. The two best-known hybrids are Surzhyk (a Ukrainian-Russian hybrid) and Trasianka (a Belarusian-Russian hybrid). Surzhyk is most prevalent in the rural areas of central Ukraine, in the area nested between the west of the country, where Ukrainian is predominant, and its east, where Russian is the language of choice. The word used in reference to this hybrid originally meant 'a blend of grains, wheat, and rye.' The idea is that the blend is not pure wheat but rather made impure by rye. That meaning of impurity or nonstandardness is present in the semantic transfer to the language form. In the linguistic blend, Ukrainian is wheat and Russian is rye. The base is Ukrainian with numerous Russian influences. These include the softening of consonants that happens in Russian but not Ukrainian, Russian case endings, and, above all, various lexical influences, for example, Russian *zavrtakat'* rather than Ukrainian *snidati* for 'to have breakfast.' Where and in which proportion this mix of Ukrainian and Russian takes place vary from one territory to another and even from speaker to speaker.

Trasianka (a Belarusian-Russian hybrid) is akin to Surzhyk in that it represents a mixture of two Slavic languages and that it is considered a nonstandard language variety. The very term for this language variety comes from the designation of low-quality hay, a mix of fresh straws with yesteryear ones. Trasianka is even more diversified in terms of the proportion of the two languages than Surzhyk. While its sound base is Belarusian, in other linguistic segments, either of the two languages can be dominant. For example, the verb for 'to work' in Trasianka is *rabotac'*, from the Russian *rabotat'* (with Standard Belarusian being *pracavac'*), but with Belarusian phonology (the Belarussian sound *c'* rather than Russian *t'* at the end).

All previously discussed Croatian, Czech, Slovene, Ukrainian, and Belarusian cases—and they are not the only ones—show how fuzzy the border between standard and nonstandard language forms is. For various reasons, speech communities the world over have the need to define the realm in which a formal use of language is desired. The marking of this realm in Slavic cultures is conducted in a considerably more overt fashion than in English-speaking cultures. This, among other things, gives more prominence to linguists, various linguistic bodies, and so on, that in effect mark the realm of formal language along with their army of teachers and (copy) editors. In the English-speaking world, the same realm is very efficiently marked by the same army of teachers and (copy) editors who do not have any linguistic field commanders. They just follow established practice the way judges follow the common law.

Now, even in the Slavic language traditions, where there is a conscious effort to conduct a demarcation of the line between standard and nonstandard, that line is not bright red. Instead, it is blurred with all these and other mixtures of wheat and chaff discussed in this section. There is no other way around it—the borderland between standard and nonstandard is a belt with countless shades of gray rather than a bright red line between black and white.

Chapter Takeaways

Slavic literary and then standard language forms have been introduced and maintained by the authority of linguists and writers. There are various ways in which this authority is asserted, ranging from broad declarations to concrete recommendations for language use. The speakers of Slavic languages generally maintain a stronger interest in the issues of their standard languages than do their English-speaking counterparts. Consequently, linguists are more prominent in the public discourse of those languages. The standard language form coexists and is used interchangeably with various other linguistic varieties, such as dialects, colloquial language forms, hybrid language forms, and the like.

Recommended Chapter Readings

Haas's text (1982) includes various studies about standard languages from all around the world. Kristiansen and Coupland (2011) present studies about standard languages in Europe. Milroy and Milroy (2012) discuss authority in language. Šipka (2019) provides a general model of the interaction between linguistic elites and the general body of speakers on the task of maintaining the standard language variety. Browne (1993) provides an excellent review of S-Cr (B/C/S), including its Chakavian dialect. Houtzagers (2013) provides information on Burgenland Croatian. A review of issues relating to Common Czech is provided by Sgall et al. (1992). An excellent account on Surzhyk is provided by Flier (1998). More information about Trasianka can be found in the texts by Kittel et al. (2010) and Hentschel (2017).

10 Slavic Language Wars

Top-Down Conflict-Building

One factor that determines how Slavs perceive each other is identity politics. More precisely, this factor includes conflicting ethnic identities and political agendas. They are projected into the sphere of language much like they are in other fields of life. Slavic linguistic elites shape distinct language policies, which then form opinions and shape attitudes. By virtue of the elites' influence over the language standards that speakers use, the politics eventually trickle down to the general body of speakers and the way they perceive other Slavs and their languages. Slavic languages and societies are a real-life laboratory of the confrontation between linguistic facts and political agendas. There is an abundance of disputes in various Slavic environments about whether a certain linguistic variety is a dialect within a language or a language of its own. For example, the claim that Macedonian is a separate language was historically countered by the contention that it is a dialect of Bulgarian. Similarly, Kashubian is considered a separate language by many scholars, but some people consider it a dialect of Polish. The ideological and political backgrounds in which the aforementioned claims and counterclaims are rooted need to be examined to understand the mechanisms behind the claims and the claims themselves. As you can imagine, this is a minefield. The review that follows is therefore provided from a critical distance, offering insight into all conflicting views so that readers can make up their own minds.

Linguistic Armies and Navies

In some cases, it is difficult to say if something is a separate language or just a variety of a language. There is a quip in Yiddish about this issue: *A shprakh iz a dialekt mit an armey un flot* 'A language is a dialect with an army and a navy.' It has been ascribed by some to the Russian Jewish scholar of Yiddish Max Weinreich. Yiddish is just one of many of the world's languages to which this saying can be applied—is it a dialect of German or a separate language? Some other examples with distinct varieties that could potentially be considered separate languages include German, Spanish, Portuguese, and, most definitely, English. The decision to declare a linguistic variety a language rather than a dialect is indeed arbitrary and greatly motivated by the ideological, and most notably political, stance of those who make that arbitration.

Although today there is a consensus that British, North American, and Australian English (and other regional Englishes) are geographical varieties of the English language rather than separate languages, some alternative theories were around in the past. In 1919, American journalist H. L. Mencken, known by his nickname "The Sage of Baltimore," published a book titled *The American Language* in which he advanced the claim that American is a separate language from British English. Obviously, words that differ from those used in British English, as in *truck* versus *lorry*, were at the crux of his line of argumentation. Years later, in 1945, Sidney J. Baker published *The Australian Language*, with chap. 1 titled "The New Language." Again, the words are what makes Australian special. Clearly, the claims about the varieties of English being separate languages are now dead and buried. Pragmatism is highly valued in mainstream English-language cultures. It is unnecessary to translate or interpret between geographical varieties of English, and it would be equally unreasonable to have the speakers of one variety learn another English-language variety as a foreign language. What sense would it then make to speak of separate languages?

In Slavic languages, the issues are not that straightforward or rational. Ethnic identity is what usually triggers disputes about language varieties. Understood the way Brubaker has proposed it—as a process rather than a state (as outlined in chapter 8)—ethnic identity has been central to the processes in the formation of Slavic literary languages. Equally, it has been at the forefront in the disputes about what should be declared a separate language and what should not. The next section discusses major current and past points of contention.

The Curious Case of Croats and Serbs

S-Cr (B/C/S) has variants, just like English. The level of linguistic differences between the two main ones, Serbian and Croatian, is lower than those between British and American English. However, the political statuses of the two S-Cr (B/C/S) variants are completely different. Linguistically, S-Cr (B/C/S) is one language, just like English. However, there are three political languages: Serbian, Croatian, and Bosnian. In public administration, schools, media, and courts, if one is a Serb, the language is called Serbian, Croats call it Croatian, and Bosniaks (formerly known as Bosnian Muslims) call it Bosnian. There are also some speakers who call their variant of the language Montenegrin (a relatively new development), but a majority of the speakers of S-Cr (B/C/S) in Montenegro still call their language Serbian.

This disconnect between the linguistic and political status of the language has led to a rather curious situation in Croatia. The 1989 movie *Rane* 'Wounds' was a rather gritty drama about the underworld of the Serbian capital Belgrade. The Croatian distributor decided to subtitle the Serbian movie, as is customary with other foreign languages. The result of this decision was that viewers all around Croatia were bursting with laughter while watching a very serious movie. Most of the time the "translation" looked like closed-captioning for the hearing impaired. The viewers found those funny, just like those instances in which there were some differences between the two varieties—even in those cases in which the words from the Serbian variety were perfectly comprehensible. Imagine having a British movie subtitled in "the American language." It should not come as a surprise that at this Croatian movie theater subtitling has been abandoned.

All this notwithstanding, a prevailing attitude in Croatia is that Croatian is a language separate from Serbian. The argument is that sociolinguistic facts are of importance, most notably the fact that the community of Croatian speakers prefer to consider it a separate language. But there is more to it—since the early 1990s, the Croatian lexicographic market has been awash with the so-called differential dictionaries, in which Croatian-specific words are confronted with their Serbian counterparts. As a rule, these dictionaries are far from depicting reality, because many words in Serbian-Croatian pairs are used in both ethnic variants, just with lower frequency in one of them, and some of them are not used at all, except in these dictionaries. The general attitude of Serbs has traditionally been that Serbian, Croatian, and Bosnian are variants of one language, and that attitude seems to be widespread among Bosniaks too. Those Serbs who are chauvinistically minded would also claim that S-Cr (B/C/S) is all Serbian and that other ethnic groups "stole" their Serbian language.

The Cause of Serbo-Croatian Divorce

These separatist Croatian and unionist Serbian attitudes formed at the time of the common Yugoslav homeland, when Croatians were a minority and Serbs a plurality ethnic group (1918–41 and 1945–92—the two periods are separated by World War II, in which Croatia was a Nazi satellite state, separate from Serbia, which was occupied by the Germans). The general political thinking in the region—as demonstrated by political preferences expressed in surveys, referenda, and elections—was that if your ethnic group is a majority in a certain territory, you want that territory to be a separate country. In the periods between 1918 and 1941 and from 1945 to 1992, Croatia, where Croatians were a majority, was a part of Yugoslavia, where Serbs were a majority. According to the aforementioned rule of thumb, most Croatians wanted Yugoslavia to disintegrate and Croatia to be a separate country, while most Serbs wanted Yugoslavia to remain. The language issue was then a tool of constructing ethnic identification: Serbs identified themselves with Yugoslavia and its main language, whereas Croats distanced themselves from the country and the common language.

Recently, the landscape of this language war has been reshaped. Although the political establishment and more conservative layers of the population in all three main ethnic groups tend to accept the reality of the existence of at least three political languages, more progressive elements in these societies tend to advocate for the idea of a common language. The cleavage in this issue seems to be shifting from the ethnic side of the debate to the ideological plane.

In April 2017, a group of over two hundred intellectuals (mostly writers and actors, but also numerous linguists—for full disclosure, I was one of them) published a declaration on the common language, which, among others, claimed that Serbian, Croatian, Bosnian, and Montenegrin are not separate languages but rather variants of the common language. The declaration was then signed by well over ten thousand people, including Noam Chomsky, probably the most famous linguist of all time, and Peter Trudgill, a global authority for the use of language in society. The declaration triggered an avalanche of criticism in all S-Cr (B/C/S)–speaking areas, but most resolutely in Croatia, including from the president and prime minister of that country. In most other countries, however, such political figures busy themselves with issues more pressing than the purely academic status of their standard language. This difference shows the prominence of linguistic issues in the circles of the social and political elites, which are considerably wider than the environment of normative linguists. All of this interest provides an additional explanation for the enormous popularity of Slavic rock star linguists and the dynamics of linguistic authorities with speakers, described in chapter 9.

An Awkward Anthem of Yugoslavia

One should say that even the concept of a Slavdom that is common to the protagonists of the S-Cr (B/C/S) language drama (Serbs, Croats, Bosniaks, and

Montenegrins), all of whom are indeed Slavs, became problematic at a particular juncture in their history. Socialist Yugoslavia, which was their common home between 1945 and 1992, had a national anthem titled "Hey, Slavs!" that started with the following lines:

Hey, Slavs, there still lives
the word (spirit) of our grandfathers
while
There lives, there lives the Slavic spirit.
It will live for ages!

This anthem was truly Pan-Slavic because the melody was a slower version of the Polish national anthem, "Mazurek Dąbrowskiego," and the lyrics were based on a Slovak patriotic song "Hey Slovaks!" The version with Slavs rather than Slovaks was an anthem of the Sokol Movement (a society that promoted healthy lifestyles among Slavic youth) in the interwar period. Yugoslav Communists embraced this anthem during World War II, and it has been used as a de facto anthem of socialist Yugoslavia since 1945, although it was only mentioned in an official document in 1977, and only as a temporary anthem of the country. Throughout the existence of socialist Yugoslavia, its rulers have tried to find a replacement. They have found it problematic that Slavdom is prominent in the anthem while socialist Yugoslavia had significant non-Slavic minorities (Albanians, Hungarians, Romani, Turks, etc.). All these attempts, including various calls for proposals for a new anthem (the most recent one in 1985, just several years before the country disintegrated), have failed. The anthem with Slavs in its name was used as an anthem until the disintegration of socialist Yugoslavia in 1992. It then continued to be used in the sized-down Federal Republic of Yugoslavia, consisting of Serbia and Montenegro, and then finally in the State Association of Serbia and Montenegro until 2006, when it was finally consigned to oblivion. So, the history of the Slavs has seen not only turf wars between Slavic nations but also confrontations in which integral Slavdom was found problematic.

The Contested Kashubian

Another interesting case of the contested status of a language form is Kashubian, aka Cassubian, spoken in northern Poland. Throughout the twentieth century, Kashubian was mostly considered a dialect of Polish. Things started to change during the last decade of the twentieth century. Today, most scholars consider it a Slavic microlanguage rather than a dialect of Polish. However, the issue of the status of Kashubian remains controversial because there are still antithetical opinions among scholars. For example, Jan Miodek, one of the Polish rock star linguists mentioned in the previous chapter, considers it a dialect rather than a language. Even when Kashubian was considered a dialect of Polish, there was an understanding that it has a special place among other Polish dialects. Terms like external dialect were used to emphasize this special status. Later, the term *ethnolect* was used to avoid calling the Kashubian language variety a language or a dialect. It is notable that the attempts to emancipate Kashubian as a separate language accelerated and acceptance for the idea gained traction after the fall of Communism in Poland in 1989, with the issue more or less tabled before this major historical event. Recently, there have been attempts to elevate the Silesian dialect of Polish to the level of a separate language. Most scholars (including the Mick Jagger of Polish linguistics, Jan Miodek) consider Silesian to be a group of Polish dialects. However, an increasing number of people disagree. Here, too, just like with Kashubian, terms like *ethnolect* have been used to avoid calling it a language or a dialect, and the issue remains controversial.

Custody Fights Consigned to Oblivion

Some disputes seem settled. Such is the case of the Macedonian language. Ever since its creation in the mid-twentieth century, the Macedonian standard has been a subject of disputes about whether it is a separate language or a dialect of the Bulgarian language. The claims about this issue were closely aligned with political orientations. The Bulgarian political and cultural elites have denied the existence of a separate Macedonian language, striving to emphasize and expand the Bulgarian national identity. Macedonians worked hard to emancipate Macedonian as a separate language as part of their general effort to underline the Macedonian ethnic identity. Eventually, structural and lexical differences between Macedonian and Bulgarian served as convincing evidence to separate the two languages. Voices that Macedonian is a dialect of Bulgarian are clear outliers these days.

Much earlier, since its formation in the nineteenth century up to the fall of the Russian Empire in 1917, Ukrainian was in a similar position as Macedonian, and Russian was in a similar position to Bulgarian. The official policy of the empire was that Ukrainians were the so-called Lesser Russians (i.e., a variety of Russians), and what they spoke was the Lesser Russian dialect of Russian. After the

1917 Bolshevik Revolution, the new authorities assumed the course of emancipation of various ethnic groups across the former empire. The view that Ukrainians
were a subspecies of Russians was consequently abandoned in the Soviet Union
(1917–91), and the scholarly community followed suit. It comes as no surprise that
sovereign Ukraine (1991–) stayed on the same course, and there are practically no
scholarly voices denying Ukrainian as a separate language.

The controversies of the past also encompass attempts to merge two Slavic
languages into one. Such is the case of Czech and Slovak. The formation of the
Czechoslovak Republic in 1918 on the rubble of the Austro-Hungarian Empire
gave rise to an attempt to create the Czechoslovak language by declaring it the
official language of the newly formed republic. The motivation behind this maneuver was obvious—it was meant to unify the newly formed country. The Constitution of 1920 stated that "the Czechoslovak language is a state, official language
of the Republic." This Constitution was in effect until the country was occupied
by the Third Reich in 1938, and the new Constitution of 1948 after World War II did
not mention the language. In practice, even when the legislation with the official
role of the Czechoslovak language was present, it was only present in letter, never
in spirit. The Czech were using Czech, Slovaks were using Slovak, and communication with the world was in Czech. Thus, the initiative died from natural causes
long before the new Constitution abandoned the language article.

The Slavic Race

Prior to this Czecho-Slovak experiment, throughout the nineteenth century there
were tendencies to see Slavs as one "race" speaking one language with multiple
dialects. A good example of this attitude is offered by the most famous Polish poet,
Adam Mickiewicz, who lectured on Slavic literatures at the prestigious Collège
de France in Paris between 1840 and 1844. In addition to Slavic unity, he promoted
what we would call today stereotypes about various Slavic languages, and he
also mentioned inter-Slavic disputes of his time. The following passages, speaking
about Slavs, illustrate the point:

> The language of such a large extended family has to be split into many dia-
> lects; but those dialects, retain a character of unity, despite all differences.
> It is one speech, which presents itself in various forms and degrees of its
> development. We see it as a dead, religious language in Old Slavic, as a
> language of jurisprudence and administration in Russian, as a language of

literature and colloquial conversation in Polish, as a language of practical skills in Czech, remaining in its primordial state of a language of poetry and music in Illyrians, Montenegrins, and Bosnians. (1860:7–8 [French ed.]; 1865:6 [Polish ed.]; see suggested readings)

and

What was that ancient common language? Which of the peoples have the dialect that is closest to that language, and hence the right to primacy.... Serbs and Illyrians have claimed primogeniture; that way the Russian language would be a grandson, whereas Polish and Czech would be further offspring of the church language. But this interpretation of the issue did not last long. Dobrovský ... has proven that the language of liturgical books was not a general language, but merely a dialect. One could not even definitively determine if the language should be called Serbian or Illyrian, or to connect these two last names. To this day, Czechs hesitantly pronounce the name of the Serbo-Illyrian language. This battle heated up so stubbornly that scholars experienced many unpleasantries, so that one ceased to walk that path to finish. (1860:122–23 [French ed.], 1865:83 [Polish ed.]; see suggested readings)

We can see from these passages that Slavic disputes are as old as Slavic philology and that one can also speak about the disputes between the Slavic past and its present, given that an overwhelming majority of today's Slavs would not go along with Mickiewicz.

All these disputes show very clearly how, in the Slavic world, language remains one of the pillars of ethnicity. Language emancipation is an integral and often a central part of ethnic emancipation. This experience is quite different from that of English-speaking nations, for which a geographical realm rather than language was the grounds for the emancipation of North Americans, Australians, and so on, who still speak the same language of their former overlords.

Cæsar non supra grammaticos

The title of this section means 'The emperor is not above grammarians,' and it comes from an incident at the Council of Constance in 1414, when the Holy Roman Emperor Sigismund tried unsuccessfully to interfere in a linguistic dispute.

However, it would seem from the review of Slavic language divorces and custody fights earlier in this section that political considerations take primacy over linguistic issues, so Caesar is above grammarians, after all.

Rather than having anything to do with languages and linguistics, Slavic language wars are tied to political attitudes. These wars have been driven by two opposing political beliefs. The first belief is construed as inclusiveness by those who advocate for it, and it is called unitarism by those who oppose it. The second is seen as emancipation by those who espouse it, and it is called separatism by those who oppose it. As a rule, majority groups embrace the former political attitude, whereas minority groups follow the latter.

The Croatian subtitling story mentioned earlier in this chapter shows that political power still has some limitations. Talking the talk about separate languages at a symbolic level is one thing. Walking the walk is an entirely different issue. The speakers will generally be inclined to reject absurd solutions that adversely affect their daily lives.

With all this in mind, another regularity can be added to the proverb that gave title to this section—not only that the emperor is not above grammarians but that grammarians are also not above the general body of speakers. Whatever solutions are proposed by linguistic authorities (including those about what should or should not be a separate language), the ultimate implementation remains the preserve of the speakers. Even in that preserve, in different contexts a variety can function differently. In courts and classrooms it can be called a language separate from another similar variety, but nobody in their right mind would translate between the two varieties the way it is done with two separate languages. It seems that speakers of Slavic languages and Slavic linguistic authorities alike are becoming increasingly aware that a top-down, authoritarian model of maintaining the standard language variety needs to be replaced with a partnership, feedback-based model.

Chapter Takeaways

In the course of their history, Slavic linguists have engaged in various disputes about what constitutes a separate language as opposed to a variety of a language. Some of these disputes are ongoing; others have been consigned to oblivion. In some cases, these disputes led to linguistic interventionism, where linguists proposed changes in language use. The ultimate measure of success for those attempts was invariably whether the speakers of the literary or standard variety in question have accepted them. Some of such attempts were highly successful; others were generally rejected by the speakers.

Recommended Chapter Readings

Langston and Peti-Stantić (2014) address the situation in Croatia. Friedman (1999) discusses language and identity in the Balkans, including S-Cr (B/C/S) and Macedonian. Shevelev (1989) discusses the emancipation of the Ukrainian language. Weinreich's text (1945) is where the quip about language versus dialect is to be found. Mencken (1919) talks about the American language, Baker (1945) about the Australian language. Garrett et al. (2003) discuss attitudes toward language varieties. The Polish poet's lectures are available in the text by Mickiewicz (1860), and the Polish translation was published in 1865.

Appendix: Transcription and Pronunciation Guide

This list represents the sounds found across Slavic languages as presented in a Roman alphabet (with diacritics) to help those unfamiliar with Cyrillic pronunciation or who are only familiar with one Slavic language understand the sounds of different languages. Consult this list whenever you want a better understanding of a word I have presented in the book.

'	When this diacritical mark appears behind a consonant (e.g., *t'*), it means there is a softening of the consonant, as if pronouncing a *y* as in *yes* very quickly after it.
ₒ	When this diacritical mark appears below a consonant (e.g., *ŗ̥, *ḷ̥, *ṃ̥, *ṇ̥), it means that it functions like a vowel.
ˌ	When this diacritical mark appears below a consonant (e.g., r̩, l̩, m̩, n̩), it means that the consonant is syllabic, meaning it forms a syllable on its own.
˰	When this diacritical mark appears below a vowel (e.g., u̯, i̯), it means that the vowel is not syllabic.
ă	The partial circle on its back above an *a* or any other vowel (e.g., ĕ, ĭ, ŏ, ŭ) means that it is pronounced as a short vowel. It is used mostly in Indo-European examples.
ā	The flat line above the *a* or any other vowel or syllabic consonant (e.g., ē, ī, ō, ū, ȳ, r̄, l̄) means that it is pronounced as a long vowel. It is used mostly in Indo-European examples.
á	The accent mark leaning right above an *a* or any other vowel or syllabic consonant (e.g., é, í, ó, ú, ŕ, ĺ) in Czech, Slovak, and Sorbian means that the vowel is pronounced longer than its counterpart without the sign.
ä	This character is pronounced *a* as in *bad*.
â	This character is pronounced as *ough* in *thought*.

ą	This character is pronounced *o* as in *hot* with the addition of what sounds like the *n* sound very shortly after the *o* sound, achieved by passing a stream of air through the nose.
aⁱ	Any combination of a regular and superscripted character (e.g., *e*ᵘ, *o*ᵘ) means that the regular character is the syllabic part of the diphthong and that the superscripted character is its nonsyllabic part. It is like in the English word *pain*, where *a* is syllabic—that is, it forms its own syllable—and *i* is not. Together, *a* and *i* are a diphthong, so there is only one syllable in this word.
č	This character is pronounced *ch* as in *cheese*. In Polish and Serbo-Croatian, a similar sound also exists but is written as *ć*, and the tongue is more tense than in the English *ch*.
č'	This character is pronounced *ch* as in *cheese* followed by a puff, the way some English speakers pronounce *p* in *part* in transcription of Armenian.
c	This character is pronounced *ts* as in *blitz*.
ch	This character is pronounced *h* as in *hit* (found in Polish and some other Slavic languages).
ć (spelled *ci* in Polish before a vowel)	This character is pronounced *ch* as in *cheese*, with the tongue more relaxed than in English.
ď	This character is pronounced *j* as in *jack*.
đ	This is character pronounced *j* as in *jack* with the tongue more relaxed.
dź (spelled *dzi* before a vowel)	This character is pronounced *j* as in *jack* with the tongue more relaxed.
ė	This character is pronounced *e* as in *bet* in the transcription of Russian.
ě	(1) *yat'*, in Proto-Slavic, is probably similar to *y* in *yes* followed by *a* in *bad* (see the discussion in chapter 3); (2) *ye, y* as in *yes*, *e* as in *bet* in Czech.
ę	This character is pronounced *e* as in *pet* with the addition of what sounds like the *n* sound very shortly after the *e* sound, achieved by passing a stream of air through the nose very shortly after the *e* sound.

ë	(1) *yo, y* as in *yes, o* as in *pot* in the transcription of Russian; (2) *ə, e* as in *better* in Albanian.
ǵ	This character is pronounced *gy, g* as in *go, y* as in *yes*.
g^u	The superscript u̯ after any consonant (e.g., *k, g*) means that a short *w* sound is added after the consonant.
^{h}	The superscript *h* after any consonant (e.g., p^h, b^h, t^h, d^h, k^h, g^h) means that a small puff (as if a very short *h*) is added after the consonant.
h_2, h_3	laryngeals, reconstructed PIE sounds made by constriction of the larynx.
ḱ	This character is pronounced *ky, k* as in *kit, y* as in *yes*.
j	This character is pronounced *y* as in *yes*. This is how it is pronounced in most Slavic languages.
ł	This character is pronounced *w* as in *word*.
l'	This character is pronounced *l* as in lip, just a bit softer.
lj	This character is pronounced *l* as in *lip, y* as in *yes*.
ń (spelled *ni* before a vowel)	This character is pronounced *ny, n* as in *no, y* as in *yes* (in Polish).
ň	This character is pronounced *ny, n* as in *no, y* as in *yes* (in Czech).
ǫ	This character is pronounced *o* as in *hot* with the addition of what sounds like the *n* sound very shortly after the *o* sound, achieved by passing a stream of air through the nose very shortly after the *o* sound.
ó	This character is pronounced *oo* as in *look*.
ř	This sound is between *r* as in *rip* and *s* as in *measure* (in Czech).
rz	This character is pronounced *s* as in *pleasure* (in Polish).
sz	This character is pronounced *sh* as in *ship*, with the tongue more tense (in Polish).
š	This character is pronounced *sh* as in *ship*.
ś (spelled *si* before a vowel)	This character is pronounced *sh* as in *ship*, with the tongue more relaxed.
t'	This character is pronounced *ty, t* as in *tip, y* as in *yes*.
ů	This character is pronounced *oo* as in *book*.
x	This character is pronounced *h* as in *hat*.
w	This character is pronounced *v* as in *vat* (in Polish).

y	(1) This sound is between *i* in *sit* and *oo* as in *pool* (in Proto-Slavic, East Slavic); (2) it also is a sound between *i* in *sit* and *e* as in *bet* in Polish; (3) it means that the previous consonant is not palatalized in Czech and Slovak.
ż	This character is pronounced *s* as in *measure*, with the tongue more tense (in Polish).
ź (spelled *zi* before a vowel)	This character is pronounced *s* as in *pleasure*, with the tongue more relaxed (in Polish).
ž	This character is pronounced *s* as in *pleasure*.
ъ	This character is a back semivowel, which sounds like an ultrashort *oo* as in *book*; if it appears in combination with *r* and *l* it means the *r* or *l* are pronounced with back pronunciation. In Bulgarian, it is an ultrashort *a* (as in *cat* in British English).
ь	This character is a front semivowel, which sounds like an ultrashort *i* as in *bit*; if it appears in combination with *r* and *l*, it means the *r* or *l* are pronounced with front pronunciation.
ə	This is a schwa, pronounced *e* as in *better*.

Bibliography

REFERENCES CITED

Allan, Kathryn, and Justyna A. Robinson. 2012. *Current Methods in Historical Semantics.* Berlin, Boston: De Gruyter Mouton.

Ammon, Ulrich, Norbert Dittmar, and Klaus J. Mattheier, eds. 2004. *Sociolinguistics: An International Handbook of the Science of Language and Society.* 2nd ed. Berlin: Walter de Gruyter.

Anderson, Benedict. 1991. *Imagined Communities: Reflections on the Origin and Spread of Nationalism.* London: Verso.

Andrews, David R. 1999. *Sociocultural Perspectives on Language Change in Diaspora: Soviet Immigrants in the United States.* Amsterdam: John Benjamins.

Augustine. 2006. *Confessions.* Indianapolis: Hackett Publishing.

Baker, Sidney J. 1945. *The Australian Language.* Sydney, London: Angus and Robertson Ltd.

Barford, Paul M. 2001. *The Early Slavs: Culture and Society in Early Medieval Eastern Europe.* Ithaca, NY: Cornell University Press.

Beekes, R. S. P. 2011. *Comparative Indo-European Linguistics: An Introduction.* 2nd ed. Amsterdam: John Benjamins.

Browne, Wayles. 1993. "Serbo-Croat." In *The Slavonic Languages*, edited by Bernard Comrie, and Greville G. Corbett, 306–87. London: Routledge.

Browne, Wayles. 2014. "Groups of Clitics in West and South Slavic Languages." In *Slavic and German in Contact: Studies from Areal and Contrastive Linguistics*, edited by Elżbieta Kaczmarska and Motoki Nomachi. Slavic Eurasian Studies, no. 26, 81–96. Sapporo: Slavic Research Center, Hokkaido University.

Brubaker, Rogers. 2004. *Ethnicity without Groups.* Cambridge, MA: Harvard University Press

Bunčić, Daniel, Sandra L. Lippert, and Achim Rabus. 2016. *Biscriptality: A Sociolinguistic Typology.* Heidelberg, Germany: Winter.

Bunin, Ivan. 1998. *Cursed Days: A Diary of Revolution.* Translated by Thomas Gaiton Marullo. Chicago: Ivan R. Dee.

Bybee, Joan. 2015. *Language Change.* Cambridge: Cambridge University Press.

Carlton, Terrence. 1991. *Introduction to the Phonological History of Slavic Languages.* Bloomington, IN: Slavica.

Clarkson, James 2007. *Indo-European Linguistics: An Introduction.* Cambridge: Cambridge University Press.

Comrie, Bernard, and Greville G. Corbett. 1993. *The Slavonic Languages.* London: Routledge.

Curta, Florin. 2001. *The Making of the Slavs: History and Archeology of the Lower Danube Region, c. 500–700.* Cambridge: Cambridge University Press.

De Bray, R. G. A. 1951. *Guide to the Slavonic Languages.* London: Dent. (3rd ed., 1980, in 3 vols.: *Guide to the South Slavonic Language, Guide to the West Slavonic Languages, Guide to the East Slavonic Languages.* Columbus, OH: Slavica.)

Derksen, Rick. 2008. *Etymological Dictionary of the Slavic Inherited Lexicon.* Leiden, Netherlands, and Boston: Brill.

Dvornik, Francis. 1956. *The Slavs, Their Early History and Civilization.* Boston: American Academy of Arts and Sciences.

Fleming, Ian. 1957. *From Russia with Love.* London: Jonathan Cape.

Flier, Michael. 1998. "Surzhyk: The Rules of Engagement." *Harvard Ukrainian Studies* 22:113–36. https://www.jstor.org/stable/41036734.

Foer, Jonathan Safran. 2002. *Everything Is Illuminated: A Novel.* New York: Harper Collins.

Friedman, Victor. 1999. *Linguistic Emblems and Emblematic Languages: On Language as Flag in the Balkans.* Columbus: The Ohio State University. Accessed April 26, 2020. https://humstatic.uchicago.edu/slavic/archived/papers/Friedman-Naylor1.pdf.

Garrett, Peter, Nikolas Coupland, and Angie Williams. 2003. *Investigating Language Attitudes: Social Meanings of Dialect, Ethnicity and Performance.* Cardiff: University of Wales Press.

Geeraerts, Dirk. 2009. *Theories of Lexical Semantics.* Oxford: Oxford University Press.

Gellner, Ernest. 1983. Nations and Nationalism. Ithaca, NY: Cornell University Press.

Golubović, Jelena, and Charlotte Gooskens. 2015. "Mutual Intelligibility between West and South Slavic Languages." *Russian Linguistics* 39 (3): 351–73.

Grant, Anthony P. 2015. *Lexical Borrowing.* Oxford: Oxford University Press.

Greenberg, Marc, et al., eds. 2020. *Encyclopedia of Slavic Languages and Linguistics Online.* Leiden, Netherlands: Brill. Accessed April 23, 2020. https://referenceworks.brillonline.com/browse/encyclopedia-of-slavic-languages-and-linguistics-online.

Greenberg, Robert D., and Motoki Nomachi. 2012. *Slavia Islamica: Language, Religion and Identity.* Sapporo, Japan: Slavic Research Center, Hokkaido University.

Gustavsson, Sven. 1998. "Sociolinguistic Typology of Slavic Minority Languages." *Slovo* (Uppsala) (46): 75–89.

Haas, William, ed. 1982. *Standard Languages: Spoken and Written.* Manchester, UK: Manchester University Press.

Hall, Edward T. 1959. *The Silent Language.* Garden City, NY: Doubleday and Co.

Hall, Edward T. 1966. *The Hidden Dimension.* Garden City, NY: Doubleday and Co.

Haspelmath, Martin, and Uri Tadmor, eds. 2009. *Loanwords in the World's Languages.* Berlin: De Gruyter.

Hentschel, Gerd. 2017. "Eleven Questions and Answers about Belarusian-Russian Mixed Speech ('Trasjanka')." *Russian Linguist* (41): 17–42.

Hill, Peter, and Volkmar Lehmann. 1988. *Standard Language in the Slavic World.* Munich: Verlag Otto Sagner.

Hobsbawm, Eric J. 1995. *The Age of Extremes: The Short Twentieth Century 1914–1991.* London: Abacus.

Hobsbawm, Eric J. 1996. *The Age of Revolution 1789–1848.* New York: Vintage Books.

Hock, Hans Henrich. 1986. *Principles of Historical Linguistics.* Berlin, New York, and Amsterdam: Mouton de Gruyter.

Hofstede, Geert. 2020. *The 6-D Model of National Culture.* Accessed March 15, 2020. https://geerthofstede.com/culture-geert-hofstede-gert-jan-hofstede/6d-model-of-national-culture/.

Hofstede, Geert, and Gert Jan Hofstede. 1994. *Cultures and Organizations: Software of the Mind.* London: HarperCollins.

Holmes, Janet, and Nick Wilson. 2017. *An Introduction to Sociolinguistics.* London: Routledge.

Houtzagers, Peter. 2013. "Burgenland Croats and Burgenland Croatian: Some Unanswered Questions." *Rasprave* (Institut za hrvatski jezik i jezikoslovlje) 39 (1): 253–69.

Huemer, Michael. 2013. *The Problem of Political Authority: An Examination of the Right to Coerce and the Duty to Obey.* New York: Palgrave Macmillan.

Jakobson, Roman. 1955. *Slavic Languages: A Condensed Survey.* New York: King's Crown Press.

Janda, Laura A., and Steven J. Clancy. 2002. *The Case Book for Russian.* Bloomington, IN: Slavica.

Janda, Laura A., and Steven J. Clancy. 2006. *The Case Book for Czech.* Bloomington IN: Slavica.

Kittel, Bernhard, Diana Lindner, Sviatlana Tesch, and Gerd Hentschel. 2010. "Mixed Language Usage in Belarus: The Sociostructural Background of Language Choice." *International Journal of the Sociology of Language* 206: 47–71.

Kristiansen, Tore, and Nikolas Coupland, eds. 2011. *Standard Languages and Language Standards in a Changing Europe.* Oslo: Novus Press.

Kuhn, Thomas S. 1962. *The Structure of Scientific Revolutions.* Chicago: University of Chicago Press.

Langston, Keith, and Anita Peti-Stantić. 2014. *Language Planning and National Identity in Croatia.* Houndmills, NY: Palgrave Macmillan.

Lehmann, Winfred P. 1952. *Proto-Indo-European Phonology.* Texas: University of Texas at Austin. Accessed April 23, 2020. https://liberalarts.utexas.edu/lrc/resources/books/piep /index.php.

Lehmann, Winfred P. 1967. *A Reader in Nineteenth Century Historical Indo-European Linguistics.* Bloomington: Indiana University Press.

Kempgen, Sebastian. 2015–16. *Slavic Alphabet Tables.* Vols. 1–3. Bamberg, Germany: Bamberg University Press.

Kempis, Thomas à. 1998. *The Imitation of Christ.* Translated by William Benham. New York: Vintage Books.

Kundera, Milan. 1981. *Kniha smíchu a zapomnění.* Toronto: 68 Publishers.

Markoviḱ, Marjan, ed. 2020. *Lingvistički atlas na makedonskite dijalekti.* Skopje, Macedonia: MANU.

Mencken, Henry Louis. 1919. *The American Language.* New York: Alfred A. Knopf.

Mickiewicz, Adam. 1860. *Cours de littérature slave I (1840–1841).* Paris: Martinet.

Mickiewicz, Adam. 1865. *Literatura słowiańska wykładana w Kolegium francuzkiem, Rok pierwszy 1840–1841.* 3rd ed. Poznań, Poland: Jan Konstanty Żupański.

Milroy, James, and Lesley Milroy. 2012. *Authority in Language: Investigating Standard English.* 4th ed. Oxford: Routledge.

OED Online. 2022. Oxford: Oxford University Press. Accessed January 20, 2023. https:// www-oed-com.ezproxy1.lib.asu.edu/view/Entry/104544?redirectedFrom=kulturny.

Picchio, Ricardo, Harvey Goldblatt, and Susanne Fusso. eds. *Aspects of the Slavic Language Question.* New Haven, CT: Yale.

Proshina, Zoya. 2012. "Slavic Englishes." In *Routledge Handbooks in Applied Linguistics: The Routledge Handbook of World Englishes,* edited by Andy Kirkpatrick, 299–315. London: Routledge.

Proshina, Zoya. 2016. "Russian and Turkic Languages in Central Asia." In *Communicating with Asia: The Future of English as a Global Language,* edited by G. Leitner, A. Hashim, and H. Wolf, 231–46. Cambridge: Cambridge University Press. https://doi.org/10.1017 /CBO9781107477186.016.

Puškin, Aleksandr S. 1990. *Eugene Onegin.* Translated by Vladimir Nabokov. Vol. 2, *Commentary and Index.* Princeton, NJ: Princeton University Press.

Saussure, Ferdinand. 1972. *Course in General Linguistics.* Translated by Roy Harris. Chicago and La Salle: Open Court.

Schenker, Alexander M. 1995. *The Dawn of Slavic.* New Haven, CT, and London: Yale University Press.

Schenker, Alexander, and Edward Stankiewicz, eds. 1980. *The Slavic Literary Languages: Formation and Development.* New Haven, CT: Yale Concilium on International and Area Studies.

Sgall, Petr, Jiří Hronek, and Aleksandr Stich, eds. 1992. *Variation in Language: Code Switching in Czech as a Challenge for Sociolinguistics.* Amsterdam: John Benjamins.

Smakman, Dick 2012. "The Definition of the Standard Language: A Survey in Seven Countries." *International Journal of the Sociology of Language* 218: 25–58.

Soglasnova, Lana. 2018. *Dealing with False Friends to Avoid Errors in Subject Analysis in Slavic Cataloging: An Overview of Resources and Strategies. Cataloging and Classification Quarterly,* no. 56: 404–21.

Spencer-Oatey, Helen. 2012. "What Is Culture? A Compilation of Quotations." *GlobalPAD Core Concepts.* GlobalPAD Open House. http://go.warwick.ac.uk/globalpadintercultural.

Surdučki, Milan. 1978. *Srpskohrvatski i engleski u kontaktu.* Novi Sad, Serbia: Matica srpska.

Sussex, Ronald, and Paul Cubberly. 2006. *The Slavic Languages.* Cambridge: Cambridge University Press.

Šipka, Danko. 2015a. *Lexical Conflict. Theory and Practice.* Cambridge: Cambridge University Press.

Šipka, Danko. 2015b. "Slavic False Cognates: A Cross-Linguistic Comparison." *Mundo Eslavo* 14: 39–50.

Šipka, Danko. 2019. *Lexical Layers of Identity. Worlds Meaning and Culture in Slavic Languages.* Cambridge: Cambridge University Press.

Thomas, George 1991. *Linguistic Purism.* London and New York: Longman.

Towsend, Charles, and Laura Janda. 1996. *Common and Comparative Slavic.* Columbus, OH: Slavica.

Triandis, Harry C. 1995. *Individualism and Collectivism.* Boulder, CO: Westview Press.

Traugott, Elizabeth Closs, and Richard B. Dasher. 2001. *Regularity in Semantic Change.* Cambridge: Cambridge University Press.

UNESCO. 2019. *UNESCO Atlas of the World's Languages in Danger.* Accessed July 9, 2019. http://www.unesco.org/languages-atlas/.

Weber, Max. 1946. *From Max Weber: Essays in Sociology.* Translated and edited by Gerth H. H. and C. Wright Mills, 77–128. New York: Oxford University Press.

Weinreich, Max. 1945. *The YIVO and the Problems of Our Time.* Speech at the Annual YIVO Conference, January 5, 1945.

Wierzbicka, Anna. 1997. *Understanding Cultures through Their Key Words: English, Russian, Polish, German, and Japanese.* Oxford: Oxford University Press.

SLAVIC COMPARATIVE GRAMMARS AND REVIEWS OF SLAVIC LANGUAGES

Arumaa, Peeter, and Jooseppi Julius Mikkola. 1964, 1976, 1985. *Urslavische Grammatik: Einführung in das vergleichende Studium der slavischen Sprachen.* 3 vols, Heidelberg, Germany: Carl Winter.

Bernštejn, S. B. 1961. *Očerk sravnitel'noj grammatiki slavjanskix jazykov.* Moscow: Izd-vo ANSSSR.

Bernštejn, S. B. 1974. *Očerk sravnitel'noj grammatiki slavjanskix jazykov: Čeredovanija: imennye osnovy.* Moscow: Nauka.

Bethin, Christina Y. 1998. *Slavic Prosody: Language Change and Phonological Theory.* Cambridge: Cambridge University Press.

Bidwell, Charles E. 1963. *Slavic Historical Phonology in Tabular Form.* The Hague: Mouton.

Bidwell, Charles E. 1969. *A Morpho-syntactic Characterization of the Modern Slavic Languages.* Pittsburgh: University Center for International Studies, University of Pittsburgh.

Bidwell, Charles E. 1970. *The Slavic Languages—Their External History.* Pittsburgh: University Center for International Studies, University of Pittsburgh.

Birnbaum, Henryk. 1987. *Praslavjanskij jazyk—Dostiženija i problemy v jego rekonstrukcii.* Moscow: Progress.

Bošković, Radoslav. 1977. *Osnovi uporedne gramatike slovenskih jezika.* Belgrade: Naučna knjiga.

Bräuer, Herbert. 1961. *Slavische Sprachwissenschaft I: Einleitung, Lautlehre.* Berlin: Walter de Gruyter.

Carlton, T. R. 1991. *Introduction to the Phonological History of the Slavic Languages.* Columbus, OH: Slavica.

Comrie, Bernard, and Greville G. Corbett. 1993. *The Slavonic Languages.* London: Routledge.

Dalewska-Greń, Hanna. 1997. *Języki słowiańskie.* Warsaw: PWN.

De Bray, R. G. A. 1951. *Guide to the Slavonic Languages.* London: Dent. (3rd ed., 1980, in 3 vols.: *Guide to the South Slavonic Languages, Guide to the West Slavonic Languages, Guide to the East Slavonic Languages.* Columbus, OH: Slavica.)

Dybo, V. A. 1981. *Slavjanskaja akcentologija. Opyt rekonstrukcii sistemy akcentnyx paradigm v praslavjanskom.* Moscow: Nauka.

Dybo, V. A., G. I. Zamjatina, and S. L. Nikolaev. 1990. *Osnovy slavjanskoj akcentologii.* Moscow: Nauka.

Franks, Steven. 1995. *Parameters of Slavic Morphosyntax.* New York: Oxford University Press.

Furdal, Antoni. 1961. *Rozpad języka prasłowiańskiego w świetle rozwoju głosowego.* Wroclaw: Ossolineum.

Garde, Paul. 1976. *Histoire de l'accentuation slave.* Paris: Institut d'Études Slaves.

Gołąb, Zbigniew. 1991. *The Origins of the Slavs: A Linguist's View.* Columbus, OH: Slavica.

Herman, Louis Jay. 1975. *A Dictionary of Slavic Word Families.* New York: Columbia University Press.

Hill, Peter, and Lehmann, Volkmar, eds. 1988. *Standard Language in the Slavic World.* Munich: Verlag Otto Sagner.

Horálek, Karel. 1962. *Úvod do studia slovanských jazyků.* Prague: Akademia.

Horálek, Karel. 1962/1992. *An Introduction to the Study of the Slavonic Languages.* Translated by Peter Herrity. Nottingham: Astra Press.

Ivšić, Stjepan. 1979. *Poredbena slavenska gramatika.* Zagreb: Školska knjiga.

Jakobson, Roman. 1955. *Slavic Languages: A Condensed Survey.* New York: King's Crown Press.

Kempgen, Sebastian, Peter Kosta, Tilman Berger, and Karl Gutschmidt. 2007. *Die slavischen Sprachen: Ein internationales Handbuch zu ihrer Struktur, ihrer Geschichte und ihrer Erforschung, Band 1.* Berlin and New York: Mouton de Gruyter.

Kempgen, Sebastian, et al. 2014. *Die slavischen Sprachen: Ein internationales Handbuch zu ihrer Struktur, ihrer Geschichte und ihrer Erforschung, Band 2*. Berlin and New York: Mouton de Gruyter.

Kondrašov, N. A. 1986. *Slavjanskie jazyki*. Moscow: Prosveščenie.

Kortlandt, Frederik. 1975. *Slavic Accentuation: A Study in Relative Chronology*. Lisse, Netherlands: Peter de Ridder Press.

Kuznecov, Petr S. 1960. *Očerki po morfologii praslavjanskogo jazyka*. Moscow: Izdatel'stvo Akademii SSSR.

Lamprecht, Arnošt. 1987. *Praslovanština*. Brno, Czechoslovakia: Univerzita J. E. Purkyně.

Lehr-Spławiński, Tadeusz, Władysłąw Kuraszkiewicz, and Franciszek Sławski. 1954. *Przegląd i charakterystyka języków słowiańskich*. Warsaw: Państwowe wydawnictwo naukowe.

Lehr-Spławiński, Tadeusz. 1946. *O pochodzeniu i praojczyźnie Słowian*. Poznań, Poland: Wydawnictwo Instytutu Zachodniego.

Liewehr, Ferdinand. 1955. *Slawische Sprachwissenschaft in Einzeldarstellungen*. Vienna: Rudolf M. Rohrer.

Mareš, František V. 1965. *Die Entstehung des slavischen phonologischen Systems und seine Entwicklung bis zum Ende der Periode der slavischen Spracheinheit*. Munich: Sagner. (English translation [1965]: *The Origin of the Slavic Phonological*.)

Meillet, A. 1924. *Le slave commun*. Paris: Champion.

Meillet, A. 1934. *Le slave commun: Seconde édition revue et augmentée avec le concours de A. Vaillant*. Paris: Champion.

Mel'ničuk, A. S., ed. 1966. *Vstup do porivnjal'no-istoryčnoho vyvčennja slov'jans'kyx mov*. Kyiv: Naukova dumka.

Mel'ničuk, A. S. 1986. *Istoričeskaja tipologija slavjanskix jazykov*. Kyiv: Naukova dumka.

Mihaljević, Milan. 2002–2014. *Slavenska poredbena gramatika*. Vols. 1 and 2. Zagreb: Školska knjiga.

Mikkola, J. J. 1913, 1942, 1950. *Urslavische Grammatik: Einführung in das vergleichende Studium der slavischen Sprachen*. 3 vols. Heidelberg, Germany: Carl Winter.

Miklosich, Franz. 1862–75. *Vergleichende Grammatik der slavischen Sprachen*. Vol. 1, *Lautlehre*; vol. 2, *Stammbildungslehre*; vol. 3, *Formenlehre*; vol. 4, *Syntax*. Vienna: Wilhelm Braumuller.

Mlacek, Jozef. 1984. *Slovenská frazeológia*. 2-é vyd. Bratislava, Slovakia: SPN.

Mokienko, V. M. 1980, 1989. *Slavjanskaja frazeologija*. Moscow: Vysšaja škola.

Nahtigal, Rajko. 1952. *Slovanski jeziki*. Ljubljana, Slovenia: Državna založba Slovenije.

Panzer, Baldur. 1996. *Die slavischen Sprachen in Gegenwart und Geschichte*. Second extended and improved ed. Frankfurt am Main, Germany: Peter Lang.

Picchio, Riccardo, and Harvey Goldblatt, eds. 1984. *Aspects of the Slavic Language Question*. Vol. 1, *Church Slavonic—South Slavic—West Slavic*; vol. 2, *East Slavic*. New Haven, CT: Yale Concilium on International and Area Studies.

Popowska-Taborska, Hanna. 2014. *Wczesne dzieje Słowian w świetle ich języka*. 3rd ed. Warsaw: Instytut Slawistyki PAN.

Rehder, Peter, ed. 1998. *Einführung in die slavischen Sprachen*. Darmstadt, Germany: Wissenschaftliche Buchgesellschaft.

Schenker, Alexander M. 1995. *The Dawn of Slavic*. New Haven, CT, and London: Yale University Press.

Schenker, Alexander M., and Edward Stankiewicz, eds. 1980. *The Slavic Literary Languages: Formation and Development*. New Haven, CT: Yale Concilium on International and Area Studies.

Seliščev, A. M. (1914) 2010. *Vvedenie v sravnitel'nuju grammatiku slavjanskikh jazykov*. Moscow: KomKniga.

Shevelev, George. 1965. *A Prehistory of Slavic: The Historical Phonology of Common Slavic*. New York: Columbia University Press.

Širokova, A. G., and V. P. Gudkov, eds. 1977. *Slavjanskie jazyki*. Moscow: Izd-vo Moskovskogo universiteta.

Stang, Ch. S. 1957. *Slavonic Accentuation*. Oslo: Universitetsforlaget.

Stankiewicz, Edward. 1986. *The Slavic Languages: Unity in Diversity*. Berlin, New York, and Amsterdam: Mouton de Gruyter.

Stankiewicz, Edward. 1993. *Slavic Accentuation*. Stanford, CA: Stanford University Press.

Stieber, Zdzisław. 1969/1973. *Zarys gramatyki porównawczej języków słowiańskich*. Part I (fonetyka [phonetics]); Warszawa; Part II, Exercise Book 2 (fleksja werbalna [verbal inflection]). Warsaw: PWN.

Stieber, Zdzisław. 1979. *Zarys gramatyki porównawczej języków słowiańskich*. Warsaw: PWN.

Stone, Gerald, and Dean Worth, eds. 1985. *The Formation of the Slavonic Literary Languages*. Columbus, OH: Slavica.

Suprun, A. E. 1983. *Leksičeskaja tipologija slavjanskix jazykov*. Minsk, Belarus: Izd-vo Belorusskogo Universiteta.

Sussex, Ronald, and Paul Cubberly. 2006. *The Slavic Languages*. Cambridge: Cambridge University Press.

Townsend, C. E., and L. A. Janda. 1996. *Common and Comparative Slavic: Phonology and Inflection*. Columbus, OH: Slavica.

Trubačev, O. N. 2003. *Ètnogenez i kul'tura drevnejšix slavjan: Lingvističeskie issledovanija*. Moscow: Nauka.

Vaillant, André. 1950–1977. *Grammaire comparée des langues slaves*. Lyon: IAC, Paris: Klincksieck.

van Wijk, Nicolaas. (1937) 1956. *Les Langues slaves. De unité a la pluralité*. 2nd ed. The Hague: Mouton.

Vondrak, Vaclav. 1906/1908. *Vergleichende slavische Grammatik*. Vol. 1, *Lautlehre und Stammbildungslehre*, vol. 2, *Formenlehre und Syntax*. Göttingen: Vandenhoeck & Ruprecht. (2nd ed. 1924–28.)

Worth, Dean S., ed. 1972. *The Slavic Word*. The Hague and Paris: Mouton.

SLAVIC ETYMOLOGICAL DICTIONARIES

Akademia. 1989–. *Etimologický slovník jazyka staroslovánského*. Prague: Academia.

Anikin, E. A. 2007–. *Russkij etimologičeskij slovar'*. Vols. 1–7. Moscow: Institut russkogo jazyka im. V. V. Vinogradova.

Bagrinovskij, Grigorij. 2018. *Kratkij étimologicheskij slovar'*. Saint Petersburg: KoLibri: Azbuka-Attikus.

BAN. 1962. *Bъlgarski etimologichen rechnik*. Sofia, Bulgaria: Ban.

Bańkowski, A. 2000. *Etymologiczny słownik języka polskiego*. I: A–K, II: L–P. Warsaw: PWN.

Bezlaj, France. 1977. *Etimološki slovar slovenskega jezika*. Prva knjiga: A–J. Ljubljana, Slovenia: Slovenska akademija znanosti in umetnosti.

Boryś, Wiesław. 1994. *Słownik etymologiczny Kaszubszczyzny*. Warsaw: Slawistyczny Ośrodek Wydawniczy przy Instytucie Slawistyki PAN.

Boryś, Wiesław. 2005. *Słownik etymologiczny języka polskiego*. Kraków: Wydawnictwo Literackie.

Brückner, Aleksander. 1927. *Słownik etymologiczny języka polskiego*. Kraków: Krakowska Spółka Wydawnicza.

Černykh, P. Ja. 2007. *Istoriko-ètimologicheskij slovar' sovremennogo russkogo jazyka: 13,560 slov*. Moscow: Russkij jazyk media (earlier ed., 1993).

Derksen, Rick. 2008. *Etymological Dictionary of the Slavic Inherited Lexicon*. Leiden, Netherlands, and Boston: Brill.

Dolukhanov, Pavel. 2013. *The Early Slavs: Eastern Europe from the Initial Settlement to the Kievan Rus*. 2nd ed. London: Routledge.

Glinkina, L. A. 2019. *Kratkij orfograficheskij slovar' russkogo jazyka s istoriko-ètimologicheskimi kommentarijami*. Moscow: Flinta.

Gluhak, Alemko. 1993. *Hrvatski etimologijski rječnik*. Zagreb: August Cesarec.

Gorjaev, Nikolaj Vasil'evich. 1896. *Sravnitel'nij etimologičeskij slovar' russkogo jazyka*. Tiflis, Georgia: Tipografija Kants glavnonach gr. ch. na Kavkaze, Loris'-Melik.

Holub, Josef, and František Kopečný. 1952. *Etymologický slovník jazyka českého*. Prague: Státní nakladateltví učebni.

Holub, Josef. 1967. *Stručný etymologický slovník jazyka českého: Se zvláštním zřetelem k slovům kulturním a cizím*. Prague: Státní pedagogické nakladatelství.

Ilarion. 1979. *Etymolohichno-semantychnyj slovnyk ukraïns'koï movy*. Winnipeg: "Volyn'."

Loma, Aleksandar, Marta Bjeletić, Jasna Vlajić-Popović, and Snežana Petrović. 2003–08. *Etimološki rečnik srpskog jezika*. Vols. 1–3, A-Bj. Belgrade: SANU.

Machek, Václav. 1971. Etymologický slovník jazyka českého. 3. vyd.n. Prague: Československá akademie v.d. (other editions 1957, 1968).

Martynoŭ, V. U., ed. 1978–. *Etymalagičny sloŭnik belaruskaj movy*. Minsk, Belarus: Navuka i texnika.

Matasović, Ranko, ed. 2016. *Etimološki rječnik hrvatskoga jezika*. Vol. 1. Zagreb: Institut za hrvatski jezik i jezikoslovlje.

Miljković, Slaviša K. 2010–. *Novi srbski etimološki rečnik*. Niš, Serbia: Serbona.

Mladenov, Stefan. 1941. *Etimologičeski i pravopisen rechnik na bŭlgarskija knižoven ezik*. Sofia, Bulgaria: Kn-vo Kh. G. Danov.

Oguibénine, Boris. 2016. *L'héritage du lexique indo-européen dans le vocabulaire russe, première série, compléments au Dictionnaire étymologique de la langue russe de Max Vasmer*. Paris: Institut d'études slaves.

Orel, Vladimir E. 2011. *Russian Etymological Dictionary*. Calgary: Theophania Publishing.

Preobrazhenskij, A. G. 1951. *Etymological Dictionary of the Russian Language*. New York: Columbia University Press.

Preobrazhenskij, A. G. 1959. *Ètimologicheskij slovar' russkogo jazyka*. Moscow: Os. izd-vo inostrannykh i nacional' nykh slovarej.

Rejzek, Jiří. 2015. *Český etymologický slovník*. Prague: Leda. (Earlier ed., 2001.)

Rudnyc'kyj, Jaroslav B. 1962–66. *An Etymological Dictionary of the Ukrainian Language*. Winnipeg, MB: Ukrainian Free Academy of Sciences.

Šanskij, N. M. 1961. *Kratkij etimologicheskij slovar' russkogo jazyka: Posobie dlja uchitelja*. Moscow: Gos. uchebno-pedagog. izd-vo (later ed. 1971).

Šanskij, N. M. 1994. *Ètimologicheskij slovar' russkogo jazyzka*. Moscow: Prozerpina.

Šapošnikov, A. K. 2019. *Ètimologičeskij slovar' sovremennogo russkogo jazyka.* Moscow: Flinta.

Skok, Petar. 1971–73. *Etimologijski rjecnik hrvatskoga ili srpskoga jezika.* Zagreb: JAZU.

Sławski, Franciszek, ed. 1974–2001. *Słownik prasłowiański,* t. 1–8. Wrocław: Ossolineum.

Snoj, Marko. 2016. *Slovenski etimološki slovar.* Ljubljana, Slovenia: Založba ZRC. (Previous ed., Mladinska knjiga 1997.)

Trubačev, O. N., ed. 1974–. *Etimologičeskij slovar' slavjanskikh jazykov.* Moscow: Nauka.

Vasmer, Max. 1986–87. *Ètimologičeskij slovar' russkogo jazyka.* Moskva: Progress.

Vasmer, Max. 1953–58. *Russisches etymologisches Wörterbuch.* Heidelberg, Germany: C. Winter.

Wade, Terence. 1996. *Russian Etymological Dictionary.* London: Bristol Classical Press.

Wolkonsky, Catherine. 1961. *Handbook of Russian Roots.* New York: Columbia University Press.

Index

Note: Information in figures and tables are indicated by *f* and *t*. Names starting with characters with diacritics are alphabetized in the place of characters without diacritics rather than in separate letter sections.

About the Author

Danko Šipka is a professor of Slavic languages and head of linguistics at Arizona State University, where he teaches in the School of International Letters and Cultures. He served as a senior linguist and consultant to numerous language industry companies. He has written thirty books, including *The Geography of Words* (2022) and *Lexical Layers of Identity* (2019).